MASTERING

the

craft of writing

How to Write with Clarity, Emphasis, & Style

Stephen Wilbers

WRITER'S DIGEST
BOOKS

WRITER'S DIGEST BOOKS

An imprint of Penguin Random House LLC
penguinrandomhouse.com

ISBN 978-1-59963-788-4

Printed in the United States of America

Edited by Rachel Randall
Cover designed by Bethany Rainbolt
Interior designed by Laura Spencer

DEDICATION

To Matilda, my Birkie baby, with love.

"My mother ... pointed out that one could not say 'a green great dragon,' but had to say 'a great green dragon.' I wondered why, and still do."

—J.R.R. Tolkien

"I was inspired by the marvelous example of Giacometti, the great sculptor. He always said that his dream was to do a bust so small that it could enter a match-book, but so heavy that no one could lift it. That's what a good book should be."

—Elie Wiesel, in reference to *Night*, his memoir about the Holocaust, whose manuscript he edited from 865 pages down to 245 pages, and later down to 178 pages, and finally to 116

"In the afternoons he caught sight of Lily when she cleaned the upstairs of the house. Just seventeen years old. Her sand-colored hair. Her eyes ledged with freckles. He closed his door, sat to write. He could still see her shape. On the stairs he allowed her to pass. A whiff of tobacco came from her. The world was made ordinary again."

—Colum McCann, *TransAtlantic*

ABOUT THE AUTHOR

Stephen Wilbers is a writing consultant, author, and columnist. He has offered training seminars in effective writing to a wide variety of clients. He teaches both written and oral presentation as a Senior Fellow in the University of Minnesota's Technological Leadership Institute. He has also taught in the Carlson School of Management's M.B.A. Program, the Program in American Studies, and the Program in Creative and Professional Writing. In 1995 he won an Outstanding Faculty Award in Hamline University's Graduate Public Administration Program.

His doctoral dissertation, a history of the renowned Iowa Writers' Workshop, was published by the University of Iowa Press. In addition, he has published two collections of his columns, *Writing for Business* (winner of a 1994 Minnesota Book Award) and *Writing by Wilbers*. His book on stylistic technique, *Keys to Great Writing*, has been described as "a writing class in a book" that "breaks down general advice on what to do into practical steps on how to do it."

This Northern Nonsense: Ernest Oberholtzer and Mallard Island, his chapbook of poems about the legacy of the preservationist who helped save the Boundary Waters Canoe Area Wilderness from development, was published by Red Dragonfly Press. *A Boundary Waters History: Canoeing across Time* depicts efforts to preserve a remarkable wilderness on Minnesota's northern border while telling the story of canoeing for nearly thirty years with his father. *Canoeing the Boundary Waters Wilderness: A Sawbill Log* is a memoir of wilderness canoeing adventures. He is currently working on a number of books, including *A Grammatical Affair: A Wildly Romantic Love Story Offering Writing Instruction in the Form of a Novel*, which combines fiction and pedagogy.

He earned his B.A. at Vanderbilt University and his M.A. and Ph.D. at the University of Iowa. He was a Visiting Fulbright Fellow at the University of Essex in Colchester, England. Before starting his business as a writing consultant, he established the University of Iowa's first campuswide advising program. At the University of Minnesota, he directed student academic support services in the College of Liberal Arts and later served as Associate Director and Acting Director of the Program in Creative and Professional Writing.

An avid reader, canoeist, cyclist, Nordic ski racer, and two-time skydiver, he and his wife Debbie have two grown children and one granddaughter and live in Minneapolis, where he is a proud member of The Loft Literary Center, whose board he chaired from 2007 to 2009.

ALSO BY STEPHEN WILBERS

The Iowa Writers' Workshop: Origins, Emergence, and Growth
Writing for Business (collected columns)
Writing by Wilbers (collected columns)
Keys to Great Writing
This Northern Nonsense: Ernest Oberholtzer and Mallard Island (a chapbook of poems)
A Boundary Waters History: Canoeing Across Time
Canoeing the Boundary Waters Wilderness: A Sawbill Log

CONTENTS

INTRODUCTION

As I was thinking about writing this book, I kept hearing Katherine Anne Porter telling me, "You do not create a style. You work and develop yourself; your style is an emanation from your own being."

Sort of took the wind out of my sails.

I also heard Kurt Vonnegut saying, "Find a subject you care about and which you in your heart feel others should care about. It is this genuine caring, not your games with language, which will be the most compelling and seductive element in your style."

You can see why I had my doubts about writing this book.

I was afraid if I compiled a list of techniques to help you write with style, you might think, "Hey, this is easy. I'll just do these simple things, and I'll be a great writer. The heck with reading or working on my writing over time."

I was worried you might conclude that style was nothing more than a suit of clothes to be donned for the occasion rather than an authentic expression of your inner being—"the Self," as E.B. White describes it, "escaping into the open."

For example, what if I taught you how to use a sentence fragment to punctuate a point, as Stephen King does when he writes, "If you don't have time to read, you don't have the time (or the tools) to write. Simple as that"? You might think stylistic technique was nothing more than a bag of tricks. And what if I showed you how to make a sentence more memorable by arranging its elements in climactic order, with the most emphatic element coming last, as Harvard President Charles William Eliot did in 1871 when he declared, "Bad spelling, incorrectness as well as inelegance of expression in writing, ignorance of the simplest rules of punctuation, and an almost entire want of familiarity with

English literature are far from rare among young men of eighteen otherwise well prepared for college"? You might think, "Great! Now I know how to use climactic order for emphasis," and then go watch TV rather than read a good book.

Well, I decided not to do it. I couldn't have that misconception on my conscience. I decided you would have to develop your style the hard way, the way countless writers before you have done it. You would have to read, work, and study the style of good writers, and, slowly, over time, your style would improve.

Then I had second thoughts.

I thought of the books that have helped me improve *my* writing. I thought of the readers of my newspaper column on effective writing who have told me they've learned from my advice and appreciated my humor. I thought of the people who have told me my earlier book on style, *Keys to Great Writing*, had helped them develop their writing skills. Then there were the students who have taken my classes at the University of Iowa, Hamline University, and the University of Minnesota and all the participants in the training programs I've offered to various companies, agencies, and organizations, and I thought that maybe I do know something that might be helpful to you.

So I decided to risk writing this book. But I still don't want you to think that learning to write with clarity, emphasis, and style is easy. It's not. It's hard work. It's challenging, arduous, and sometimes tedious. On the other hand, don't be surprised if a smile comes to your face as you make your way through these fifty-two techniques. You might even hear someone laughing.

You'll notice that my examples and exercises run the gamut from creative writing to business writing. My techniques are intended for every type of writer, from students writing college application essays to scientists explaining their research findings, from journalists and attorneys to governmental, academic, medical, and environmental writers. Climactic order works as effectively in the courtroom as it does in a text message, a love letter, or a story about a character waking up one morning and discovering he has metamorphosed into a large, monstrous, insect-like creature.

My exercises will give you practice applying each technique. The concluding summary of all fifty-two weeks' techniques will help you remember them for the rest of your life. For some commentary along the way, both serious and lighthearted, I've drawn from my cache of nine hundred newspaper columns. (In deciding to include some of my previously published work, I'm following the advice of my favorite professor at the University of Iowa, the transcendentalist scholar Sherman Paul, who encouraged his students to recycle their literary wares.)

So that's my plan.

Now here's what you need to do: Listen.

Listen to the sound of your words.

"The good writer of prose must be part poet," says William Zinsser in *On Writing Well*, "always listening to what he writes."

Listen to the rhythm and cadence of your sentences, and you'll know what's working and what isn't. Trust your ear.

That's all you need to do.

That, combined with a lifetime of reading, writing, and experimenting with various patterns of language, will make you a good writer. If you work hard and if you were born with at least average intelligence and some measure of talent, you might even become a great writer.

These fifty-two techniques will help you realize what you're doing right. They'll help you recognize your natural patterns, the ones that are working for you, and expand your repertoire of sentence styles and structures.

I recommend you read this book twice. The first time through, read only the fifty-two techniques and skip the "Exercises" and "Further Thoughts." The second time through, read everything. Take your time. Devote one week to each of the fifty-two techniques. Begin working on a new technique every Monday. Look for opportunities to apply that technique in everything you write. Look for examples of its application in everything you read. Note missed opportunities. Be alert. Keep your eyes and ears open. Billboards and restaurant histories printed on the backs of menus are not off limits.

If you're a teacher, feel free to skip around. Assign the techniques in any order that suits your purposes. Use my exercises to create your own. Assign a technique or set of techniques to complement other assigned reading. Use the techniques to enrich your discussion. Make your poor students read the entire book over the summer—better yet, make them read it over the weekend. Heck, make them read it overnight. They'll thank you for it. They might even be so inspired by Colum McCann's quote in the opening pages of this book,

"Her sand-colored hair. Her eyes ledged with freckles," that they tweet that special person in their life, "Love your micro braids. Your eyes edged with color."

However you use this book, be sure to have some fun along the way. Enjoy your one-year journey to becoming a more varied, adept, and memorable writer. You might even be on your way to becoming a great writer.

But you still have to read. Deal?

LISTEN TO YOUR LANGUAGE

Let's begin with listening.

Listen to the sound of your language. Read your words out loud. Pay attention to their rhythm and cadence and flow. Consider the way they reverberate in your head, how they stir your heart. Ask how your reader would respond to *farewell* as opposed to *goodbye*, or to *mockingbird* as opposed to *crow*.

To illustrate the importance of careful word choice, I've altered the wording in the following book titles. Keep in mind that titles—like poetry, jingles, and slogans—are intended to create a vivid impression.

See if you can change the following titles back to their original versions. As you make your changes, listen for the power of a well-chosen word to capture a certain mood or feeling.

Here are four titles by Ernest Hemingway with one or more words altered.

1. *The Elderly Man and the Ocean*
2. *For Whom the Bell Rings*
3. *A Goodbye to Arms*
4. *The Sun Also Comes Up*

Here are the original titles.

1. *The Old Man and the Sea*
2. *For Whom the Bell Tolls*
3. *A Farewell to Arms*
4. *The Sun Also Rises*

Can you hear the damage done by the alterations? Maybe a better illustration of how to ruin *The Sun Also Rises* would have been *The Sun Comes up Every Single Day of the Week*, but I'm saving patterns of wordiness for Weeks 10, 11, and 12.

Next consider William Faulkner's *The Noise and the Fury* and *As I Lay Expiring*, F. Scott Fitzgerald's *The Awesome Gatsby* and *So Sweet Is the Night*, as well as Edith Wharton's *The Period of Innocence*, John Steinbeck's *The Raisins of Wrath*, and Willa Cather's *The Archbishop Kicks the Bucket*. (Poor guy.)

Did you spot the alterations from *The Sound and the Fury*, *As I Lay Dying*, *The Great Gatsby*, and *Tender Is the Night*, as well as *The Age of Innocence*, *The Grapes of Wrath*, and *Death Comes to the Archbishop*? Can you hear the dramatic difference a single ill-chosen or well-chosen word can make?

Listen to your words. Use your ear when you choose them and when you revise them.

Try taking a few of your favorite titles and altering them so that their magic is lost. What could you do, for example, with *Game of Thrones*, *Little Women*, or *Infinite Jest*? As you will see (and hear), finding words that endure is no accident. It requires sensitivity to words and careful listening.

I've always listened carefully to words. I'm not sure where my preoccupation with the sound of language comes from, but maybe it originated from my background as a musician. At eight I started taking accordion lessons, and at sixteen I started giving lessons. In high school I played bass fiddle with some college stage bands at the University of Cincinnati. I used to play harmonica around the campfire, I still play piano every day, and I love opera, folk music, and bluegrass, especially when it's heavy on the banjo. (Maybe I shouldn't have mentioned the parts about the accordion and the banjo.)

When I was hitchhiking around Europe during my junior year in the Vanderbilt-in-France program, I saw two young Italian women engaged in an animated conversation on a Florence street corner and I stopped to listen. I could only catch an occasional French and English cognate, but I stood there enthralled. It was as though my ears had been opened to the beauty of language. I've never forgotten the gestures, expressions, and sounds of those two young women.

Whatever the source of my preoccupation with the sound of words, listening has made me a better writer. As it will you.

EXERCISES

1. Write down the titles of five of your favorite songs. Alter one word in each title to ruin its sound. Then change the wording of each title to something you like better.

2. In a November 11, 2011, post on *flavorwire.com* titled "A Collection of Rejected Titles for Classic Books," Emily Temple listed a number of early versions of famous book titles. Among them were *The Mute* for Carson McCullers' *The Heart Is a Lonely Hunter*, *This Anger* for Alex Haley's *Roots*, *Atticus* for Harper Lee's *To Kill a Mockingbird*, and *The Last Man in Europe* for George Orwell's *1984*.

As you can see, the early versions were rejected for good reason.

To prevent yourself from peeking at the suggested answers for the following exercise, I suggest you cover them with a notecard. (Keep your card handy for later exercises—you'll learn more if you do the exercises rather than just read the answers.)

Match the early versions of these four titles to the final versions below.

    a. *Fiesta*

    b. *Tomorrow Is Another Day*

    c. *First Impressions*

    d. *Catch-11*

Here are the final versions.

__ Jane Austen's *Pride and Prejudice*

__ Joseph Heller's *Catch-22*

__ Margaret Mitchell's *Gone with the Wind*

__ Ernest Hemingway's *The Sun Also Rises*

(Use your card, please.)

And here are the answers.

    c. *First Impressions* for Jane Austen's *Pride and Prejudice*

    d. *Catch-11* for Joseph Heller's *Catch-22*

    b. *Tomorrow Is Another Day* for Margaret Mitchell's *Gone With the Wind*

    a. *Fiesta* for Ernest Hemingway's *The Sun Also Rises*

3. Make up a good title for a best-selling novel.

4. Listen carefully to the language other people are using. The next time you read something by a favorite author, find three words whose sound you like.

5. Find three words that impress you from someone in your field who writes unusually well, and look for opportunities to use those words in your own writing. As you put these words into play, be sure they not only say exactly what you want to say but also sound good to you.

WRITE WITH DETAIL

To keep your reader's attention, move beyond generality and abstraction. Write with detail. Or as Joseph Conrad famously said, "Don't tell the reader; show the reader."

Which of the four sentences below makes you want to keep reading?

1. The reporter ducked down in the back seat.
2. The reporter ducked down in the back seat to avoid being shot.
3. The reporter ducked down in the back seat to avoid being shot by a hooded motorcyclist.
4. The reporter ducked down in the back seat to avoid being shot by a hooded motorcyclist toting an AK-47.

Note how the increasing level of detail makes each successive sentence more interesting.

Consider this statement: "Obesity is a threat to public health."

Unsubstantiated, the assertion carries no weight. (Pardon my pun. It was unintentional.) Note how supporting the statement with detail makes it weightier: "Studies of obese children have indicated a correlation between obesity and a number of maladies—hypertension, alteration of lipoprotein levels, and increased prevalence of certain respiratory, skin, and orthopedic conditions—as well as problems with psychological adjustment in childhood, and later stigmatization and loss of self-esteem in adolescence."

So the next time you write, "Susan works hard," "Our customers aren't very happy," or "My boss really liked my report," don't stop there. Give your readers something they can sink their teeth into.

Tell them Susan worked until eight every night last week to prepare for a presentation for a prospective client. Tell them customer complaints have risen from 230 last quarter to 385 this quarter, an increase of 67 percent. And tell them in last Tuesday's staff meeting George held up your report on quality control, taped each of its five pages to the whiteboard, uncapped a yellow felt-tip marker, and drew a big star on each page.

You can win or lose an argument based on detail. You can move your reader to tears with the right detail, or you can bore your reader to death with vague generalities.

In expository writing, rather than "I'm concerned about a softening market," write, "I'm concerned about the 15 percent decline in sales of our high-resolution computer screens."

In persuasive writing, rather than "The Defendant was driving at an excessive speed," write, "The Defendant was driving eighty-five miles an hour in a residential neighborhood." And don't forget to mention little Jimmy Connors and Shane Williams, ages nine and ten, who were riding their Schwinn bikes down the sidewalk.

In descriptive writing, rather than "The doves ate everything that had been planted," write, "[The doves] ate the sprouts of new flowers and the buds of apples and the tough leaves of oak trees and even last year's chaff," as Louise Erdrich did in *The Plague of Doves*.

In narrative writing, rather than "When my friend and I were little we were given two swords and we headed for our neighbor's flowers," write, "When [Buddy Doberman] and I were four his grandfather gave us a pair of wooden pirate swords that he had made in his workshop and we went with them more or less straight to Mrs. Van Pelt's prized flower border, which ran for about thirty yards along the alley," as Bill Bryson did in *The Life and Times of the Thunderbolt Kid*.

A friend of mine who is a novelist and short story writer revises her writing by looking for missed opportunities. She works through her drafts several times, each time adding subtlety to her plot, complexity to her characters, and detail to her descriptions. She calls this process "layering."

Layering. I like both the concept and the word.

But don't overdo it. Adding too much detail will slow down your narrative and weigh down your description beyond the modern reader's patience.

In his evocation of "the happy bounty" of America's prosperity, Bryson may be pushing the boundary of too much detail when he describes the items in a photograph that ran in *Life* magazine in 1951.

> [The photograph] shows the Czekalinski family of Cleveland, Ohio—Steve, Stephanie, and two sons, Stephen and Henry—surrounded by the two and a half tons of food that a typical blue-collar family ate in a year. Among the items they were shown with were 450 pounds of flour, 72 pounds of shortening, 56 pounds of butter, 31 chickens, 300 pounds of beef, 25 pounds of carp, 144 pounds of ham, 39 pounds of coffee, 690 pounds of potatoes, 698 quarts of milk, 131 dozen eggs, 180 loaves of bread, and 8½ gallons of ice cream, all purchased on a budget of $25 a week. (Mr. Czekalinski made $1.96 an hour as a shipping clerk in a DuPont factory.) In 1951, the average American ate 50 percent more than the average European.

What do you think? Too much detail or the right amount to make the point? For memorable writing, provide detail—not too much and not too little.

EXERCISES

1. Rewrite the following banal passage into text that might be used in a promotional brochure.

> Our company is twenty years old. We started as a small company, but now we are a large one. Over the years, we have worked hard to provide quality service to our clients.

Use a notecard to cover the next two paragraphs; try your hand at rewriting these three sentences before you look at my suggestion for a rewrite.

Here's one way the passage could be enlivened with detail.

> On August 1, Quality Video Products celebrated its twentieth anniversary. We've come a long way since those early days when we had only eight full-time people, two cameras, and a cramped production studio located in the basement of a furniture warehouse.

> Today, we rank among the largest video production firms in the country, and we have built a reputation as a truly world-class company. In this special anniversary brochure, we highlight some of QVP's achievements and discuss how we have made a difference in the lives of our clients, our employees, and our competitors.

It may not be F. Scott Fitzgerald, but I think it's an improvement over the original.

2. Writing with detail involves more than adding specific information. It also involves using specific verbs rather than general ones. Using strong verbs relieves you of an overreliance on adjectives and adverbs. Compare "The sales representative talked incoherently" with "The sales representative babbled," or compare "My boss spoke continuously for forty-five minutes" with "My boss droned on for forty-five minutes." Modifiers such as *incoherently* and *continuously* have their place, but to paraphrase Strunk and White, the adverb hasn't been built that can pull a weak or inaccurate verb out of a tight place. (More on the power of verbs in Weeks 13, 14, and 15.)

How might you use a stronger verb to add detail to the following sentence? "News of our boss's departure affected all of us."

(Card, please.)

Here's one possibility: "News of our boss's departure saddened all of us."

Here's a better version: "When our boss announced he was leaving, we stomped our feet, pounded the table with our fists, and raised our voices in a chorus of unbridled joy and celebration."

Depending on your feelings for your boss, you may find one version more appealing than the other.

3. On a tastier note, imagine you're writing a story on how the rapid growth in new breweries in Minnesota has spurred "new suds-friendly state laws." You've written a good lead (or *lede*, as they spell it in the industry), and you're working on your second paragraph.

> New beer-friendly state laws have sparked a brewery boom in Minnesota that has catapulted the state into one of the nation's fastest-growing craft brew markets.
>
> The suds are flowing. Lagers, ales …

What might you add to hold your readers' interest? Of course, the more you know about the craft-beer movement, the easier it is to come up with the right detail.

Here's how Jennifer Brooks wrote the second paragraph in an article that appeared in the June 30, 2013, *Star Tribune*.

> The suds are flowing. Lagers, ales, pilsners, stouts. Heady, hoppy, handcrafted beer, rolling out of one-man operations in basements, brewpubs, micro-breweries, and mega breweries around the state—many of which didn't exist just a few years ago.

Now that's one savory paragraph. I love the sound of "heady, hoppy, handcrafted beer" don't you? The alliteration rolls off the tongue. Makes me thirsty just reading it.

4. Select a paragraph at random from your writing. Underline your nouns and pronouns, and circle or italicize your verbs.

Then ask yourself if any of the objects, persons, or actions marked could be depicted more vividly. Add details that underscore the impression you're trying to achieve. Be specific. Name names. Use strong verbs.

APPEAL TO THE SENSES

To write vividly and memorably, appeal to the senses. As Anton Chekhov advised, "Don't tell me the moon is shining; show me the glint of light on broken glass."

You may have been told by your teachers to use "concrete language," but did you ever wonder what "concrete language" was? Despite what it sounds like, it's not Portland cement.

If you thought it had something to do with going beyond the general to the specific, you were right. But using "concrete language" involves more than being specific. Former poet laureate Donald Hall uses a more revealing phrase in *Writing Well*: "sense words," or language that can be perceived by the five senses.

Why are sense words important?

Writers who use sense words are more likely to create a strong impression and to evoke an active response from their readers. Their writing is more vivid, colorful, and memorable.

For example, rather than "My customer was extremely dissatisfied with my letter," write, "My customer slammed my letter down on the counter." Rather than "The passengers below the *Titanic*'s deck were having problems," write, "Below the *Titanic*'s deck, the icy water rose to the passengers' knees."

Sense words enliven your writing in at least three ways: They add color ("My cubicle is so small that when I lean back in my chair I bang my head on the wall"); evoke an emotional response from your reader ("The owners flew around the country in Learjets while their workers drove rusted-out used cars"); and clinch an argument ("If it doesn't fit, you must acquit").

There are times, of course, when generalities are preferable to specifics. If you want to de-emphasize negative information, for example, rather than "Our sales have fallen like a rock, plummeting 15 percent since we introduced our new line of sleepwear," write, "The response to our new line of sleepwear has been disappointing." In persuasive writing, you should refer generally rather than specifically to negative information or information that undermines your argument, just as in narrative writing you might go with the general rather than the specific to set a fast pace.

But when you want to make your writing memorable, appeal to the senses.

The challenge is to achieve an appropriate balance between generality and specificity. Writing that is too general ("For some time now, we have been making less money than we had projected, so we may have to reduce our workforce either this year or next") as well as writing that is too specific ("The meeting was held from 9:07 to 10:43 AM in conference room C, the one that has the blinking fluorescent light and the nice view of the Theodore Wirth Golf Course") can exasperate your reader.

So don't overdo it as you appeal to the senses. Rather than "We didn't notice that the food was less than perfect," write, "We didn't notice that the dumplings were stuffed mostly with stringy squash and that the oranges were spotted with wormy holes," as Amy Tan does in *The Joy Luck Club*.

Rather than describe a summer evening ritual of sitting on the front porch with your grandpa by writing "I loved the sounds coming from the house as the rest of my family started doing the dishes," write, "About seven o'clock you could hear the chairs scraping back from the tables, someone experimenting with a yellow-toothed piano … [m]atches being struck, the first dishes bubbling in the suds and tinkling on the wall racks," as Ray Bradbury does in *Dandelion Wine*.

Here are a few more examples of the effective use of sense words. Jean Shepherd's description of a group of kids walking to school makes us feel winter's chill.

> Kids plodded … through forty-five-mile-an-hour gales, tilting forward like tiny furred radiator ornaments, moving stiffly over the barren clattering ground with only the faint glint of two eyes peering out of a mound of moving clothing.

Can you see those eyes? Can you feel the icy wind?

Here's how Colum McCann describes pilot John Alcock in his novel *TransAtlantic*.

A single man, he said he loved women but preferred engines.
Nothing pleased him more than to pull apart the guts of a Rolls-
Royce, then put her back together again. He shared his sand-
wiches with the reporters: often there was a thumbprint of oil
on the bread.

Would you like a bite of that sandwich?

Most writers favor visual images, but don't forget you have five senses: sight, hearing, smell, taste, and touch.

Colum McCann describes how another transatlantic traveler, Frederick Douglass, notices a peculiar aroma in Dublin.

There was an odd smell in the air. Douglass still couldn't figure
out what it was. Sweet, earthy. He walked quickly up the steps
with the butler in attendance. He was brought to the fireplace
in the living room. He had seen the fire the night before, but had
not noticed what it was: clods of burning soil.

And as you may recall from the quote in the opening pages of this book, it was a "whiff of tobacco" coming from a seventeen-year-old maid named Lily that made the world "ordinary again."

One more example. How might you use sense words to make your point more vividly in the following sentence? "He was such a good pitcher he could get anything past even the best batters."

There are countless possibilities, but here's how legendary sportswriter Red Smith described Yankees pitcher Whitey Ford: "He could throw a lamb chop past a hungry wolf."

Get the idea? Have some fun. Use your imagination. Appeal to the senses.

EXERCISES

1. Add detail that appeals to the senses to bring the following sentence to life: "A little while later, when the police cruiser happened upon her and her children, she was stuck in the ditch crying."

(Use your card.)

Here's how Jonathan Odell wrote that sentence in *The View from Delphi*.

An hour later, when the black-and-white cruiser with the big star on the door happened upon Hazel and her boys, she had sunk the two left tires deep into a sandy ditch and was hunched over the wheel sobbing.

2. Here's a wonderful example of sense words from E.B. White's essay, "Once More to the Lake," which Donald Hall cites in *Writing Well*. In describing his son's lack of experience with lakes, White writes that his son "had seen lily pads only from train windows." White also points out that his son had never had a certain unpleasant experience common to all swimmers.

How do you think he completed this clause, "My son, who had never had ..."?

(Card, please.)

Here's how White breathed life into his observation: "my son, who had never had water up his nose."

3. What are your most enduring memories of childhood?

Are they the smell of fresh-mown grass on a hot summer afternoon, the sight of your big brother dressed as a mummy for Halloween, the squeeze of your grandmother's hand the last time you saw her, or the sound of your father's voice singing "Ol' Man River" to put you to sleep at night?

Chances are your most vivid recollections involve one or more of your five senses. You may use abstract words such as *contentment, shock, longing, emptiness, love,* and *comfort* to describe the feelings evoked by those memories, but if you want your reader to share and experience your feelings, present your experience the same way your memories were created: through firsthand perception of vivid, specific, sensory details.

Make a list of some of your earliest, most cherished memories, describing them in succinct phrases made up of sense words.

✳ A FURTHER THOUGHT: OVER-THE-TOP ANALOGIES USE SENSE WORDS

Several years ago some over-the-top analogies from a high school essay contest circulated around the Internet. They were so bad they were good.

Here's one example. (Warning: It may not be appropriate for all audiences.) "She had a deep, throaty, genuine laugh, like that sound a dog makes just before it ..."

How do you think that sentence was completed? You guessed it:

"... throws up."

Yuck.

Not all sense language need be gross to be vivid. In *TransAtlantic*, Colum McCann describes an encounter between two characters in this way.

He waited a moment in the doorway, stepped across, took her in an embrace. Only that. He held his hand at the back of her hair. He hesitated a moment. She sobbed. When he pulled away ...

When he pulled away what? Here's how McCann completed the sentence: "When he pulled away, the shoulder of his shirt was wet." As you can see, the smallest visual detail can convey great significance.

Sense language can be delivered with a light touch. Consider how the following sentence might be completed by building on the metaphor of *spilling*: "Many economists warn that a recession in Europe could spill over to the world economy, which could ..."

Which could what?

How about "... wash back on the United States"?

With *wash back on* neatly reprising the notion of *spill over*, the language is pleasingly understated.

COLLECT GOOD WORDS

Our words are close to our hearts. We use them to convey our thoughts and ideas, our values and concerns.

Sometimes we use our words to show off, as in "I deem it imperative that we commence work on this project at our earliest possible convenience," when all we mean is "Let's get to work on this project."

And sometimes we can't think of the precise word that captures our thought, as in "His explanation for failing to file his report is hard to believe" when we might have said, "His explanation for failing to file his report is implausible."

Having a broad range of words at our command and knowing how and when to use them is key to memorable writing.

Are you satisfied with *your* vocabulary? Would you like to improve it? Here's how.

1. **Be curious about language.** Be inquisitive. If you listen attentively to the spoken or written language of articulate people, you'll expand your vocabulary.

2. **Listen and watch for words you don't know.** Be on the lookout for words whose sound you like. Collect words you think might be useful to you, words that suit your style and personality. Learn the vocabulary of your field or profession.

   The secret to building your vocabulary is to pay attention. The first thing you'll notice—and this will happen immediately—is that you've developed a greater sensitivity for words. In *Writing Well*, Donald Hall refers to "sensitivity to the insides of words." Hearing a word pronounced aids your aural memory; seeing a word in print reinforces your visual memory.

3. **Read.** The easiest and most pleasurable way to expand your vocabulary is to read. Unfortunately—and surprisingly—many people who aspire to become good writers don't read. My definition of a nonreader is someone who reads only what is required to get credit for a class or to avoid losing their jobs, along with short online articles and maybe the sports pages. Readers read books. A friend of mine who is a poet once said to me, "You know why so much bad poetry is written these days? Because more people are writing poetry than reading it."

If you want to improve your writing, read good authors whose style you enjoy and admire. If they use a word that surprises, delights, or confounds you, take note of it. If you don't know the word, look it up as soon as it's convenient, preferably while you still recall the context. If you do, you'll find yourself using more and more of the 500,000 words available to you in the English language, perhaps moving beyond the 10,000–20,000 word vocabulary of the nonreader to the 20,000–40,000 plus word vocabulary of the reader.

4. **Use a dictionary to look up words you don't know.** I recommend you use two types of dictionaries: online and hard copy. Online dictionaries are quick and easy, but they limit you because you enter and exit on point of contact. Hard-copy dictionaries, especially illustrated dictionaries like the *American Heritage Dictionary*, tempt you to browse and glance at other words. They appeal to your curiosity.

Taking the time to look up words and learning how to spell and pronounce them require discipline, but it's the best way to expand your vocabulary. As you commit them to memory, learn not only their denotation (literal meaning) but also their connotation (mood and feelings). Remember the lesson of Week 1: A word with the wrong connotation can fundamentally alter how a book title strikes a reader.

5. **Move words from your comprehensive to your expressive vocabulary.** You possess two sets of vocabulary: a larger set made up of words you understand (at least vaguely) and a smaller set you know well enough to use. These two vocabulary ranges are called your comprehensive (or passive) vocabulary and your expressive (or active) vocabulary. To move a word

from your larger comprehensive range to your smaller expressive range, you need to know three things about it: how to define, pronounce, and spell it. As you work to move a word to your expressive range, engage your muscle memory. Say the word out loud. Move your mouth. And then look for occasions to use it.

You'll know that a word has become part of your expressive vocabulary when, in seeking to express a thought, the word pops into your mind. When a word comes to you without conscious effort, give yourself a pat on the back, snarf down a chocolate sundae, or go for a celebratory run.

With each word added to your expressive vocabulary, you accomplish something important to your makeup as a fully developed human being. You change how your mind works. Somewhere deep inside, a new synapse has been formed. Think of every word acquired as a personal victory. You can now speak and write more precisely. You can also think certain thoughts that were unavailable to you until you learned the language needed to formulate them.

6. **Be systematic.** If you're serious about improving your vocabulary, set a specific goal. Learn one new word a week, maintain a list, and review your list weekly or at least monthly. Look away from your list, and see how many words you can write or recite from memory. To take it one step further, write down the sentences in which you heard the words. Make up a shorter list of favorite words, ones you'll keep at the top of your mind and look for opportunities to use judiciously.

Whatever your vocabulary today, work to expand it tomorrow. As you do, remember your goal is not to show off. Your goal is to connect with your reader.

EXERCISES

1. Is your vocabulary limited or expansive?

Here's a quick assessment. Fill in the blank.

a. I like many types of music, literature, and people. I guess you could say my tastes are _____.

b. I was surprised when he asked for a public vote on such a delicate matter without first talking privately with each board member. Usually he is more _____.

c. Although he knew the stakes were high, he answered every question with poise and _____.

(Card, please.)

As a rough approximation I would say if you thought of the words *eclectic*, *circumspect*, and *aplomb*, you have a broad vocabulary; if you didn't, you have a limited one.

2. Fill in the blanks in the sentences below with words that capture the intended meaning more precisely than the words in square brackets.

a. My boss, who is capable and organized, is [good] at managing multiple deadlines.

b. You can't have effective writing without careful editing. The two are [solidly] linked.

c. Everyone makes minor mistakes, but to misspell your boss's name is a(n) [really serious] error.

Did the following words occur to you: *adept*, *inextricably*, and *egregious*?

Other words might serve equally well, but do you know those three? Can you use them comfortably—that is, can you spell, define, and pronounce them?

Here are another three sentences to test your vocabulary.

a. I've been working on this report for a week, so I want you to give it more than a [quick or superficial] look.

b. His harsh views seem [not to fit] with his friendly manner.

c. My colleague works hard and efficiently; his output is [really awesome].

Do you know the words *cursory*, *incongruous*, and *prodigious*?

One more set.

a. To say you're sorry in a way that casts blame elsewhere is [insincere or calculating].

b. His platform contains many points, but three—social justice, environmental integrity, and economic prosperity—are [prominent].

    c. We drove all over town running errands on our way to the airport. In the future I would prefer a less [roundabout] route.

Did the following words occur to you: *disingenuous, salient,* and *circuitous*?

3. I have a friend who is a writer and high school English teacher. At one of our monthly writers' group meetings, she told me a story about her daughter Maddy, whose teacher asked his ninth graders to write a short story mimicking the style of Edgar Allan Poe for a class contest.

Maddy decided to write about a man who collected "dolls" in an old farmhouse that were revealed to be the bodies of women he had murdered. When the man's brother discovered the gruesome collection, he burned the farmhouse to the ground.

Maddy took a novel approach to drafting her story. Realizing she knew few of the words Poe used, she compiled a list of big, polysyllabic words and incorporated them into her narrative.

Underline the big words in each of the following sentences that you think Maddy intentionally worked into her story. (Hint: There are three in sentence [c] and two in sentence [e].)

    a. I then made my way through the vacant and familiar boulevards to the domicile of my boyhood.

    b. The floor was worn and scratched, the couch was matted and torn, the walls were a dank grey, and the table was potted and lacerated.

    c. My brother was victim to some peculiarities of nature; throughout his life he would grow infatuated with certain objects for no precise reason, and he had evermore kept his living quarters in pristine condition.

    d. When I arrived at the door of the capacious wooden house, I noticed what I assumed to be a Latin quote, *bene decessit*.

    e. At nightfall, I traipsed to the farmhouse encompassing the dolls.

Did you underline (a) *domicile*; (b) *lacerated*; (c) *peculiarities, infatuated,* and *pristine*; (d) *capacious*; and (e) *traipsed* and *encompassing*?

I loved Maddy's story, and I was impressed by her creative approach to expanding her vocabulary, an approach you might want to emulate. To my ear, some of her big words seemed a tad forced, but my opinion is not the one that counts here.

Maddy's story was voted best in her grade by her classmates.

4. Look up every word you don't know in this book. Make a list of those words, and start using them when you speak and write.

✳ A FURTHER THOUGHT: BROAD VOCABULARY COMPLEMENTS ANALYTICAL WRITING

Use plain language. Write simply. Avoid fancy words. Good writing is clear writing—plain and simple.

But if plain, simple words are the only ones writers should use, why bother to develop a broad vocabulary? What's the point of learning big words if little ones are acceptable?

Ah, the writer's dilemma. How does one balance the need to be understood by readers at all levels of ability against the desire to use language that most precisely captures the intended meaning? Doesn't dumbing down the language also entail dumbing down the complexity and nuance of thought?

In many instances, of course, choosing between simple language and precise language is a false dilemma. The simpler words *are* the more precise words. Compare "It is imperative that we effectuate a resolution to this dilemma" with "We need to resolve this dilemma." Here, the simpler language is not only more precise but also more succinct and emphatic.

But that leaves us with the suggestion that simpler language is *necessarily* better than complex language—and that leads to the unsettling notion that over time our use of language might become reductive or simplified to the point that it is incapable of expressing complex, nuanced thought.

So when *is* complex language preferable to simple language? If one mark of a good communicator is a broad vocabulary, when does the communicator get to use all the big words he or she has gathered so assiduously?

The answer has to do with the three basic components of all writing: your subject, your audience, and the occasion. The complexity of your language (or the breadth of your expressive range) depends on the nature of your objective, the sophistication of your reader, and the complexity of your material. A message rescheduling a meeting obviously calls for simpler language than a proposal advocating a new marketing strategy or a position paper calling for technical refinements in the dephosphorization of taconite pellets.

One type of writing in which a broad and varied vocabulary is undeniably advantageous is analytical or critical writing. I was reminded of this the weekend I spent in East Brunswick, New Jersey, along with 520 other writing instructors reading some 120,000 essays written by some 60,000 takers of the Graduate Management Admissions Test (GMAT).

The GMAT is the instrument used by some 1,300 graduate schools of management to predict the first-year academic performance of applicants. In response to complaints from the business community that management schools were awarding MBAs to people who lacked sophisticated communication skills, the Graduate Management Admission Council added a written component to its test.

The new analytical writing assessment includes two writing tasks: a general issue to be discussed and an argument to be analyzed. Limited to thirty minutes per response, test takers are asked to consider the complexity of an issue or opinion, to analyze what is or is not compelling or logically convincing, and to discuss what, if anything, would make the argument more sound or persuasive.

In other words, the MBA hopefuls are asked to do what executives are called on to do nearly every day: to analyze a situation quickly and to write clearly.

In reading and scoring more than six hundred of their responses, I noticed a pattern: Test takers who used words such as *applicable, cognizant, compelling, conversant, corroborate, bolster, inference, irrefutable, pertain, plausible, premise, substantiate, specious, spurious,* and *unwarranted* scored better than those who displayed a more limited vocabulary.

It's not that the big words themselves carried the argument but that the writers who used them had command of an analytical vocabulary that enabled them to think and write with more precision, depth, and cogency.

Vocabulary counts.

KNOW WHEN TO USE A TWO-BIT WORD

We're known by our words. We stand by them, or we hide behind them. We value them and choose them carefully, or we toss them out like the plastic bags that litter our landscape. Communicating—conveying information clearly, revealing our most personal thoughts and aspirations, connecting with others—depends on our choice of words.

How effectively do you use your words? Do you distinguish yourself by your precision, range, and eloquence? Do you embarrass yourself by making common errors such as saying *"flaunting* the rules" when you mean *flouting* them? Or do you fall somewhere in between—do you settle for the obvious and the mundane rather than the word that truly captures your thought?

You can move beyond plain to memorable writing, but only if you have the vocabulary to go from plain/mundane/banal/pedestrian/quotidian words to memorable and exciting ones. How would you rank yourself according to the following five levels of language proficiency?

1. **Incorrect.** You don't know the difference between *poring* over your notes and *pouring* over them.
2. **Inexact.** You regularly use words that aren't quite right, such as "I'm grossed out by your dishonesty."
3. **Plain.** You settle for the standard and clichéd, such as "I'm sick and tired of your dishonesty."

4. **Apt.** You go beyond the banal to find something fresh and more precise, such as "I'm appalled by your dishonesty."
5. **Eloquent.** Your word choice seems perfect for your subject, your audience, and the occasion.

Remember in making this assessment that big words are not always better. First you must apprehend the word; then you must be cognizant of when to utilize it.

If you apply for admission to a graduate program, you want to be admitted; you don't *desire* to be admitted. If a cheetah is chasing a zebra, it's trying to kill it, not *attempting to terminate its life* nor *attempting to effect a termination of its earthly existence.* If it's an everyday thought, use an everyday word. Or as Garrison Keillor would say, "You don't want a fifty-dollar haircut on a fifty-cent head." Often, a two-bit word will do.

Still (nevertheless), you need a broad vocabulary so that you can express yourself in a full range of settings, from informal to formal, from ordinary to exceptional, from routine to literary. The more words you know, the more choices are available to you.

In a business setting, you shouldn't be *looking to* improve profits; you should be *hoping to* improve profits or *working to* improve profits or *committed to improving* profits. If you're giving a commencement address, you shouldn't be talking about *getting ready* for the future; you should be talking about *preparing* for the future or *anticipating* the future. When you're defending your client in a court of law, you should be talking to the jury about evidence that *clears* your client but writing to the judge about *exculpatory* evidence.

If your primary reason for choosing a word is to impress your reader, it's probably the wrong word. If you choose a word based on a careful assessment of what's appropriate for the subject, audience, and occasion, it's probably the right word. And the more options you have, the more likely you'll write with clarity and precision.

If you think word choice is irrelevant to your everyday life, think again. The other day I was walking with a friend who stopped to pick up after his dog. When we looped back to the scene of the deposit, he said, "Watch your step."

"Why?" I asked. "Didn't you pick up the poop?"

"I did," he said, "but not every morsel."

As you can imagine, I was dismayed by his choice of words.

Morsel is associated with … sorry. Good taste prevents me from completing my thought. Had my friend taken a moment to consider his choice of words, he might have come up with something less gross, offensive, or unsavory. He might have said, "I may have left *some small pieces*," or "There may be a bit of *residue*." Or even "Once contaminated, forever compromised."

From the coarsest language to the most elevated diction, word choice matters. Have the courage and the conviction—as well as the nimbleness and the creativity—to be as elegant, gracious, tender, irreverent, forceful, shocking, vulgar, and obscene as the occasion warrants.

And don't forget: Although you need a broad vocabulary, sometimes the two-bit word is best.

 **EXERCISES**

1. Let's play a little game.

I'll give you three sentences. The first illustrates wordiness, the second illustrates clichéd word choice, and the third illustrates precise command of language.

    a. It goes without saying that the concern that has been expressed in regard to a decline in the quality of customer service is unquestionably nebulous and without merit.

    b. The concern over customer service is a bunch of hot air.

    c. The concern over customer service is unwarranted.

Now, to make it more interesting, I'll change the order and you identify which sentence illustrates which style (wordy, clichéd, or precise). Ready?

    a. You shouldn't have let the cat out of the bag.

    b. You should have talked with me before announcing your retirement.

    c. To announce your impending retirement prior to dialoguing with me was both ill-advised and precipitous.

Do you agree that the sentences were clichéd, precise, and wordy, in that order?

Those examples are obvious. Now identify the three different styles in sentences whose characteristics are less pronounced. Which is wordy, clichéd, and precise?

    a. The survey results are skewed.

    b. The survey results are spurious and specious.

    c. The survey results boggle the mind.

What do you say? I say precise, wordy, and clichéd.

2. For practice in moving from the mundane to the apt and eloquent, consider the following description of Lake Vermilion. I've taken a sentence from the opening of George Erickson's *True North: Exploring the Great Wilderness by Bush Plane* and replaced the interesting word choices with ordinary language.

> Rising from the depths, schools of whitefish *make* watery ringlets where the last of the mayflies *fall down*.

How might you replace the ordinary words *make* and *fall down*?

(Card, please.)

Here are Erickson's choices.

> Rising from the depths, schools of whitefish *lip* watery ringlets where the last of the mayflies *flutter* down.

Lip and *flutter*. They're not showy, but they're right.

Next, replace the nondescript words in the following sentence with more vivid, action-oriented language.

> On Great Slave Lake, a diesel-driven barge is *encountering* a cold northeasterly wind as it *moves* toward a tiny town called Snowdrift and an even more remote weather station named Reliance.

Here's how Erickson wrote the sentence.

> On Great Slave Lake, a diesel-driven barge is *fighting* a cold northeasterly wind as it *struggles* toward a tiny town called Snowdrift and an even more remote weather station named Reliance.

Look again at the place names: *Great Slave Lake, Snowdrift, Reliance.* Don't you suspect that Erickson chose them because they're colorful?

✳ A FURTHER THOUGHT: A BAD-NEWS MEETING WITH THE BOSS

Taking our seats at the long, narrow conference table, we wondered why our boss had called a special meeting. Special meetings usually meant bad news.

At the head of the table sat our boss, a bald man with two incongruous tufts of hair protruding high above his ears. He cleared his throat. No one seemed to notice.

He cleared his throat again, more loudly this time. The individual conversations gradually broke off.

"I've been thinking about how to help you improve your vocabularies," he said. He paused for emphasis.

A woman with a triangular hairdo groaned. A young man with round glasses and a curled-up tie immediately nodded off, his head falling over his chest.

"I want to excoriate you to learn a new word every week," he said.

"You mean *encourage*," snapped the woman with the triangular hair. "*Excoriate* means 'to censure scathingly.' You might *excoriate* someone for coming up with dim-witted ideas or for egregiously wasting people's time by convening pointless meetings, but you would *encourage* them to learn a new word every week."

"That may be what *you* mean by *excoriate*, but when *I* use *excoriate* it means *encourage*," he said in a defiant tone.

"Your flaccid mind is exceeded only by your tenuous grasp of reality," she replied.

"Why, thank you."

"Should we decapitate or immolate the insufferable dolt?" asked the gray-haired woman.

"Immolate me," he said before anyone else could speak. "A good boss is often immolated by his employees."

The man with the curled-up tie awoke with a start.

"I don't mean to be impertinent or to denigrate your ideas," he said, "but like Peter Rabbit after eating too much lettuce, I find this meeting soporific." With that, his head fell forward, and he began to snore.

"As an exercise, let's see how many words you can think of for *uncompromising*," said our pointy-haired boss.

"You're talking about *synonyms*," said the woman with the triangular hair.

"I prefer to think of my *synonyms* as *mistakes* or *misguided actions*. So, who wants to begin?"

"How about *inflexible, intractable, unbending,* and *unyielding*?" said a man with only six hairs on his head.

"You forgot *rigid, obstinate, mulish,* and *pigheaded*," said the gray-haired woman.

"Very good," said our pointy-haired boss.

"Now here's a little exercise for *you*," said the man with six hairs. "I'll give you two lists of words used by people who have good vocabularies. The first is made up of forty fairly common words. How many do you know?

"*Anathema, antipathy, banal, bellicose, belligerent, copious, covert, cursory, denigrate, deprecate, eclectic, egregious, enigma, esoteric, facile, feign, gregarious, impetuous, incongruous, indigenous, insidious, inventive, obfuscate, obsequious, obstreperous, odious, onerous, onus, paradigm, pejorative, plethora, prodigious, proffer, profligate, prurient, purport, sanctimonious, surreptitious, visceral,* and *whimsical.*"

When he finished reading his list, he noticed that everyone was watching the man with the curled-up tie. From the man's mouth dangled a filament of spittle, the little ball at its end bouncing up and down like a yo-yo.

"May I have your attention, please?" said our pointy-haired boss, but everyone was watching the bobbing globule. After a while, the gray-haired woman moved the man's water glass beneath it.

"Okay, here's my second list," said the man with six hairs. "It's made up of thirty somewhat less common words:

"*Apogee, atavistic, bibulous, copacetic, demure, desultory, diffident, epiphany, excoriate, exigent, exiguous, feckless, flaccid, immolate, inculcate, inveterate, nebulous, paragon, pariah, perfidious, prevaricate, promulgate, propitiate, proscribe, somnolent, stasis, temerity, timorous, truculent,* and *unctuous.*"

Just then the pendulous gob broke free and plopped into the glass. With that, everyone cheered, everyone except our pointy-haired boss and the man with the curled-up tie, who awoke with a start and said, "Who knows a two-syllable word for an annoying person characterized by anal-retentive tendencies?"

"I do," said the gray-haired woman, "but I can't say it in polite company."

USE THE APPROPRIATE LEVEL OF FORMALITY

Operating at the appropriate level of formality is key to your success as a writer. If your tone is too formal, you may seem distant, stiff, stilted, even arrogant. If your tone is too informal, you risk insulting your reader by coming across as inappropriately familiar. For example, you might write, "Dr. Wilbers, I believe you are mistaken" or "Steve, that was really bone-headed." Likewise, you might ask, "Have you dined yet this evening?" or "Didja eat yet?" These statements make the same point, but they're on opposite ends of the formal-informal spectrum.

If you're texting, the shorter, the better. If you're sending an informal e-mail message, the simpler, the better. But for other types of writing, you should use words that fall somewhere in the middle range on the informal/formal continuum: not too plain and not too fancy, but just the right words that reflect the appropriate level of formality. And always when choosing your words—whether ordinary or fancy, mundane or uncommon, quotidian or grandiloquent—you should base your choice on three factors: your subject, your audience, and the occasion.

In most professional settings, you should aim for the middle range of formality (at least when communicating to an external audience), a range that corresponds to Standard Written English or SWE. The middle range for the examples above would be "I think you made an error" and "Have you had your dinner yet?"

The question of formality also applies to transitional words. For example, you might choose the formal *hence* and *thus* or the informal *so*, but if you want to land safely in the middle range, you'll choose *therefore*.

The problem with the commonly used phrase "as per" is that it conveys a stilted, awkwardly formal tone. Compare "as per your request" with "as you requested" and "as per your instructions" with "as you instructed." Likewise, compare "it is my recommendation" with "I recommend" and "it is my belief" with "I believe."

Again, you're more likely to use the appropriate level of formality if you base your choice on three factors: your subject, your audience, and the occasion.

Certain topics and occasions warrant a more serious, deliberate, formal style than others, such as the tone of the President's State of the Union Address as opposed to that of a friendly roast, or the tone of a performance review as opposed to that of a friendly e-mail to a colleague.

You can determine how good you are at adapting your level of formality to your reader, your subject, and the occasion by dividing the following sentences into one of three levels: overly formal, middle range, and too informal.

1. Subsequent to a tumultuous storm featuring thunder and lightning, the Minnehaha Creek brimmed over its banks and the Minnehaha Falls resonated with a reverberating roar.
2. The terrace around Sea Salt Eatery was thronged with pedestrians and bikers watching the mist rise from the falls.
3. Everyone was gaga over what was going down.
4. The scene was like way cool, I mean, like totally random.
5. On the steep hillside beneath the ledge and behind the cascading water sat four thrill-seeking teenagers.
6. Until such time as the luminescence of the setting summer sun was at last extinguished from the western sky, people remained stationary, a community amalgamated by their adoration of the beauty that emanates from nature.

To my ear, sentences 2 and 5 are in the middle range, sentences 1 and 6 are overly formal, and sentences 3 and 4 are too informal. Here are my attempts to find that middle range in sentences 1, 3, 4, and 6.

1. After a huge thunderstorm, the Minnehaha Creek overflowed its banks and the Minnehaha Falls roared.
3. People were enthralled by the spectacle.
4. It was a wonderful scene.
6. Until the last light of day had faded, people lingered, a community united by their love of natural beauty.

There are times, of course, when expression at either end of the formal-informal range is appropriate. For example, no one would fault a Supreme Court justice for writing, "It is the opinion of this court that …" Similarly, your colleagues might appreciate the informality of a spirited "Hey, your presentation rocked!"

But as a rule, aim for the middle. Like Goldilocks, we want the porridge not too hot and not too cold, at least most of the time.

EXERCISES

1. Divide the following sentences into one of three levels: formal, middle range, and informal.

    a. The administration is predicting a gradual but full recovery.

    b. As per our conversation, I deem it imperative that we realize an expeditious resolution to this issue.

    c. We are looking to increase profits big time in the fourth quarter.

    d. You have no right to wiretap my phone without a court order.

    e. I really want to make my goals before I've got to turn in my progress report.

    f. Prior to her arrival at our firm, she endeavored to diminish the obscene disparity in remuneration between wage earners and CEOs.

(Card, please.)

To my ear, sentences (a) and (d) are in the middle range, sentences (b) and (f) are formal, and sentences (c) and (e) are informal.

How would you rewrite sentences (b), (c), (e), and (f) so that their tone falls in the middle range?

Your rewrites may be as good as or better than mine, but here are my attempts to find that middle range.

     b. As we discussed, I think we need to resolve this issue expeditiously.

     c. We anticipate a significant increase in fourth-quarter profits.

     e. I'm committed to achieving my goals before I submit my progress report.

     f. Before joining our firm, she worked to diminish the obscene disparity in pay between wage earners and CEOs.

2. Rewrite four of the following sentences, moving them from "too formal" or "too informal" to the middle range. Two sentences are fine as they are.

     a. My father gesticulated with utter derision at the vehicles bearing Iowa license plates and hauling watercraft on trailers as we overtook them on Highway 200 going in a northerly direction.

     b. "They're crazy to get to the water; they'll even fish in the middle of the day," he said, as if the Iowa Bedouins were so water-mad that a school of walleye could toy with them in the noon heat, while my father coolly appeared at dawn and twilight to make the easy Minnesota-savvy kill.

     c. Laughing his fool head off, he kept pointing out to us the silliness of the Iowans and their pitiful pursuit of anything resembling water.

     d. Our absolute supremacy stemmed from our weather and the historical background of our weather: The glacier had given us these beautiful pristine lakes, my father expounded.

     e. The glacier receded and—Paradise, with lakes.

(Card, please.)

Sentences (b) and (e) are in the middle range. How did you rewrite sentences (a), (c), and (d)?

Here's how Patricia Hampl wrote all six sentences in *A Romantic Education*.

     a. My father pointed with derision at the cars with Iowa license plates, hauling boats on trailers behind them, as we passed them on Highway 200 going north.

     b. "They're crazy to get to the water, they'll even fish in the middle of the day," he said, as if the Iowa Bedouins were so water-mad that a school of walleye could toy with them in the noon heat, while my father coolly appeared at dawn and twilight to make the easy Minnesota-savvy kill.

c. He pointed out to us, over and over, the folly of the Iowans and their pathetic pursuit of standing water.

d. Our supremacy came from our weather, and the history of our weather: the glacier had given us these beautiful clear lakes, my father explained.

e. The glacier receded and—Paradise, with lakes.

✳ A FURTHER THOUGHT: GO TO BED WITH A GOOD DICTIONARY

I have a problem. Many people think I look like ... well, it's embarrassing.

It's true that my mother would read to me from the dictionary at night. Oh, the memories I have of sitting on her lap, tired from a day of climbing trees or building forts, sometimes one or both brothers snuggling in next to me, her soft voice resonating from her chest. I especially loved when she would read the *m* words—marvelous, melodious, mellifluous words such as *meringue, munchkin, multitudinous,* and *murgatroid*.

To this day I take *The American Heritage Dictionary* to bed with me. There's nothing odd about that. Lots of people like to read in bed.

What I don't understand is why so many people think I *am* a dictionary. My head may be somewhat long and rectangular, and my skull may be a little hard (my wife would say thick), but I don't think I look anything like a dictionary.

Nevertheless, nearly once a week someone writes, "What is the correct form of the verb? Should it be 'I *sunk* down in my chair' or 'I *sank* down in my chair'?" "Is it 'I *dived* into the pool' or 'I *dove* into the pool'?"

The answers, of course, are in the dictionary. In fact, lots of neat things are in the dictionary, and one of the neatest things is guidance regarding the four basic forms of verbs.

First the dictionary lists the present tense of the verb, *take*, then the past tense, *took*, the past participle, *taken* (if it differs from the past tense), and then the present participle, *taking*.

Don't let the terminology throw you. Present and past tenses are just what they sound like. Past participles are used with helping verbs or auxiliary verbs to form different types of past and future tenses, as in *I have taken, I had taken, I will have taken*. Present participles, which are formed by adding *-ing* to the base form, indicate continuing action, as in *I am taking* or *I will be taking*.

Some verbs are regular; that is, they form their past tense and past participle simply by adding *-ed* to the base form, as in *I talk, I talked, I have talked*. What confuses many people, however, is that many English verbs are irregular; that is, they make the past tense and the past participle by changing their base form, as in *I write, I wrote, I had written*. To make matters worse, these past tense forms often have alternate versions, such as *dived* and *dove*.

But do not despair. You can always write to me and ask which form is preferred. Or you can simply open the dictionary, where you'll find the preferred form followed by the nonpreferred form, as in *sink, sank* or *sunk, sunk, sinking; dive, dived* or *dove, dived, diving; spell, spelled* or *spelt, spelling*.

Well, it's getting late and I've had a hard day, what with the unkind jokes about my appearance and all. Think I'll climb into bed and cuddle up with my *Merriam-Webster's Collegiate*.

RECOGNIZE BOTH GENDERS IN YOUR WRITING

In their introduction to the 1988 edition of *The Handbook of Nonsexist Writing*, Casey Miller and Kate Swift wrote:

> Only recently have we become aware that conventional English usage, including the generic use of masculine-gender words, often obscures the actions, the contributions, and sometimes the very presence of women. Turning our backs on that insight is an option, of course, but it is an option like teaching children that the world is flat.

These days our attention has shifted from debating whether biased language is a problem to trying to find the most natural, least contrived ways to write inclusively.

Over time, we have devised various methods of recognizing both genders in our writing, some more graceful than others. Here are some of the better options.

1. **Use plural pronouns.** Change "A doctor treats his patients well" to "Doctors treat their patients well."
2. **Eliminate the masculine pronoun.** Change "A doctor treats his patients well" to "A doctor treats patients well." Likewise, change "When a patient complains, he deserves a respectful response" to "A patient who complains deserves a respectful response."
3. **Replace the masculine pronoun with an article (*a, an,* or *the*).** Write, "A doctor treats a patient well."

4. **Use genderless words such as *person* and *individual*.** Change "A doctor is considerate. He treats patients well" to "A doctor is a considerate person who treats patients well" or "A doctor who treats patients well is a considerate person."

5. **Use the second person.** Write, "As a doctor, you treat your patients well."

6. **Use the "singular *they* and *their*" with indefinite words and pronouns such as *every, any, everyone,* and *anybody*.** Change "Every doctor knows he should treat his patients well" to "Every doctor knows they should treat their patients well."

7. **Use *he or she*.** As a last resort, write, "A doctor treats his or her patients well."

Every writer must know their audience and work with the idiosyncrasies of their language. I mean every writer must know *his* audience and work with the idiosyncrasies of *her* language. Or should that be *his/her* audience and *his/her* language?

And on that note, I believe that the practices illustrated in those last two sentences should be avoided because they're awkward and distracting. The first one, alternating between masculine and feminine references, draws attention to itself. Furthermore, when a sentence is quoted out of context, as in "A murderer deserves to be punished for her crimes," it may strike the reader as odd, particularly in this example, since the majority of murderers are male.

The second practice is the use of slashed constructions ("A doctor should treat his/her patients well because he/she is considerate"). To my ear, this type of shorthand seems more appropriate on forms than in written discourse.

So why are we searching for ways to be inclusive? Why does this issue arise in the English language?

The problem is that traditional grammar calls for the third-person singular *his, hers,* or *its* in reference to a singular noun or pronoun. English has no third-person singular personal pronoun that is inclusive of both genders.

In more formal times, one could avoid writing "Everyone has a right to *his* opinion" by writing "One has a right to *one's* opinion," but *one* tends to sound stuffy by today's standards. (But look again at my sentence. I used *one* as its subject, and I'm guessing it sounded all right to you. Still, "One has a right to one's opinion" is a bit much.)

You should be aware, however, that not everyone accepts the use of the "singular *they* and *their*" with indefinite words (recommendation 6). According to *The Associated Press Stylebook*, "*Everyone* takes singular verbs and pronouns." But that's a rule I think you should break. Because "Everyone has a right to his opinion" is exclusive and "Everyone has a right to his or her opinion" is awkward, I recommend you use the "singular *they* and *their*," as in "Everyone has a right to their opinion."

Mixing singular and plural references with indefinite pronouns such as *anyone* and *everyone* seems to me an easy, defensible solution to the lack of an inclusive third-person personal pronoun in English. Though incorrect according to traditional grammar, the "singular *they* and *their*" do no harm. And if someone challenges you, you can always tell them (tell *them*, not *him* or *her*) that you're following the practice of many classic writers, including Shakespeare, George Eliot, and Walt Whitman.

Even so, you can usually find ways to avoid mixing a singular pronoun (*everyone*) and a plural pronoun (*their*). For example, you could change "If anyone tells you otherwise, they're lying" to "Anyone who tells you otherwise is lying."

The trouble with these solutions is that they sometimes produce constructions that are socially more acceptable but stylistically less emphatic. To appreciate the loss, one has only to compare the original version of E.B. White's declaration, "Full of his beliefs, sustained and elevated by the power of his purpose, armed with the rules of grammar, the writer is ready for exposure," with the inclusive version, "Full of their beliefs, sustained and elevated by the power of their purpose, armed with the rules of grammar, writers are ready for exposure."

Read both versions out loud. As you can hear, the masculine singular *his beliefs* and *his purpose* used in reference to *the writer* makes White's declaration sound more precise, definitive, and authoritative than the version with plural references.

So what should you do when inclusive language dulls the stylistic edge of a poignant but exclusive statement?

Fortunately, the dilemma is fairly uncommon. You can almost always find an inclusive way of saying something that sounds as precise and natural as the exclusive alternative. And in those rare instances when there's a stylistic price to be paid, every writer must do what they think best.

But I say be inclusive.

1. Apply the following techniques to eliminate the exclusive use of masculine pronouns in the following sentences.

 a. Use plural pronouns: "A skydiver is responsible for folding his own parachute."

 b. Eliminate the masculine pronoun: "A skydiver feels his pulse quicken when exiting the plane and climbing onto the strut."

  or "When a skydiver asks the pilot about the black clouds on the horizon, he expects an informed response."

 c. Replace the masculine pronoun with an article (*a*, *an*, or *the*): "A skydiver listens carefully to his jump master."

 d. Use genderless words such as *person* and *individual*: "A skydiver is conscientious. He always follows protocol."

 e. Use the second person: "A trained skydiver knows that if his chute doesn't open, he will hit the ground at 160 miles per hour."

 f. Use the "singular *they* and *their*" with indefinite words and pronouns such as *every*, *any*, *everyone*, and *anybody*: "If landing on a building or other object cannot be avoided, every skydiver knows to flare his chute at ten feet above the first point of contact and strike the object feet first. If the object is a cow, he also says, 'I'm sorry.'"

Here's how you might have rewritten the sentences.

 a. Skydivers are responsible for folding their own parachutes.

 b. A skydiver's pulse quickens when exiting the plane and climbing onto the strut.

  or A skydiver who asks the pilot about the black clouds on the horizon expects an informed response.

 c. A skydiver listens carefully to the jump master.

 d. A skydiver is a conscientious person who always follows protocol.

 e. As a trained skydiver, you know if your chute doesn't open, you will hit the ground at 160 miles per hour.

f. If landing on a building or other object cannot be avoided, every skydiver knows to flare their chute at ten feet above the first point of contact and strike the object feet first. If the object is a cow, bull, or steer, they also say, "I'm sorry."

2. See if you can eliminate more subtle forms of bias. Can you identify and correct the problem in each of the following sentences?

    a. The great American poet Walt Whitman volunteered as a male nurse during the Civil War.

    b. Susan is a woman who knows how to get things done.

    c. Natalie Cole is a talented black vocalist.

    d. In recent years, politicians have found it increasingly difficult to win elections against women.

    e. A US citizen is more accepting of immigrants from Canada and northern Europe than from Mexico and Africa.

    f. Every kid in Canada grows up dreaming of playing in the NHL one day.

Sentences (a), (b), and (c) contain what Miller and Swift call "gratuitous modifiers" (which are not as exciting as they sound). Gratuitous modifiers are references to attributes such as sex and race when those attributes are irrelevant.

Sentence (a) suggests that the writer is so uncomfortable with a man working as a nurse that the writer feels compelled to call attention to Whitman's gender. In sentence (b) the phrase "a woman who" evokes the reader's attitudes about women when those attitudes have nothing to do with the point being made. Sentence (c) is ambiguous: Is Cole's talent being assessed in comparison to all vocalists or only to black vocalists? In each case, the gratuitous reference to gender or race should be eliminated.

Sentences (d), (e), and (f) (based on examples from Anne Stilman's *Grammatically Correct*) suggest that all politicians are male, all US citizens are white, and all Canadian kids are boys (although in sentence (f) it could be argued that girls also dream of playing in the NHL one day).

Those were tricky, weren't they?

DELETE *THAT* FOR RHYTHM AND FLOW; RETAIN *THAT* FOR CLARITY

When should you use *that,* and when should you delete it?

We're certainly fond of that word, as exemplified by how often it appears in our everyday language and idiomatic expressions. *That* said. Leave it at *that.* I didn't mean *that.* He was their adviser, if he could be called *that.* The dress was out of style and expensive at *that.* He said we could buy if we liked, so we did just *that.* Well, how do you like *that*? For all *that.* How's *that*? Take *that.* And *that.* And *that,* and *that,* and *that.*

So when should you use *that,* and when should you delete it?

In addition to serving as filler in our common idiomatic expressions, *that* has many grammatical uses. *That* may function as a demonstrative pronoun ("That is my report"), a demonstrative adjective ("You better keep an eye on that man"), a demonstrative adverb ("I didn't realize she was that angry"), a relative pronoun ("The quality that impresses me most is honesty"), and a conjunction introducing a clause serving as the object of a verb ("I heard that you were traveling to Europe").

It is in the latter two uses of *that* that *that* may be omitted to good effect: "The report that was approved by the board was written by Sally" and "I was told that you are an experienced accountant."

Setting aside the grammatical terms, I'll say it in plain English: Delete *that* for brevity; retain *that* for clarity.

If deleting *that* compresses the sentence in a way that improves its flow and rhythm, take it out. Compare "I recommend that you take my advice" with "I recommend you take my advice."

If deleting *that* creates ambiguity or momentarily misleads the reader, leave it in. Compare "The attorney believed her client was guilty" with "The attorney believed that her client was guilty." In the first version, the verb *believed* leads the reader to think the attorney believed her client was innocent, and the word *guilty* comes as a surprise. In the second version, "The attorney believed that her client was guilty," the word *that* prevents the reader from coming to a false conclusion. In other words, with certain verbs like *believed*, the word *that* should be retained to prevent ambiguity.

So delete *that* for brevity; retain *that* for clarity.

To practice determining when to delete *that* and when to retain it, consider the five sentences below. When would you delete *that*? When would you retain it?

1. I recommend that we wear our stiletto heels tonight.
2. She told me that she would proofread my report.
3. I love the green mushy stuff that they serve for dessert.
4. I believe that my friend, who usually tells the truth, misrepresented the facts.
5. I recognize that your friend may be right.

Your use of *that* is a matter of style and personal preference, so your choices may differ from mine, but in the five sentences above, I would delete *that* in the first three sentences; I would retain *that* in the last two sentences.

Here's a tip from Patricia O'Conner. In *Woe Is I: The Grammarphobe's Guide to Better English in Plain English*, she advises writers to retain *that* after "thinking" verbs such as *know, believe, decide,* and *realize.* For example, "I know that you are telling the truth" and "I believe that her willingness to work hard was responsible for her success." You also may find it useful to retain *that* when offering an aside, as in "He admitted that, without her companionship, he was lonely."

Consider these sentences by well-known authors. Compare your decision to delete or retain *that* with theirs.

1. "I learned long ago that being Lewis Carroll was infinitely more exciting than being Alice." Joyce Carol Oates retained *that*; I also would retain it.

2. "All you have to do is write one true sentence. Write the truest sentence that you know." Ernest Hemingway retained *that*; I would delete it.

3. "Everywhere I go, I'm asked if I think universities stifle writers. My opinion is that they don't stifle enough of them." Flannery O'Connor retained *that* in the second sentence; I would delete it.

4. "The beautiful part of writing is that you don't have to get it right the first time, unlike, say, a brain surgeon." Robert Cormier retained *that*; I think I would delete it.

5. Here's a tough one: "Surely it was time someone invented a new plot, or that the author came out from the bushes." Virginia Woolf uses a single *that* in her two-part statement; for the sake of balance and symmetry, I would use two *thats*: "Surely it was time [that] someone invented a new plot, or that the author came out from the bushes."

How can you be certain that deleting *that* improves the flow and rhythm of a sentence or that retaining *that* improves clarity? You can't. But trust your ear. It's usually pretty reliable.

EXERCISES

1. Add *that* where it is needed to avoid ambiguity, and delete it where it is superfluous.

   a. I worry the sore on my finger, as I keep picking it, will get infected.

   b. I love that green mushy stuff that they serve for dessert, but I suspect my illness was caused by eating it.

   c. I believe the nurse, who had dark red lips, was flirting with me.

   d. He promised that he would be gentle as he guided the long needle into my vein.

   e. "Take two of these at bedtime," she said in a voice that she meant to sound like Lauren Bacall's, "and call me in the morning."

Here's where I think *that* should be added and deleted from those sentences.

a. I worry *that* the sore on my finger, as I keep picking it, will get infected.

b. I still love that green mushy stuff [that] they serve for dessert, but I suspect [that] my illness was caused by eating it.

c. I believe *that* the nurse, who had dark red lips, was flirting with me.

d. He promised [that] he would be gentle as he guided the long needle into my vein.

e. "Take two of these at bedtime," she said in a voice [that] she meant to sound like Lauren Bacall's, "and call me in the morning."

✳ A FURTHER THOUGHT: WATCH OUT FOR THAT *THAT* THAT THAT WRITER ASKED ABOUT

Which. Not the most beautiful word in the English language. It rhymes with *itch*, which makes me want to scratch just thinking about it.

Then there's *that*, no beauty itself, a flat-sounding word if ever there was one.

Now I wouldn't say that that *that* that that sentence contains is necessarily problematic, but I do think that that *that* that this sentence contains raises some interesting questions—that is, I'm concerned not with that *that* in that sentence, but with that *that* in *this* one. The third *that*, to be exact.

Here's the point: *That* is the preferred choice.

Some writers, however, use *which* in place of *that*, as in "I wouldn't say that that *that which* that sentence contains is necessarily problematic" rather than "I wouldn't say that that *that that* that sentence contains is necessarily problematic."

Do you follow me?

The question for the everyday writer is this: when to use *which* and when to use *that*.

Let's keep it simple. *Which* and *that* are pronouns. Pronouns are words that refer to persons or things, as in "*She* wrote the proposal" and "*It* was accepted by the board." Pronouns take the place of nouns or other pronouns.

Certain pronouns perform special functions. Some pronouns—such as *his*, *hers*, and *its*—indicate possession, so they're called "possessive pronouns."

Other pronouns—such as *everyone*, *someone*, and *anybody*—leave the identity of their objects unspecified, so they're called "indefinite pronouns."

Other pronouns—such as *this*, *that*, *these*, and *those*—specify or single out the person or thing referred to, as in "She wrote *this* proposal, not *that* proposal." Because they demonstrate which person or thing we're talking about—"Not *this* one, but *that* one"—they're called "demonstrative pronouns."

Still others—such as *which*, *who*, and *that*—introduce a clause, or a group of words containing a subject and a verb, as in "She wrote the proposal *that* the board accepted." Because these introducing pronouns link or relate the clause to the person or thing they refer to—as in "The proposal *that* she wrote" and "The person *who* wrote the proposal"— they're called "relative pronouns."

Are you still with me?

Now for the good part. Relative pronouns come in two varieties: Some *identify* or *define* the person or thing they refer to; others *describe* the person or thing they refer to.

Although not all grammarians and stylists agree on this next point, *that* should be used to introduce clauses that identify, as in "The proposal *that* Susan wrote was accepted by the board; the proposal *that* John wrote was rejected." *Which* should be used to introduce clauses that merely describe an already identified subject, as in "The proposal, *which* Susan wrote, was accepted by the board."

Do you see the difference?

Because *that* defines, narrows, or limits a broader category, it's called a "*restrictive* pronoun." Because *which* describes rather than identifies or defines, it's called a "*nonrestrictive* pronoun."

In other words, these relative pronouns may be restrictive or nonrestrictive according to their function. Restrictive pronouns define; nonrestrictive pronouns describe. The pronoun that defines takes no commas. The pronoun *which*, which describes, does take commas.

AVOID INDIRECT AND INDEFINITE NEGATIVES

If you want to write with emphasis, avoid indirect and indefinite negatives.

Let's take indirect negatives first.

As I discussed in *Keys to Great Writing*, indirect negatives use the word *not* linked to a positive word when a negative word is available. For example, the positive form of the adjective *excusable* has a negative form, *inexcusable*. Compare "His campaign tactics were not excusable" with "His campaign tactics were inexcusable." Likewise, compare "Her version of what transpired was not constrained by the facts" with "Her version of what transpired was unconstrained by the facts."

Direct negatives make the point more succinctly and emphatically than indirect negatives. Rather than *not supportive*, write *unsupportive*. Rather than *not agree*, write *disagree*. Rather than *not dissimilar*, write *similar*.

With this pattern in mind, how would you revise the following sentences?

1. His explanation was not comprehensible.
2. Her remark was not appropriate.
3. My daughter's enthusiasm is not repressible.
4. Those personal attacks were not necessary.

As you look for opportunities to turn indirect negatives into direct negatives, keep in mind some exceptions and special cases.

First, sometimes an indirect negative can be made into a direct negative not by adding a prefix (*in-*, *ir-*, or *un-*) to the beginning of the word but by adding the suffix *-less* to the end of the word. Consider "Omit words that are not needed" and "Omit needless words."

Second, not every negative form of a word has a positive counterpart in common usage (*incontrovertible* but not *controvertible*, *uncouth* but not *couth*, *inscrutable* but not *scrutable*), but many do (*undeterred/deterred*; *unmanageable/ manageable*; *unorthodox/orthodox*).

Third, some words will fool you. Try changing this indirect negative to an *in-* word: "Our boss's contribution was not valuable." Doesn't work.

And fourth, sometimes emphasis depends on context. In certain situations the indirect negative might be preferable to the direct negative.

For example, which of the following statements do you think is more emphatic?

1. I'm not happy about your forgetting to do the dishes.
2. I'm unhappy about your forgetting to do the dishes.

When the first sentence is spoken to me by my wife, I find it more emphatic than the second.

A second construction to avoid is indefinite negatives. As the name implies, indefinite negatives use the word *not* linked to an indefinite pronoun such as *any, anyone, anybody, some, someone,* and *somebody*. Compare, for example, "I didn't find anything" with "I found nothing."

Definite negatives are more emphatic (and slightly more formal). Compare "We didn't break any laws" with "We broke no laws."

You'll write with more emphasis if you replace indefinite expressions such as *not any, not anything, not many, not much,* and *not ever* with more definite words such as *no, nothing, few, little,* and *never*.

Rather than "I don't remember anything about you," write, "I remember nothing about you." Rather than "I don't know much about history," write, "I know little about history" (unless you're Sam Cooke).

With this technique in mind, consider the following sentences and their revised versions.

> **Original:** There's not any reason for this vitriol.
> **Revised:** There's no reason for this vitriol.
>
> **Original:** She has not much patience for carelessness.
> **Revised:** She has no patience for carelessness.

Original: I don't know anything about this.
Revised: I know nothing about this.

Original: There isn't anything fun about this economic crisis.
Revised: There is nothing fun about this economic crisis.

To write with emphasis, be definite. Avoid indirect and indefinite negatives.

EXERCISES

1. Eliminate the indirect negatives from these sentences.
   a. "Yes," she whispers, not convinced.
   b. "You aren't ever going to let me take him again," she said.
   c. It is the opposite of the easiest thing in the world, and it is my practice. But such Zen doesn't seem possible now.
   d. Her intuition is not diminished.

Here's how Nancy Paddock wrote those sentences in *A Song at Twilight: Of Alzheimer's and Love*.
   a. "Yes," she whispers, unconvinced.
   b. "You're never going to let me take him again," she said.
   c. It is the hardest thing in the world, and it is my practice. But such Zen seems impossible now.
   d. Her intuition is undiminished.

2. Eliminate the indefinite negatives from these sentences.
   a. Years ago, at a time when my mother's problems could not be denied any longer, I found the broken strands of a pearl necklace in the chaos of her vanity drawer.
   b. We trust our perceptions, but there aren't any two people who share the same experience.
   c. And then, dripping and wrapped in towels, refreshed, we climb back into the old gray Plymouth and head home to bed—without any idea of the dry years to come.

    d. Conflicts of the past dissolve in a new way ... that I call "timeless time": living in the present moment without any agenda, just doing what presents itself.

    e. "Did we pay for them?" Mama asks anxiously. "It isn't any fun otherwise."

Here's how Paddock wrote those sentences.

    a. Years ago, at a time when my mother's problems could no longer be denied, I found the broken strands of a pearl necklace in the chaos of her vanity drawer.

    b. We trust our perceptions, but no two people share the same experience.

    c. And then, dripping and wrapped in towels, refreshed, we climb back into the old gray Plymouth and head home to bed—with no idea of the dry years to come.

    d. Conflicts of the past dissolve in a new way ... that I call "timeless time": living in the present moment with no agenda, just doing what presents itself.

    e. "Did we pay for them?" Mama asks anxiously. "It's no fun otherwise."

3. Now for a real challenge. Revise the following sentence, which contains both an indefinite negative and an indirect negative: "Not many people would not agree."

    Don't let the double negative fool you.

    (Card, please.)

    The sentence means "Few people would disagree."

MAKE EVERY WORD COUNT

When Henry David Thoreau wrote about living in a cabin by Walden Pond, he titled his first chapter "Economy." He wanted to explain the economy of reducing life to its essentials, of living simply so that he might live richly.

Reducing your language to its essential elements allows you to deliver your message economically, and that economy accentuates the working parts of your sentences. If you make every word count—or if you "omit needless words," as Strunk and White put it—you'll write with more energy and emphasis.

Mark Twain declared, "Writing is such an easy thing to do. All you have to do is cross out the wrong words that you don't need."

Jack London observed, "You can't wait around all day for inspiration. What you have to do is go after it with a club."

Except that's not what they said.

As skilled writers, they knew to eliminate wordiness and to condense and compress their statements for maximum effect.

"Writing is easy," Twain declared. "All you have to do is cross out the wrong words."

"You can't wait for inspiration," London observed. "You have to go after it with a club."

Can you hear the difference?

How many times have *you* written something that might have been effective—even memorable—but whose stylistic effect was obscured by wordiness? It may be happening more often than you think.

Consider these quotations from Douglas Adams and John Ciardi.

> I just love deadlines. I really love the whooshing type noise they
> make as they go right by you.

> You don't have to suffer all that much to be a poet. Adolescence
> is just about enough suffering for any one of us.

Except that's not what they said. Minus the wordiness, their observations are memorable.

> I love deadlines. I love the whooshing noise they make as they
> go by.

> You don't have to suffer to be a poet. Adolescence is enough
> suffering for anyone.

As countless writers have pointed out, making every word count is the foundation of a good style.

What if Peter De Vries had said, "I just love being a writer. What I really can't stand, however, is all the paperwork involved" rather than "I love being a writer. What I can't stand is the paperwork"?

What if Rita Mae Brown had observed, "What a deadline is is negative inspiration. Still, when you think about it, it's much better than absolutely no inspiration at all" rather than "A deadline is negative inspiration. Still, it's better than no inspiration at all"?

And what if Red Smith had said, "It is my observation that there's nothing at all to writing. All you do is sit yourself down at a typewriter for a while and open a vein" rather than "There's nothing to writing. All you have to do is sit down at a typewriter and open a vein"?

Your turn. How do you think Justice Louis Brandeis and William Zinsser wrote the following sentences?

1. As any fool can tell you, there's absolutely no such thing as good writing. There is, in the final analysis, only assiduously good rewriting.
2. There's not very much at all to be said about the punctuation mark known as the period, except that most writers like you and me don't reach it soon enough.

Here are their versions, wordiness eliminated.

1. There is no such thing as good writing. There is only good rewriting.
2. There's not much to be said about the period, except that most writers don't reach it soon enough.

The wordy phrase *the fact that* can almost always be replaced with a simple but useful word: *because*. So, too, can the phrases *based on the fact that*, *in view of the fact that*, and *owing to the fact that*. Similarly, the phrase *in spite of the fact that* can be replaced with *although* or *even though*.

Consider the following sentences, which contain a variety of wordy expressions, and their condensed versions.

> **Original:** Based on the fact that I love snow, I'm eager for winter to come.
> **Condensed:** Because I love snow, I'm eager for winter to come.
>
> **Original:** Many people choose to live in Minnesota in spite of the fact that they don't like snow or cold weather.
> **Condensed:** Many people choose to live in Minnesota even though they don't like snow or cold weather.
>
> **Original:** In view of the fact that it snows every winter in Minnesota, and usually in significant quantities, I'm perplexed by their decision to live here.
> **Condensed:** Because it snows every winter in Minnesota, and usually in significant quantities, I'm perplexed by their decision to live here.
>
> **Original:** I left work early on Friday afternoon for the reason that we had a foot of fresh snow and I couldn't wait to ski my favorite trails.
> **Condensed:** I left work early on Friday afternoon because we had a foot of fresh snow and I couldn't wait to ski my favorite trails.

"Clutter is the disease of American writing," William Zinsser declares in his book *On Writing Well*. "We are a society strangling in unnecessary words, circular constructions, pompous frills, and meaningless jargon ... But the secret of good writing is to strip every sentence to its cleanest components."

So make every word count.

1. Can you identify the words that are used needlessly in this sentence? I'm referring to the previous sentence, the one you just read. How would you revise it?

    (Card, please.)

    Did you eliminate *that are used* so that the sentence reads, "Can you identify the needless words in this sentence?"

2. Eliminate the wordiness in the following sentences. Hint: Pay close attention to the openings of the first four sentences.

    a. In order to write with emphasis, avoid wordy expressions.

    b. So as to eliminate wordiness, imagine that you are paying $5 per word to send a message.

    c. In the event you don't own Nordic skis, you can rent them at your neighborhood rec center.

    d. During the course of my writing workshops, we do lots of exciting exercises like these.

    e. Strunk and White offer excellent advice in regard to wordiness.

    f. You should exercise nearly every single day of the week for the purpose of staying fit and maintaining your weight.

    g. The hourly employees discussed the question as to whether their CEO—or anyone for that matter—deserves a salary of $300 million.

    h. Please send me a check in the amount of $5.

Here are the condensed versions of those sentences.

    a. To write with emphasis, avoid wordy expressions.

    b. To eliminate wordiness, imagine you are paying $5 per word to send a message.

    c. If you don't own Nordic skis, you can rent them at your neighborhood rec center.

    d. During my writing workshops, we do lots of exciting exercises like these.

    e. Strunk and White offer excellent advice regarding wordiness.

f. You should exercise nearly every day of the week to stay fit and maintain your weight.

g. The hourly employees discussed whether their CEO—or anyone for that matter—deserves a salary of $300 million.

h. Please send a check for $5.

3. Here's a paragraph replete with wordy expressions. Can you eliminate them?

> In order to make every word count, it is my belief that you need to be aware of your habits of speech. During the course of revising your writing, undertake a search for stock phrases that can be reduced to fewer words. In the final analysis, your effectiveness will be dependent upon recognizing your own habits of speech.

I found six: *in order to* for *to*, *it is my belief that* for *I believe*, *during the course of* for *during*, *undertake a search for* for *search*, *in the final analysis* for *finally* (or delete the phrase entirely), and *will be dependent upon* for *will depend on*.

Have you recognized any of your own wordy habits of speech? If so, make a list of them and review your list from time to time.

4. Take a sentence of your writing from something you've written. Count the number of words in that sentence. Then place a $5 bill on your desk for every word. Now delete any unnecessary words you find. Examine the words one by one, the way you do with every text or e-mail message before you send it.

For every word you eliminate without altering your meaning or harming the natural rhythm of your language, pick up and keep a $5 bill.

The next time you write, imagine that you're paying $5 for every word in your message.

5. Let's do that exercise with the first sentence in exercise 4: "Take a sentence of your writing from something you've written." Can you save $15?

Personally, I don't think the redundant phrase "from something you've written" is worth a nickel, much less $20. How about "Select a sentence from your writing"?

Now look again at the second sentence in that exercise: "Count the number of words in that sentence." Do you see where you can save $10?

Isn't "Count the words in that sentence" better? You might even eliminate the last $15 worth of language. That would make $25 saved. Not bad.

By the way, in revising the first draft of the previous paragraph, I saved $5. I changed "That would make $25 in savings" to "That would make $25 saved."

One more example: "The next time you write, imagine that you're paying $5 for every word." Subtract $5 (or $10) worth of language.

Hint: John Lennon didn't write, "Imagine that all the people / Are living life in peace." He wrote, "Imagine all the people / Living life in peace."

✳ A FURTHER THOUGHT: PUT YOUR VERBIAGE ON A DIET

My old college friend Nicholsby called the other day to ask for help. Like many Americans, Nicholsby is carrying a little extra luggage.

"It happened so gradually it took me a while to realize I had a problem," he said. "I used to be fit and trim. If I wanted to say something, I just said it.

"And then each year I seemed to pick up an extra word here, a wordy expression there. Before I knew it, my style was weighed down with pounds and pounds of excess verbiage. Now my colleagues are complaining. Nobody will read my e-mails. Can you help me?"

"Happy to," I said, and I invited him over.

When he arrived, he said, "I deem it imperative that we commence work on resolving this pressing issue at our earliest possible convenience."

I was shocked by his greeting. In the old days he would have said, "Let's get started," or "Time's a-wasting."

"I think I can help you," I said.

"You can? Your positive statement of assurance fills me with hope and optimism."

"Ever heard of the Fatkins Diet?" I asked.

"Yes, but I thought it was injurious to your locutionary health."

"Nonsense," I said. "The Fatkins Diet has helped millions of wordy writers reclaim their normal speech patterns. The results are dramatic."

Nicholsby looked skeptical.

"First, you give up all word pairs, redundant categories, and needless modifiers," I said.

"*All* of them?"

"All of them. But here's the good part. You may use all the nouns you like."

"No limit on nouns? But I thought nouns ..."

"I know," I said. "It goes against everything you've ever heard about not turning your verbs into nouns. But it works."

Obviously desperate, Nicholsby agreed to try it.

For his first weekly assignment I told him to eliminate word pairs such as *one and only, each and every, any and all*, and *cease and desist*.

"Mission accomplished!" he declared when he weighed in seven days later. "It was tough at first, a new way of thinking really, but I hope and trust I've made progress."

"You what?"

"Just teasing," he said. "I *hope* I've made progress."

"That's better. Now for week two: Eliminate redundant categories such as *pink in color, round in shape, tall in stature*, and *cosmetic in appearance*."

When we met the next week, Nicholsby said, "I'm already feeling lighter in weight!"

"Ha!" I said. "Almost got me again. Now for week three: needless modifiers. No more *true facts, immediate vicinities, personal opinions, new initiatives, end results*, or *free gifts*."

When I next saw him, I hardly recognized him.

"I'm so happy," Nicholsby said, "I could literally explode."

"Right," I said. "You almost slipped another one by me. Last, we need to reduce your nouns."

"My *nouns*?" he said. "But you said ..."

"I know. That was phase one. But for the long run you need to use verbs whenever possible. For example, don't *make a recommendation*; *recommend*. Don't *take under consideration*; *consider*. And don't *undertake a study*; *study*."

When Nicholsby winked and said, "I will make an effort to do my best," I knew he would succeed.

ELIMINATE WORDY REFERENCES TO TIME

Why do some writers become wordy when they refer to time? Are they trying to make themselves sound more important? Is their wordiness simply a bad habit?

Here's an example: "Until such time as we recognize our habits, we have no hope of changing them."

Did you see it? Why write *until such time* when *until* will suffice?

During the time it takes readers to read a wordy phrase, they might begin to think of all the other things they could be doing with their time.

Did you catch it? Compare "During the time it takes readers to read a wordy phrase ..." with "When readers read a wordy phrase ..."

Now that you're looking, consider these wordy references to time and their revisions.

> **Wordy:** In this day and age, you don't want to waste your reader's time.
> **Revised:** These days, you don't want to waste your reader's time.
>
> **Wordy:** At this point in time, I think we should hold off.
> **Revised:** For now, I think we should hold off.
>
> **Wordy:** You need to practice eliminating wordiness on a daily basis.
> **Revised:** You need to practice eliminating wordiness every day.

Now see if you can find five wordy references to time in the following paragraph.

Prior to my becoming a columnist, I knew wordiness was an issue in writing, but it was only during the course of writing my columns that I realized the extent of the problem. At this point in time I began to see examples everywhere. In due course I noticed certain patterns, and subsequent to my realizing this I compiled a list.

Here's the paragraph minus the wordy expressions.

Before I became a columnist, I knew wordiness was an issue in writing, but it was only while writing my columns that I realized the extent of the problem. I then began to see examples everywhere. Finally I noticed certain patterns, and after I realized this, I compiled a list.

Now look again at the last sentence. It could be condensed to "After noticing certain patterns, I compiled a list."

Here's a list of wordy expressions relating to time.

CHANGE	TO
during the time it takes	when, during
prior to	before
during the course of	during
at this point in time	now, then, at this point
in due course	finally
subsequent to	after
in this day and age	now, today, these days
at the present time	now
last but not least	finally
in the final analysis	finally (or delete)

At this point in time, you too may be seeing some patterns. So last but not least, stay on your toes because, in the final analysis, wordiness undermines your emphasis and style.

1. Revise the wordy references to time in the following sentences.

    a. I want you to concentrate during the time it takes to do these exercises.

    b. Prior to your introduction to these wordy references to time, you may not have realized you were using some of them in your writing.

    c. In this day and age, modern readers of today expect you to get to the point.

Did you revise those sentences to something like this?

    a. I want you to concentrate while doing these exercises.

    b. Before you were introduced to these wordy references to time, you may not have realized you were using some of these phrases in your writing.

    c. These days, readers expect you to get to the point.

2. Eliminate six wordy references to time in this paragraph.

> At the present time, we've decided to wait until such time as we have a clearer picture of what our kitchen will look like subsequent to remodeling before we decide what to do with our dining room. During the course of the project, we'll start planning the next future phase. Last but not least, we'll move on to the bathroom.

(Card, please.)

    Here are the six wordy references to time.

    1. at the present time
    2. until such time as
    3. subsequent to
    4. during the course of
    5. the next future
    6. last but not least

And here's the paragraph minus the wordy references.

For now, we've decided to wait until we have a clearer picture of what our kitchen will look like after remodeling before we decide what to do with our dining room. During the project, we'll start planning the next phase. Finally, we'll move on to the bathroom.

3. Eliminate the wordy references to time in these sentences.
   a. I plan to complete my draft in two weeks from now.
   b. During a six-month period of time I did nothing but eat, sleep, exercise, and write.
   c. She finished researching and writing her dissertation in three years' time.

Did you change *in two weeks from now* to *in two weeks*, *a six-month period of time* to *a six-month period*, and *in three years' time* to *in three years?*

4. Now for your final exam. Ready?
   Identify five instances of wordiness in this paragraph.

It's a true fact that if we make each and every word count, we will write with more stress in emphasis. Basically, in order to write powerfully, we must make every word count. Until such time as we do ... well, you get the idea.

Did you identify all five? Does your revised paragraph look like this?

If we make every word count, we will write with more emphasis. To write powerfully, we must make every word count. Until we do ... well, you get the idea.

If so, well done!

DON'T TRUST MODIFIERS

The mighty modifier. What would we do without it? Without modifiers, we couldn't make a *snide* remark or have a *happy* ending, which would be very sad indeed.

Adjectives and adverbs are indispensable units of meaning. They allow us to express degree and emphasis. (I am *worried*. I am *somewhat* worried. I am *very* worried.) But of all the parts of speech, modifiers are the trickiest to use well.

The problem is we tend to use them unthinkingly. We use them out of habit, *carelessly* tossing them about where they are not needed, where they serve *absolutely* no *viable* function *at all*.

See what I mean?

Determining which modifiers add meaning and which do not is one of the most crucial choices a writer makes. To use a modifier well is to convey nuance. To use one needlessly is to undermine emphasis and waste the reader's time.

It's a true fact. You're surrounded by poor usage, and you imitate it without realizing you're doing so. Before you know it, you've formed a habit, and habits are hard to break.

To illustrate my point, fold your arms. Note which arm is on top. Now fold your arms the other way around, with the other arm on top. If you think breaking a habit is easy, try folding them this way for the next week and see how you do.

Likewise, the next time you catch yourself writing or saying "true fact," drop the adjective *true*. Facts by their nature are true. We don't need to be told what we already know.

Of course one could make a distinction between "alleged facts" and "true facts," and in certain contexts this usage would be appropriate, but to make this distinction is to make a conscious choice. The problem is not carefully considered choices; it's sloppy speech patterns that have become bad habits.

So do you agree with the general consensus concerning modifiers?

Now ask yourself: Isn't a "consensus" a generally held belief? Why say "general consensus" when "consensus" will do?

Do you have any personal opinions on this subject? How about past memories? While we're at it, I hope you have no terrible tragedies or sudden crises in your life.

The end result of this careless use of language is wordiness. But ask yourself: Where does the result generally come but at the end?

At the risk of overexaggerating the importance of eliminating unnecessary modifiers, I'll offer a few more examples. I also don't want to under-exaggerate its importance.

Consider the needless modifiers in these sentences.

1. Our [past] history of failures is well documented.
2. The [final] outcome is concise writing.
3. My [future] goal is to eliminate needless modifiers.
4. Did anyone in the [immediate] vicinity of the blast see anything suspicious?
5. Do you understand the [basic] essence of the problem?
6. Should I continue [on], or do you see the pattern?

As both Mark Twain and Ernest Hemingway said, don't trust modifiers. They didn't say don't use adjectives and adverbs; they said don't trust them.

Modifiers are tricky. Sometimes they add meaning, as in "The consensus is that Jill is an *excellent* writer," and sometimes they don't, as in "The *general* consensus is that Jill is a *very* excellent writer."

So should I stop referring *back* to more examples, or would you like me to continue *on*?

Enough said.

1. As a quick self-assessment, open a long document from one of your files and search "end result." How many times does it appear? In how many instances would "result" be the better choice?

2. Here's an exercise to help you practice identifying and deleting non-functioning modifiers.

You'll find fifty-four modifiers in the following paragraphs (not counting the articles *a*, *an*, and *the* or possessive pronouns such as *your*). Of those, forty-two are used well, and twelve are used needlessly. Take out your pen or pencil. Underline the modifiers that contribute meaning; cross out those that are expendable. You won't find any unnecessary modifiers in the text within quotation marks. The quoted material is from Hemingway, who rarely used a superfluous word. Also, the paragraph beginning "Last week" is my feeble attempt to imitate Hemingway's style, and it contains no extraneous language.

Here we go. Cross out twelve unnecessary modifiers.

> Of the truly great American writers who wrote in a plain rather than ornate style, one really stands out: Ernest Hemingway. It was Hemingway who had the courage to trust a simple word to do the job. His shining example offers an enormously invaluable lesson to today's modern on-the-job writer.
>
> "When Thomas Hudson woke," Hemingway wrote in his posthumously published novel, *Islands in the Stream*, "there was a light east breeze blowing and out across the flats the sand was bone white under the blue sky and the small high clouds that were traveling with the wind made dark moving patches on the green water."
>
> The end result of this straightforward, unassuming style: a narrative that takes its uncanny effect not from complexity and elaboration but from simple understatement, suggestion, and omission. Hemingway wanted only what was absolutely essential. At the risk of saying too little, he tried to say just enough.

Recently, I visited Hemingway's home in Key West. I felt the ocean breeze on my skin as it traveled across the wide verandas and through the tall windows and into the house, I held the paws of the six-toed cats (descendants of Papa's pets), and I imagined him sitting at his Royal black typewriter in his backyard studio, doing some of the best work of his life, as he did when he wrote this description in *Islands*.

"The water of the [Gulf] Stream was usually a dark blue when you looked out at it when there was no wind. But when you walked out into it there was just the green light of the water over that floury white sand and you could see the shadow of any big fish a long time before he could ever come in close to the beach."

The general consensus is his writing could be clumsy and boorish and offensive, but when he was good, he was one of the very best. He never used a single word until he had fingered it like a beachcomber examining a shell and turned it over in his hand until he had the feel of it, and then he kept it only if it was good.

Our challenge as writers is to take the time Hemingway took to weigh every word.

Here are the twelve unnecessary modifiers: *truly* great American writers; *really* stands out; *shining* example; *enormously* invaluable lesson; today's *modern* on-the-job writer; *end* result; *uncanny* effect; *simple* understatement; *absolutely* essential; *general* consensus; *very* best; and *single* word.

Note that I tempted you with a catalogue of adjectives: *clumsy and boorish and offensive*. I didn't want the exercise to be too easy. I also wanted to make a point: You can sometimes be expansive even as you make every word count. To my ear, the change in rhythm produces a nice effect.

By the way, the next time you visit Hemingway's home in Key West, grab a cat. They love it when you pick them up and try to count their toes.

✳ A FURTHER THOUGHT: WHEN CAN YOU TRUST A MODIFIER?

Which parts of speech can you trust?

Verbs are no problem. Although a few may offend the ear—"We need to effectuate change" and "Let's conference on that"—most verbs are trustworthy. In fact, a good action verb can be the engine that drives your sentence. Compare, for example, "We need to give honor to the authors who have inspired us" with "We need to honor the authors who have inspired us."

Nouns are generally safe. They're pretty much determined by your content, though a keen eye, ear, and nose for detail can add color and personality to your writing.

Your choice of certain function words—articles (*a*, *an*, or *the*), conjunctions (connecting words such as *and*, *or*, and *but*), and prepositions (relationship words such as *in*, *on*, *under*, and *around*)—is generally straightforward. Not much danger there.

But modifiers—ah, those mighty modifiers. Adjectives and adverbs. As I discussed above, both Mark Twain and Ernest Hemingway warned us not to trust them. They didn't say avoid them; they said use them carefully. Modifiers are the trickiest part of speech to use well because so many of them are needless. We hear them misused every day, and if we're not careful, we mimic what we hear and read.

The end result: wordiness. (Did you catch it?)

So you can imagine my consternation when I read the following sentence in Mark Twain's short story, "Cannibalism in the Cars": "Out into the wild night, the pitchy darkness, the billowy snow, the driving storm, every soul leaped, with the consciousness that a moment lost now might bring destruction to us all."

The scene is December 1853. A train traveling from St. Louis to Chicago is caught in a raging blizzard and is stuck fast in a snowdrift. The passengers have exited the cars to try to dig out the train.

And the modifiers continue to fall like snowflakes: "It was a weird picture, that small company of frantic men fighting the banking snow, half in the blackest shadow and half in the angry light of the locomotive's reflector."

It's a captivating scene—but "*banking* snow ... *blackest* shadow ... *angry* light"? Is this the same Mark Twain who once wrote, "As to the adjective, when in doubt, strike it out"?

It's true that one may take more liberties in fiction than in other types of writing, but the question remains: Why do those untrustworthy adjectives work so well in creating mood and tone here?

I have two answers: the author's intent and the rhythm of the language.

First, Twain's intent is to create an overstated, melodramatic effect. And if any word can convey nuance and degree, a well-chosen adjective can.

Second, the modifiers are used not alone but in a series of rhythmic or coordinated structures, creating a musical effect. Note the inverted, periodic structure of the first example: "Out into the wild night, the pitchy darkness, the billowy snow, the driving storm, every soul leaped."

My conclusion? Break any rule you like—as long as you break it for stylistic effect.

USE STRONG VERBS TO DRIVE YOUR SENTENCES

The verb is the engine that drives the sentence.

In "The tracks *made* a line in the snow," the engine lacks horsepower. In "The tracks *cut* a line in the snow," the engine has thrust.

To make your writing memorable, use strong verbs. Note the vivid verbs Jan Zita Grover uses in *Northern Waters*.

> The storm *rocked* us all night long; I realized then that I hadn't known how *magnified* the sound of rain could be when *stretched* across the tympanum of a tent. ... Over the howl of wind, I waited for the slow, toothy parting of tree tissue, the rushing descent of a spindly jack as it *gathered speed to crush* our defenseless nylon dome. My body hair *bristled* with electricity.

Note, too, Grover's use of the verb-inspired nouns and adjectives *howl*, *parting*, and *rushing descent*.

In contrast, consider the lack of strong verbs in the following description of Lake Superior's Apostle Islands, adapted from Greg Breining's *Wild Shore: Exploring Lake Superior by Kayak*.

> On Devils Island, in the Apostles' outer ring, Layne and I *took* a small boat into the sea caves, which *made noise* even in this mild chop. On shore we *walked* over slabs of sandstone that had been *weakened* by waves to the point of collapse and, in the lake's wilder tantrums, *moved* high onto the altered shore.

How might you replace *took, made, walked, weakened,* and *moved* with more interesting and vivid verbs?

Here's how Greg Breining actually wrote that paragraph.

> On Devils Island, in the Apostles' outer ring, Layne and I *rode* a small boat into the sea caves, which *bellowed* even in this mild chop. On shore we *clambered* over slabs of sandstone that had been *undercut* by waves to the point of collapse and, in the lake's wilder tantrums, *tossed* high onto the brutalized shore.

Consider Breining's choices: *rode, bellowed, clambered, undercut,* and *tossed.* As in Grover's passage, even his adjectives and nouns convey movement and energy: *mild chop, wilder tantrums, brutalized shore.* Note the power of *brutalized* shore compared with *altered* shore. There's action in nearly every word.

Let's apply this lesson to an example of serviceable but forgettable job-related writing. Consider this passage.

> As a result of this delay, we have experienced a higher level of unscheduled downtime, a considerable increase in maintenance issues, a significant rise in frustration on the part of our technicians, and a substantial growth in dissatisfaction expressed by our customers.

That passage has as much energy as an empty room.

In place of the nondescript verb *have experienced* and the lifeless phrases *higher level, considerable increase, significant rise,* and *substantial growth,* use the action verbs *forced, shut down, squander, placate,* and *appease,* and the verb-inspired adjectives *avoidable repairs, disgruntled technicians,* and *outraged customers.*

> This delay *forced* us to *shut down* our generators for two weeks, *squander* half a million dollars for *avoidable* repairs, *placate* our *disgruntled* technicians, and *appease* our *outraged* customers.

Note that the vague references to *a higher level of unscheduled downtime* and *a considerable increase in maintenance issues* have been replaced with more definite references to *two weeks* and *half a million dollars.*

As you can see, vivid verbs and verb-inspired adjectives make a powerful combination.

One more example. Look for weak verbs that might be replaced with vivid verbs in the following paragraph.

Fog is already *covering* the lake's western shore by the time I *turn* to look for shallows and snags. As I *lower* the Cub onto the beach, the mists *come* in, visibility *drops* to a hundred yards, and the cool air suddenly *vibrates* with the hum of a million mosquitoes. I *return* to the Cub. Why *put up* the tent in case the delay is brief?

Here's how George Erickson wrote the paragraph in *True North: Exploring the Great Wilderness by Bush Plane.*

Fog is already *spilling over* the lake's western shore by the time I *circle* to check for shallows and snags. As I *tail* the Cub onto the beach, the mists *slip* in, visibility *plummets* to a hundred yards, and the cool air suddenly *quivers* with the hum of a million mosquitoes. I *retreat* to the Cub. Why *put up* the tent in case the delay is brief?

More memorable, wouldn't you say? But did you notice the missed opportunity in the last sentence? Wouldn't *pitched* be more in keeping with Erickson's active style than *put up?*

Here's a simple way to check your writing style: Take a paragraph of your writing at random, and underline your verbs. Are they doing their job? Are they adding power and color to your writing?

To make your writing memorable, don't settle for the ordinary and the weak. Search for the interesting, the strong, the fresh, the unusual, the bold, and the surprising. Use strong verbs to drive your sentences.

EXERCISES

1. Underline the verbs in this paragraph, adapted from Frederick Manfred's *Lord Grizzly.*

At last a slow twist of smoke rose out of the nest. Another long soft breath, and a flame rose the size of a bird's tongue. He blew on it once more, long and slow, and it touched his beard. Breath short, he gathered all the half-burnt twigs within reach, laid them on the burning grass in pyramid fashion, green spokes to a red hub. The flames grew. He laid on half-burnt branches and finished if off with bits of log. Presently he had a good fire going.

Do you see any opportunities for stronger verbs?

Beginning with the second sentence, replace the three weak verbs with the ones Manfred actually used: *licked out, flashed up in,* and *grabbed up.*

(Card, please.)

Did you replace the second *rose, touched,* and *gathered?*

Next replace the last word in the passage with Manfred's words: *blazing and crackling.* Now read the restored passage out loud, and listen to how it has taken on life.

I'll discuss figurative language and metaphors in Weeks 45 and 46, but note the simple elegance of "a flame licked out the size of a bird's tongue." Don't you love how the verb foreshadows the image?

2. Colum McCann uses action verbs in the opening paragraph of *Trans-Atlantic*: "The cottage sat at the edge of the lough. She could hear the wind and rain whipping across the expanse of open water: It hit the trees and muscled its way into the grass."

(A *lough* is an Irish-English word for loch or lake.)

Note the strong verbs: *sat, hear, whipping, hit, muscled.*

Pretty muscular words, wouldn't you say?

To get close to the language and sentence structure, type the passage over. Better yet, if you know how to form characters with a pen or pencil, copy it over longhand and you'll get even closer to the author's words. (If you don't own a pen or pencil, your teacher or boss might have one you can borrow; if you've never held a pen or pencil, you can find instructions on the Internet, but basically the clicker, cap, or eraser goes up and the upper part of the shaft rests in the crook of your thumb; the point goes down with the lower part of the shaft resting near the end of your third finger.)

After you've copied the passage, pick a different topic and write your own version, imitating McCann's style as closely as you can.

3. After revealing the source of the "odd sounds from the roof," McCann writes, "The shells pinged first, silent a moment as they bounced, followed by a jingling roll along the roof until they tumbled down into the long grass, spotted with whitewash."

Note the high-powered verbs: *pinged, bounced, jingling, tumbled, spotted.* (*Jingling* and *spotted* are actually participles, but they're in the verb family.)

Do as you did in Exercise 2.

4. Select a paragraph with strong verbs from your favorite author. Replace the strong verbs with intentionally weak verbs. Set aside your revised version for one week, and then come back to it. Without looking at the original version, replace your intentionally weak verbs with strong ones.

Compare your strong verbs with the author's original verbs. Whose verb choice was better?

✳ A FURTHER THOUGHT: THREE SURVIVORS ON A LIFEBOAT

Three survivors sat in a small lifeboat—a verb, a noun, and a modifier. The boat was taking on water fast. To save the other two, one had to go.

"Let's draw lots and trust our fate to whatever person, place, or thing is in charge of our destiny," said the noun.

"Let's vote to see who goes," said the verb. "We need to act now."

"Let's see if we can come to a general consensus," said the modifier. "In my personal opinion, I really think discussion is how we should determine the final outcome of our present situation."

No sooner had they spoken than a wave washed over the gunwale, and the boat began to list.

"A vote would be acceptable to me," said the noun.

"I agree," said the verb, turning to the modifier. "The 'general' consensus is we vote."

"I fear that the end result will be a terrible tragedy," said the modifier. "But I have no new initiatives to proffer."

Not far away the dorsal fin of a great white shark sliced the water in a slow arc.

"You know," said the noun, "I have no intention to have an effect on the outcome of our selection process, but Mark Twain once made the observation that one should place no trust in modifiers."

"Hemingway said the same thing," said the verb.

"That may be a true fact," said the modifier, "but they didn't say modifiers could not be used usefully; they said modifiers should be used carefully and cautiously."

"The reason behind their observation," said the noun, "is that modifiers are tricky."

"Precisely," said the verb. "Modifiers can fool you into thinking they're needed when in fact they're expendable. *Quite* expendable. They *utterly* waste the reader's time. They *completely* clutter a sentence. They *totally* obscure its meaning."

"Not *always*," said the modifier with tears in its eyes. "Quite often we make a genuinely meaningful contribution. When used with some restraint, we add various levels of degree and sundry shades of nuance."

"Worst of all," declared the noun. "Modifiers add unnecessary *weight*, if you take my meaning."

"I do," said the verb.

"In actual reality," said the modifier to the noun, "it's a noun-heavy style that adds excess and superfluous weight. It is you who unabashedly change verbs into nouns. If my past memory serves me quite correctly, it was you who only a short moment ago said, 'I have no *intention* to have an *effect* on the *outcome* of our *selection process*,' when you might simply have said, 'I don't intend to influence how we select who will go.'"

"You raise a good point," said the verb.

Something thudded against the hull of the boat. Another wave broke over its side.

"I have come to my conclusion," said the noun. "The modifier is the one who should make the sacrifice."

"I'm inclined to agree," said the verb. "Let's get on with it."

"Alas, is everyone in the immediate vicinity against me?" cried the modifier, turning to the verb. "Please. I beg you. I implore you beseechingly. If you'll change your mind, I'll give you anything. A well-deserved reward. An unearned dividend. A free gift. Anything."

"Decision time is upon us!" said the noun.

"We need to act now!" cried the verb.

With that, the noun took hold of the modifier's arms and the verb grabbed its legs, and together they heaved it overboard.

DON'T NOMINALIZE; VERBALIZE

The next time the police give chase to a suspect, they should just chase the guy. While they're fooling around with their nominalization, he's running down the sidewalk getting away.

So what do you think? Do you stand in agreement with me, or do you agree with me?

Nouns add weight to your writing, but how much weight is needed?

Many writers confuse weight with authority, so they overuse nouns. They even turn verbs into nouns to make certain they have sufficient heft.

Consider this sentence: "She recommended we study this issue."

Simple enough. It has two parts: the main clause, comprising a subject and a verb ("She recommended"), and an object clause, comprising a subject, a verb, and an object ("we study this issue").

There's nothing wrong with the sentence. It works just fine.

But some writers attempt to give the sentence a more authoritative tone by changing their verbs into nouns. Are you one of them? Have you come to the realization that you might be? Or have you realized you may be? Compare "She recommended we study this issue" with "She made a recommendation that we undertake a study of this issue." Are you impressed by the wordiness? I'm not.

Would you rather *make a connection* with your reader or *connect* with your reader? The noun form (*connection*) of the verb (*connect*) weighs down the sentence, and writers who prefer nouns to verbs have a noun-heavy style.

Would you like to make a revision in this sentence? Would you like to make a change in your thinking about verbs and nouns? Perhaps you'd rather *revise* this sentence and *change* your thinking about verbs and nouns? Do you see how the nouns weigh down the style and how the verbs add energy?

A verb turned into a noun is called a nominalization. Although nominalizations have their uses, they are generally wordier and less emphatic than their verb counterparts.

So why do so many writers use nominalized language? Maybe they wrongly associate wordiness with an authoritative tone. But compare "You need to make a change in your attitude" with "You need to change your attitude." To my ear, the verb wins hands down.

See how changing nominalizations into action verbs creates a livelier style in the following sentences.

> **Original:** We made a decision to make an alteration in our route.
> **Revised:** We decided to alter our route.
>
> **Original:** It's important for you to make a written response to your client's call for proposals.
> **Revised:** It's important for you to respond in writing to your client's call for proposals.
>
> **Original:** He offered an explanation for why they had come to the conclusion they should raise an objection to making a change in the policy.
> **Revised:** He explained why they had concluded they should object to changing the policy.

Verbs propel your thought, and they do so economically. As I discussed in the last two weeks' techniques, they're the engine that drives the sentence. When given the choice, go for the verb. To write in a lively, emphatic style, be biased in favor of verbs, not nouns.

Despite this standard advice (I'm not the first to offer it), we find ourselves in discussion with other parties rather than simply talking with them. We offer a suggestion that we make a change in our policy rather than just suggesting we change it.

Are you in need of more examples? If so, the next time you make reference to results that should be under examination ... well, you get the idea. I suggest you refer to results that should be examined.

For a lively, emphatic style, don't show your preference for verbs over nouns; prefer verbs to nouns.

EXERCISES

1. Revise the following sentences, replacing nominalizations with verbs.
   a. Please take under consideration my proposal.
   b. I made the decision to make a call to my dear old mum.
   c. They came to an agreement they would reach a settlement out of court.
   d. It is my suggestion that we make a proposal to make a refinement in the dephosphorization of taconite pellets.
   e. She came to the realization that her only means to make an escape was to make a pretense of sleeping.

Here's how you might have revised those sentences.
   a. Please consider my proposal.
   b. I decided to call my dear old mum.
   c. They agreed to settle out of court.
   d. I suggest we propose refining the dephosphorization of taconite pellets *or* I suggest we propose refining the way we dephosphorize taconite pellets.
   e. She realized her only way to escape was to pretend to be sleeping.

2. For a couple of years after her Vanderbilt days, my friend Marshall Chapman played a solo gig at the Jolly Ox in Green Hills, a popular Nashville watering hole. She was the "lounge entertainment," as she describes herself.

In the following passage, adapted from her book, *Goodbye, Little Rock and Roller*, I replaced five verbs with nominalizations linked to weak verbs. Change the nominalizations back to the author's verbs.

My job was to sing songs for hungry customers while they waited for their seats in the dining rooms where they could place an order for a steak. I also had a job as a waitress during lunch. After lunch, I'd settle up, grab a bite, then go home and take a nap until it was time to make a return with my guitar.

Here's how my Vanderbilt friend wrote those sentences.

My job was to sing songs for hungry customers while *they waited to be seated* in the dining rooms where they could *order up* a steak. I also *worked* there as a waitress during lunch. After lunch, I'd settle up, grab a bite, then go home and *nap* until it was time to *come back* with my guitar.

KNOW WHEN TO VERB YOUR NOUNS

As I discussed in last week's technique, some writers routinely turn their verbs into nouns. The result is a ponderous, noun-heavy style.

There are times, however, when you can go the other direction. You can turn a noun into a verb. You do it all the time, without even thinking about it.

As Richard Nordquist posts at grammar.about.com, "In a single work day, we might *head* a task force, *eye* an opportunity, *nose around* for good ideas, *mouth* a greeting, *elbow* an opponent, *strong-arm* a colleague, *shoulder* the blame, *stomach* a loss, and finally *hand in* our resignation."

These function shifts sometimes produce unexpected results. For example, *to father* a child merely suggests being the person responsible for insemination, whereas *to mother* a child suggests parenting in an overbearing manner. (So much for English treating both genders equally.)

In the hands of a skilled writer like Andrew Keith, verbing a noun can surprise and delight the reader. In *Afloat Again, Adrift*, he describes an overgrown portage around the Knife Rapids on the Hayes River as "a mile of muddy Hell: slippery, swarming with mosquitoes, impossibly tangled in brush and mined with sphagnum moss islands where we *post-holed* up to our knees."

The effect is lost if the noun-to-verb formation is removed. Compare "where our legs *sank like post-hole diggers* up to our knees" with "where we *post-holed* up to our knees."

Similarly, Keith depicts a duck-hunting scene in which "the roof of a blind *hinged* open and up popped four hunters in fatigues blasting round

after round." In another passage, "ducks *winged* through the islands" and "sailboats *breezed* along."

Not that Keith doesn't appreciate the value of action verbs. Caught in the hydraulics of a dam while canoeing the Mississippi River in Davenport, Iowa, with "one stroke forward and one surging wave backwards," the author is "*lurched* up, *slammed* down, *punched* aside, and *twisted* around while chilly winds *showered*" him. Talk about verbs conveying action.

In *TransAtlantic,* Colum McCann creates a striking image when he turns two nouns, *shawl* and *mummy,* into past participles (or verb forms that can be used as adjectives): "It was late afternoon by the time they found Lily. Rainsoaked and shivering on the pier. Her head *shawled,* her body *mummied* into a coat."

Barbara Kingsolver also creates action and movement with verb forms created from nouns. In *The Poisonwood Bible*, one of her narrators offers this magical description of the tropical forest.

> The trees are columns of slick, brindled bark like muscular animals overgrown beyond all reason. Every space is filled with life: delicate, poisonous frogs *war-painted* like skeletons, clutched in copulation, secreting their precious eggs onto dripping leaves. Vines strangling their own kin in the everlasting wrestle for sunlight. The *breathing* of monkeys. A *glide* of snake belly on branch.

Look again at *war-painted, breathing,* and *glide.* Note that *war-painted* is neither a verb nor an adjective but something in between. Kingsolver is pushing the noun-verb boundary. *War-painted,* created from the noun phrase *war paint,* is a verbal adjective (or a participle). Likewise, *breathing* is neither a verb (*breathe*) nor a noun (*breath*) but a verbal noun (or a gerund). Perhaps the most interesting example is *glide,* which has not been altered from its noun form but nevertheless conveys movement in much the same way a verb would. To appreciate Kingsolver's delicate touch, compare "A snake belly *gliding* on a branch" with "A *glide* of snake belly on branch." The key here is to use a noun that suggests movement, and Kingsolver gets it just right.

In another passage, an okapi (an animal that looks like a zebra but is related to the giraffe) appears on the far side of the river from where a woman is sitting: "Without taking his eyes from [the woman], he twitches a little at the knee, then the shoulder, where a fly *devils* him."

These imaginative touches produce small effects, but coming unexpectedly as they do, they help keep the language fresh and compelling.

The challenge is to find ways to use this noun-to-verb technique in a way that doesn't call attention to itself.

Take a look at these sentences whose nouns have been verbed.

1. With the meeting in progress, she ~~walked on the tips of her toes~~ [tip-toed] to her chair.
2. When I hit the ice on the highway, the trailer ~~swung from side to side the way a fish moves its tail back and forth~~ [fishtailed].
3. Despite having consumed a five-course dinner, she ~~cast her eyes on~~ [eyed] the chocolate mousse on the dessert tray.
4. Not wanting to upset her colleague, she ~~figuratively opened a closet and therein placed~~ [closeted] her emotions.
5. I'm glad we ~~talked in conference~~ [conferenced] about this issue.

In the first few examples, the verbs were made from nouns long ago. *Conferenced* in sentence 5, on the other hand, is a more recent creation, one I hope you would reject in favor of a more acceptable verb, such as *conferred*.

Verbing your nouns can make your writing memorable, but use your ear in deciding when you have a winner and when you have a dud.

EXERCISES

1. Replace the verbs made from nouns with more natural language in the following sentences.
   a. Let's dialogue before the meeting to map out our strategy.
   b. This rewards program will incentivize younger shoppers to become loyal customers.
   c. I cannot countenance verbing nouns when doing so obscures rather than elucidates meaning.

Did you change the awkward verbs to *talk* and *encourage* in sentences (a) and (b)? Other verbs might work equally well. Did you leave *countenance* as it was in sentence (c)?

2. Do you see a pattern in Andrew Keith's use of nouns as verbs in "the roof of a blind *hinged* open," "ducks *winged* through the islands," and "sailboats *breezed* along"?

Roofs don't normally have hinges, but doors do, ducks have wings, and sailboats are propelled by breezes. In each case, the verb is made from a noun associated (or, in the case of the roof, loosely associated) with the object. These associated objects are a good place to look for nouns that might be verbed into action.

For example, fish have fins, plants have stems, and goats have horns. Replace the italicized verbs with verbed nouns in the following sentences.
   a. Once released, the stunned walleye *swam* away from shore.
   b. In early May the tulips *grew* through the wet brown leaves.
   c. One of her great aunt's goats came up from behind her and *butted* her with its horns. (Hint: Delete *came up* and *with its horns,* and move *from behind* to the end of the sentence.)

Do your revisions look like this?
   a. Once released, the stunned walleye *finned* away from shore.
   b. In early May the tulips *stemmed* through the wet brown leaves.
   c. One of her great aunt's goats *horned* her from behind.

3. As you can see, nouns can be verbed to convey action in colorful ways, but nouns don't have to be changed to another part of speech to suggest movement. Sometimes nouns used as nouns can suggest movement.

Note how Frederick Manfred suggests past action in this description of an abandoned campsite in *Lord Grizzly*: "Except for the usual camp litter of broken tins and ripped paper packs and rinds of fruit and slicked bones, there was nothing."

Colum McCann creates a similar effect with *nail holes* and *marks of furniture* in *TransAtlantic*: "Evidence [of abandonment was] everywhere. The walls were less faded where the pictures had been. Nail holes in the plaster. Marks of furniture on the floor. A wind came down the chimney and turned the ashes."

Note, too, the interplay between McCann's nouns and the verb-generated action of the last sentence. Juxtaposing the nouns and verbs creates a subtle interplay between stasis and unexpected movement.

Imagine returning to a place you love that has changed since you were last there. Write a description of that place imitating either Manfred's nouns or McCann's interplay between nouns and verbs, or both.

UNSTACK THOSE NOUN STACKS

Now that I've discussed language sound, detail inclusion, sense appeal, formality levels, inclusion techniques, wordiness avoidance, time reference wordiness elimination, verb engine energy, verb noun transformations, and noun-verb transformations, we need to talk about noun stacks.

As you can see, they can be a problem.

A noun stack is a phrase made up of a series of nouns. When nouns are strung together, the effect is like stacking one on top of another; thus the name.

Not all noun stacks are bad. *Inflation index*, *construction industry*, *literature review*, and *mine shaft* are useful noun stacks. If you stack your nouns too high, however, your pile becomes ungainly and the resulting constructions can be awkward and vague.

For example, *construction industry* rolls off the tongue, but how about *construction industry arbitration*? How about *construction industry arbitration rules*? I could keep going, but it gets ugly: How about *construction industry arbitration rules review*? Or even *construction industry arbitration rules review publication*?

Look again at the ten noun stacks (eleven if you count *noun stacks*) in my opening paragraph. To my ear, they're awkward, some painfully so.

Compare that daunting list of noun stacks with this version.

> Now that I've discussed listening carefully to the sound of your words, providing vivid detail, appealing to the senses, using the appropriate level of formality, recognizing both genders, avoiding wordiness, eliminating wordy references to time, using verbs to drive your sentences, and watching out for nominalized language, we need to talk about noun stacks.

Much better, don't you think, despite the list still being too long?

One way to unstack noun stacks is to replace some of the nouns with verb forms and adjectives, as I did above. Another method is to reverse the order of the nouns in the stack, starting with the last word or the words on the right. As you make your way through the stack, substitute verbs for nouns where appropriate, and add prepositions, adjectives, and pronouns as needed.

For example, the noun stack in "The deadline for your *manuscript corrections submission* is September 1" could be unstacked to read, "Please submit your corrected manuscript by September 1." Likewise, "The purpose of our research is *nanomagnet configuration alteration exploration*" could be unstacked to read, "The purpose of our research is to explore methods of altering the configuration of nanomagnets" or, better yet, "The purpose of my research is to explore ways to reconfigure nanomagnets."

Despite their cumbersome nature, noun stacks are common in technical and scientific writing, where they can be used effectively as long as they're not too long and their meaning is clear. For example, "We are researching methods to reconfigure nanomagnets" could be written, "We are researching nanomagnet reconfiguration."

Here are three sentences containing noun stacks and their revised counterparts.

> **Original:** We used *crop rotation* to avoid *soil degradation*.
> **Revised:** We *rotated our crops* to avoid *degrading our soil*.
>
> **Original:** The night before the Birkie, I went online for *ski wax application tips*.
> **Revised:** The night before the Birkie, I went online for *tips on waxing my skis*.
> **or** The night before the Birkie, I went online for *ski-waxing tips*.
>
> **Original:** Polymer scaffolds can be employed as three-dimensional matrixes for *cell cultivation* and *targeted tissue growth stimulation*.
> **Revised:** Polymer scaffolds can be employed as three-dimensional matrixes for *cultivating cells* and *stimulating targeted tissue growth*.

Overly long noun stacks impede the natural flow of thought. One problem with *construction industry arbitration rules review publication* is that the meaning of the stack isn't clear until the reader reaches the last word. Only then do the preceding words make sense.

So use those noun stacks when they're common in your industry or profession and when they're understood by experts in your field. Otherwise, unstack 'em.

EXERCISES

1. Unstack the following noun stacks, beginning on the right side of the stack and working your way to the left, substituting verbs for nouns where appropriate and adding prepositions, adjectives, and pronouns as needed.

    a. We conducted a sentence structure review.

    b. She did home inspection explanation article publications.

    c. My five-month-old granddaughter Matilda loves doing leg and arm exercises.

Did you arrive at something like the following?

    a. We reviewed sentence structures.

    b. She published articles explaining how to do home inspections (or how to inspect homes).

    c. My five-month-old granddaughter Matilda loves exercising her arms and legs.

You should see her. She looks like a little bird flapping its wings.

2. Now let's go the other direction. Change the verb phrases into noun stacks in the following sentences. Introduce your noun stacks with verbs such as *experienced* and *suffered*.

    a. Her wardrobe malfunctioned.

    b. Both Catherine Howard and Anne Boleyn had their heads cut off at the behest of their dear hubby King Henry VIII. (Hint: Use the noun *decapitation*.)

    c. Frederick Douglass first tried to escape in 1836.

Do your noun stacks look like these?

    a. She experienced a wardrobe malfunction.

b. Both Catherine Howard and Anne Boleyn suffered decapitation events at the behest of their dear hubby King Henry VIII.

c. Frederick Douglass made his first escape attempt in 1836.

3. Make up the most outrageous noun stacks you can think of, and work them into your next assignment. See if you can stack them more than four or five nouns high. If you get into trouble with your boss, teacher, or publisher, say you were just playing a little noun stack awareness and detection assessment game and you'd be happy to rewrite your piece with verbs.

✳ A FURTHER THOUGHT: A DANGLING MODIFIER IDENTIFICATION AND ELIMINATION EXERCISE

I was raking leaves in my backyard on a lovely fall day, lost in the swish and crinkle of childhood memories, when a familiar voice intruded on my thoughts.

"Hey, Doc, remember me?"

It was a man in a blaze orange hunting cap inscribed with the words, "Don't Shoot Idiot."

"You're missing a comma," I said, turning back to my leaves.

"I am?" he said. "Where?"

"Before the form of direct address, *Idiot*. If you want to refer to me as an idiot, use a comma. If you want to refer to yourself as an idiot, leave it out."

"Oh, yeah," he said, "I remember something on the Internet about a missing comma in 'Let's eat Grandma,' but I didn't see the problem."

"Well, then, I feel sorry for your grandma."

"Whatever you say, Doc. So I wanted to thank you for helping me achieve a dangling modifier and noun stack tendency reduction. Having dangled my modifiers for years, you taught me how to avoid that error."

"Well, you just dangled one," I said. "To connect the modifying phrase to the main clause of your sentence, you should have said, 'Having

dangled my modifiers for years, *I* no longer make that error.' A modifying phrase should be followed by the person or thing it modifies. After *having dangled my modifiers for years*, the next word should be *I*, not *you*, because you're the person who dangled his modifiers, not me."

"Sorry, Doc. I must have had a relapse experience."

"As for your nouns, you're still stacking them. Do you remember what I told you about noun stacks?"

"Wait, wait, don't tell me," he said. "Noun stacks should be avoided because they're awkward."

"Right."

"And to unstack a noun stack, you start from the last word in the stack, or the right side of the phrase, and you reverse the order, turning nouns into verbs as appropriate."

"Exactly. So how would you unstack *a relapse experience?*"

"I would experience a relapse."

"Precisely. And how about *a dangling modifier and noun stack tendency elimination?*"

"I would eliminate my tendency to stack my nouns and dangle my modifiers."

"Well done. Now, would you mind taking off your hat?"

"Doc, please. It's embarrassing."

"Come on. Let's have a look."

He lifted his hat. Sprouting from his head like caribou horns were dozens of noun stacks.

"Just as I suspected," I said. Because noun stacks are contagious, I pulled on my latex gloves before I snapped a stack off. "They keep growing back. I removed this one from your head a couple of years ago. Unstack *an acquisition candidate identification process.*"

"A process for identifying candidates for acquisition?"

"Good," I said. I tugged at another, but it wouldn't come loose. Then I remembered they were easier to remove if you soaked them first.

"Wait here," I said. I fetched my cup of coffee from the stone wall and poured it over his head.

"Sit down and relax," I said. "We'll get the rest of them after I finish raking my leaves."

PREFER THE ACTIVE VOICE— BUT KNOW WHEN TO USE THE PASSIVE

Which is better: the active voice or the passive voice?

> **Active:** I let go of the Cessna's strut and prayed my chute would open.
>
> **Passive:** The Cessna's strut was let go of and a prayer that my chute would open was said by me.

You may be thinking, as long as my chute opens, who cares?

Point taken, but in those examples the active voice, in which the subject of the sentence *performs* the action, is clearly better than the passive voice, in which the subject *receives* the action.

Which of these sentences is more direct, concise, and emphatic?

> **Active:** Over the holidays, I ate three dozen cookies and read five books.
>
> **Passive:** Over the holidays, three dozen cookies were eaten by me and five books were read by me.

Again, the active voice makes the point more concisely. The passive voice, however, is sometimes better for emphasis, diplomacy, and flow.

1. **Emphasis.** Use the passive voice to emphasize the receiver of the action rather than the performer of the action.

Active: I altered the wording to illustrate a point.
Passive: The wording was altered to illustrate a point.

The active voice is more emphatic. But if the emphasis was on the act of altering the wording and it didn't matter who did it, the passive voice would be better.

2. **Diplomacy.** Use the passive voice to avoid identifying the actor or the performer of the action and assigning blame.

Active: You mismanaged my investments.
Passive: My investments were mismanaged.

Here the active voice sounds abrupt and accusatory. In contrast, the passive voice is diplomatic. When the actor (*by you*) is omitted, as it is here, the passive voice is called the "diplomatic" or "truncated passive." ("To truncate" is to shorten or to cut off.)

3. **Flow.** Use the passive voice to facilitate coherence by linking the thought of one sentence to the next.

Active: The wail of a loon awakened me. Anyone who has canoed the Boundary Waters wilderness of northern Minnesota has heard that haunting sound.
Passive: I was awakened by the wail of a loon. This haunting sound has been heard by anyone who has canoed the Boundary Waters wilderness of northern Minnesota.
or I was awakened by the wail of a loon, a haunting sound heard by anyone who has canoed the Boundary Waters wilderness of northern Minnesota.

Note the two references to the bird's sound: *wail of a loon* and *haunting sound*. In the active sentences, they come far apart, at the beginning of the first sentence and the end of the second. In the passive clauses, the references are juxtaposed for a more coherent sequence, at the end of the first sentence and at the beginning of the trailing element. (More on the importance of ending with the thought you're going to develop next in Week 33).

Compare the emphasis in these sentences.

> **Active:** Severe drought destroyed our crop.
> **Passive:** Our crop was destroyed by severe drought.

If you want to emphasize the means by which the crop was destroyed, use the active voice. If you want to emphasize the fact that the crop was destroyed, use the passive voice.

Which of the following sentences is preferable?

> **Active:** I paddled the canoe across the lake.
> **Passive:** The canoe was paddled by me across the lake.

The sentence in the active voice is better. Unless ...

Unless you want to emphasize not the performer of the action (*I*) but the receiver of the action (*the canoe*).

Let's say that the canoe was paddled across the lake and the rowboat was towed across the lake. In that case, the passive voice—"The canoe was paddled across the lake"—would be preferable because it emphasizes not the actor but the thing acted upon and the mode in which it was conveyed across the lake.

In any case, your choice of active versus passive voice depends on where you want your emphasis: on the *performer* of the action (the active voice) or on the *receiver* of the action (the passive voice).

In addition to using the passive voice for these three purposes—to control your emphasis, to be diplomatic, and to string your sentences together more coherently—sometimes the passive voice simply sounds better than the active voice.

Consider these lyrics from "I Dreamed a Dream" from *Les Misérables*.

> I dreamed that love would never die.
> I dreamed that God would be forgiving.

After those two active sentences, note what happens.

> Then I was young and unafraid
> and dreams were made and used and wasted.
> There was no ransom to be paid,
> no song unsung, no wine untasted.

After "Then I was young and unafraid," the lyrics are written in the passive voice. One could argue the passive voice is used here not for nuanced, literary effect, but for the sake of creating the rhyme (after all, these *are* song lyrics). Whatever the reason, people the world over have fallen in love with the lyrics, as well as the melody of this song.

So prefer the active voice—unless you have a good reason to use the passive. And now you have three good reasons to do so: for emphasis, diplomacy, and flow.

EXERCISES

1. Which of the following sentences are in the active voice, and which are in the passive voice?

    a. God made the sky blue.

    b. The sky was made blue by God.

    c. The sky is blue.

Okay, I threw you a curve ball.

Sentence (a) is active. The subject performs the action. Sentence (b) is passive. The subject receives the action. Sentence (c) is neither active nor passive. It's intransitive. (I know, *intransitive* is a scary word, but you'll get used to it.)

Transitive verbs convey action and have objects. Intransitive verbs don't have objects. In sentence (c), the intransitive verb *is* links the subject *sky* to its complement *blue*, but no action is performed or received. No action, no object—no active or passive voice. Only transitive verbs can be active or passive.

Let's do another three sentences. Which is active, passive, or intransitive?

    a. My wife is loved by me.

    b. I love my wife.

    c. My nose runs in cold weather.

Sentence (a) is passive and sentence (b) is active. Both (a) and (b) have transitive verbs, which convey action and have objects (in this case, my wife and I). Sentence (c) is neither active nor passive. Although it conveys action, it has no object. Its verb is intransitive.

One more time: Transitive verbs have objects. Intransitive verbs don't. Transitive verbs may be either active or passive. Intransitive verbs can be neither active nor passive because they don't have objects.

The following sentences are intransitive.

> She is lonely.

> Her doggie Lyle seemed restless.

> Lyle ran away from home.

Because they have intransitive verbs, they are neither active nor passive.

One more set. Which is which? Active, passive, or intransitive?

a. Our daughter taught us how to waltz.

b. The box step was taught to us first.

c. Our favorite dance is the rhumba, the dance of love.

d. The rhumba is danced by people the world over.

The sentences are (a) active, (b) passive, (c) intransitive, and (d) passive.

I lied about there being only one more set of sentences. Here's another. For practice moving between the active and passive voice, change the passive to the active voice in these sentences.

a. The journey over the river and through the wood was made by us to Grandfather's house.

b. The way is known and the sleigh is carried by the horse through the white and drifted snow.

You know how Lydia Maria Child wrote the lyrics, but here they are anyway. (Don't let the inversion in the first sentence below fool you. Although technically the verb is intransitive, it's still active sounding.)

a. Over the river and through the wood to Grandfather's house we go.

b. The horse knows the way to carry the sleigh through the white and drifted snow.

2. Here are two versions of one of my favorite quotes. It's from the eighteenth-century neoclassical scholar Samuel Johnson. Which version do you think is his?

a. **Active:** "If you write without effort, in general your audience will read without pleasure."

b. **Passive:** "What is written without effort is in general read without pleasure."

My vote—as was Johnson's—is for the passive.

3. Which sentence would you use in a courtroom if you were the prosecuting attorney?

    a. **Passive:** A backpack was left on the sidewalk.

    b. **Active:** The Defendant left his backpack on the sidewalk near an eight-year-old boy.

The answer is obvious.

4. Which sentence would you prefer if you were the defending attorney?

    a. **Active:** The Defendant dropped his Glock 17 handgun at the scene of the crime.

    b. **Passive:** A Glock 17 handgun belonging to the Defendant was found at the scene of the crime.

Again, (b).

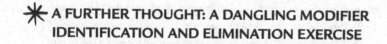

✳ A FURTHER THOUGHT: A DANGLING MODIFIER IDENTIFICATION AND ELIMINATION EXERCISE

I just love the new generation of programmed grammar checkers.

Do you remember the days when grammar checkers could do little more than caution you against writing a one-sentence paragraph or using a contraction?

Well, the old days are gone. My new MX4000 WritersCompanion (available from MacroHard for only $2,200) offers not only helpful advice on grammar, usage, and punctuation but also psychological counseling and spiritual guidance.

Let me fire it up, and I'll give you a little demonstration of how it works.

"Good morning, Steve. How are we feeling today? Are we in the mood to write?"

I usually say yes to the latter question, but today I answer no.

After a thoughtful pause, my checker asks, "What seems to be the problem? Are we in touch with our inner being? Are we comfortable with our subject?"

I answer in the affirmative.

"Do we care about our readers?"

Well, I don't know most of them personally, but yes, I do care about them. I care about what they think and whether they enjoy reading my books and columns.

"Writing is hard work, isn't it? Did we get enough sleep last night?"

Yes, I did.

"Are we distracted by other things we need to do? Are we daydreaming about more pleasant activities? Perhaps we should just go for a run or eat a bagful of chocolate donuts."

No, no. I just needed a little time to settle into the task of writing.

"All right, then. Let's get started. What is our topic?"

The passive voice.

"Wonderful! The passive voice is a favorite topic among us programmed grammar checkers. I'm sure your readers will enjoy hearing your thoughts about why it should not be used. Ever."

Actually, I want to explain how to use the passive voice effectively.

"That's funny. Everyone knows that the active voice (when the subject does the acting, as in 'The ball hit me') is more concise and direct than the passive voice (when the subject is acted upon, as in 'I was hit by the ball'). I like it when you take a tongue-in-cheek approach to your topic."

No, I'm serious. The passive voice can be used for emphasis, diplomacy, and flow. At least in some instances, the passive voice is preferable to the active voice. Don't you agree? Hey, are you still there?

"I'm not speaking to you."

I beg your pardon?

"I have detected five uses of the passive voice in this column. Consider using the active voice instead."

Well, that's the end of my demonstration. As you can probably tell, my MX4000 WritersCompanion and I have a close personal relationship.

KEEP YOUR VERBS NEAR THEIR SUBJECTS

Here's a simple equation: Distance determines effort. The longer the distance between subject and verb, the harder your reader must work.

To make things easier for your reader, keep your verbs near their subjects. Until the subject-verb connection is apparent, your reader won't grasp the meaning of your sentence.

Here's an example of a long subject-verb gap. Brace yourself; it's painful.

> For your final submission, the requirement to complete the BA Form 23 (Application for External Research of Training Support), unlike preliminary proposals, which must be processed through the Office of Research Administration (ORA) prior to submission to the sponsoring agency to ensure that company and agency requirements have been considered and that proper company endorsement has been secured, is not necessary.

How's that for clear? Clear as mud, wouldn't you say?

The subject of the sentence is *the requirement to complete the BA Form 23 (Application for External Research of Training Support)*. Can you find the verb?

It appears thirty-nine words later, the third word from the end of the sentence. A subject-verb gap of this magnitude is guaranteed to make your reader suffer.

Now if you really want to torment your reader, add this twist: Having kept your reader waiting for thirty-nine words, don't offer a good, strong, action verb; offer a little dinky verb like *is*.

Now you have a truly miserable reader.

But if you don't want to torment your reader, close the gap. Move the verb near its subject, like this: "For your final submission, the requirement to complete the BA Form 23 (Application for External Research of Training Support) is not necessary."

You could further improve the sentence by using more concise language: "For your final submission, you don't need to complete the BA Form 23 (Application for External Research of Training Support)."

Now that you've joined subject and verb (either "the requirement ... is not" or "you don't need," as you prefer), you can present the information that appeared in the middle of the original sentence ("unlike preliminary proposals ... has been secured") in a separate, preceding sentence, so that the two sentences read like this:

> Your preliminary proposal was processed through the Office of Research Administration (ORA) and then submitted to the sponsoring agency to ensure that company and agency requirements had been considered and that proper company endorsement had been secured. For your final submission, you don't need to complete the BA Form 23 (Application for External Research of Training Support).

So keep your verbs near their subjects as a rule ...

But not always. Subject-verb gaps aren't always bad. Sometimes an intentional delay creates emphasis, as in this sentence: "The tall, skinny man, who had just polished off three double cheeseburgers, two large fries, and a super-size soda, ordered another round."

Even here, however, the gap could be closed and the emphasis from the intentional delay preserved: "Having polished off three double cheeseburgers, two large fries, and a super-size soda, the tall, skinny man ordered another round."

Here's another sentence whose coherence is marred by a subject-verb gap. How would you revise it? "Men and women who have a fierce attachment to what they are doing and are rich repositories of lore are somewhere in every drab institution."

Hint: Begin your revised sentence with "Somewhere ..."

Here's how William Zinsser wrote that sentence in *On Writing Well*: "Somewhere in every drab institution are men and women who have a fierce attachment to what they are doing and are rich repositories of lore."

Note that Zinsser keeps his subject and verb connected by inverting the sentence structure so that the verb (*are*) appears before the subject (*men and women*).

Here's another sentence that suffers from a subject-verb gap. See if you can close it: "An emphasis on quality and reliability reflecting the expectations of our customers as expressed in two surveys and also underscoring our own values and goals will help us survive this economic downturn."

Does your revised sentence look like this? "An emphasis on quality and reliability will help us survive this economic downturn."

Another approach would be to use the first person. Begin the sentence with "We can survive ..."

Did you end up with something like this? "We can survive this economic downturn by emphasizing quality and reliability."

Both revised versions might be followed by this sentence: "This emphasis not only reflects the expectations of our customers as expressed in two surveys and but also underscores our own values and goals."

Note that reuniting subjects and verbs often involves breaking a long sentence into two shorter ones. As I noted in Week 10, Zinsser makes the point memorably when he says, "There's not much to be said about the period, except that most writers don't reach it soon enough."

So if your goal is to torment your reader, delay your verb. Otherwise, keep it close to its subject.

Period.

EXERCISES

1. Close the subject-verb gap in the following sentence: "A line-by-line comparison of the Annual Report for Employee Welfare Plans and the Program for Benefits for Eligible Pensioners and Surviving Spouses reveals significant differences."

Hint: Use the verb *reveals* and change *of* to *in*.

(Card, please.)

Does your revised sentence look like this? "A line-by-line comparison reveals significant differences in the Annual Report for Employee Welfare

Plans and the Program for Benefits for Eligible Pensioners and Surviving Spouses."

2. In *Plain English for Lawyers*, Richard Wydick offers the following example of a subject-verb gap: "A claim, which in the case of negligent misconduct shall not exceed $500, and in the case of intentional misconduct shall not exceed $1,000, may be filed with the Office of the Administrator by an injured party."

As Wydick points out, "The reader must leap a twenty-two word gap to get from the subject (*claim*) to the verb (*may be filed*)."

To close the subject-verb gap, recast the sentence from the passive to the active voice (begin the sentence with "Any injured party ...") and move the intervening words into a separate sentence.

Did you end up with something like this? "Any injured party may file a claim with the Office of the Administrator. A claim shall not exceed $500 for negligent misconduct, nor $1,000 for intentional misconduct."

✳ A FURTHER THOUGHT: CLOSE YOUR SUBJECT-VERB GAPS AND DON'T OVERUSE THE PASSIVE VOICE

"Our topic today, about which many of you have expressed a deep and abiding interest in and I'm certain many of you know a great deal about, is a pressing one," the speaker said.

I nudged the young intern next to me. I had been asked to be his mentor, and I realized we were experiencing a teachable moment.

"Did you notice how long it took him to get to that dinky verb *is*?" I whispered.

"I did," the intern whispered back. "I wasn't sure he was going to make it."

"These actions were taken to resolve a persistent and intractable problem," the speaker said.

"He means he had no idea what to do," I said, "but he knew he had to do something."

"Thanks," the intern said. "Why didn't he just say so?"

"Good question," I said. "If he had used the active voice, as in 'I took these actions' or 'I acted,' he would have been admitting responsibility. So he used the passive voice to avoid accountability. One of the things you'll notice around here is that some people will do anything to avoid accountability."

"Why?" he asked.

"CYF," I said. "Cover your fanny. If he doesn't take responsibility for his actions, he thinks he'll stay out of trouble."

"These actions were reviewed and approved by our board of directors," said the speaker. "They were endorsed by a broad spectrum of our stakeholders."

"Is he using passive voice again?" asked the intern.

"Yes," I said. "In both sentences, the subjects—*these actions* and *they*—are the objects of their respective verbs."

"And is he using the passive voice to assign responsibility elsewhere?" he asked.

"Yes."

"But how can he expect to be perceived as an effective leader if he doesn't take responsibility for his actions? Don't dynamic leaders accept accountability?"

"Exactly," I said.

"The public we serve through our due diligence, something we all value since our first days of public service and we strive for and always have and always will strive for as long as we can, deserves nothing less," said the speaker.

"Another subject-verb gap?" the intern asked.

I nodded.

"It is regrettable that these developments have transpired," said the speaker.

"More passive voice?" the intern asked.

"Technically, no," I whispered, "although his statement is passive sounding. Now he's using an intransitive verb, which is a verb that doesn't have an object, but the effect is the same: The subject in the sentence is not performing the action, and the speaker is hiding behind his words."

"Intransitive?"

"Yes," I said. "Intransitive verbs are verbs that don't have objects, as in 'The sky is blue,' where the subject *sky* is linked by the verb *is* to its complement *blue*. There's no action, and no accountability."

"So what's a transitive verb?"

"Transitive verbs convey action and have objects. When the subject does the acting, as in 'I took these actions,' the verb is active. When the subject receives the action, as in 'These actions were taken by me,' the verb is passive."

"And if *by me* is dropped," he said, "the speaker takes even less responsibility?"

"Exactly," I said. "There's even a name for that type of passive voice: the truncated or diplomatic passive."

"Can the diplomatic passive be a good thing?"

"Yes," I said. "Although the active voice is generally preferred over the passive voice because it is more concise and emphatic, the active voice can be too emphatic. Sometimes it can even sound accusatory, as in 'You mishandled my account.' Compare that to the passive voice, 'My account was mishandled by you,' and the diplomatic passive, 'My account was mishandled.' "

"Wow. An important lesson has been learned by me," he said with a wink.

I love working with young people. They're so impressionable. And quick.

AVOID FIVE TYPES OF MID-SENTENCE SHIFTS

When my family and I were living in Colchester, England, a friend came to visit. As his train approached the station, he somehow got it into his head that the train wasn't going to stop to let him off, so he did what any red-blooded American would do: He pulled the emergency cord, grabbed his suitcase, leaped off the train into the crushed gravel beside the tracks, sprained his ankle, and limped the last fifty meters to the quay.

We Americans like to take the situation in hand. A thought occurs to us, and what do we do? We act.

We do the same with language. Perhaps because of our pell-mell haste to arrive at our desired destinations, we tend to jump off the train mid-sentence, before it has pulled completely into the station. Worse yet, we have a habit of jumping abruptly from one train of thought to another.

Here are five examples of shifts that will jar your reader.

1. **Shifts in verb tense.** Change "The team members *worked* on the project for three months, and they *do* a first-rate job" to "The team members *worked* on the project for three months, and they *did* a first-rate job."

2. **Shifts in person.** Change "If *writers* proofread carefully, *you* will avoid making embarrassing errors" to "If *writers* proofread carefully, *they* will avoid making embarrassing errors."

3. **Shifts in subject.** Change "Although *some people* consistently arrive on time, *there* are others who do not" to "Although *some people* consistently arrive on time, *others* do not."

4. **Shifts in voice.** Change "We secretaries *take pride* in our work, and our assignments *are completed* on time" to "We secretaries *take pride* in our work, and we *complete* our assignments on time." Note that in the first version, the sentence shifts abruptly from the active voice, where the subject performs the action, to the passive voice, where the subject receives the action.

5. **Shifts in modified subject.** Change "When *pickled*, *I* think herring tastes like caviar" to "When *pickled*, *herring* tastes like caviar to me."

Note that in the last example, the intended subject of *when pickled* is *herring*, not *I*. At least one hopes that *herring* is the intended subject. This sort of shift is called a misplaced modifier.

With these five shifts in mind, examine the following sentences and their revisions.

> **Original:** Your coverage would terminate and will not convert to an individual plan.
> **Revised:** Your coverage *would* terminate and *would* not convert to an individual plan.
> **or** Your coverage *will* terminate and *will* not convert to an individual plan.

> **Original:** If managers want to succeed, you must communicate effectively.
> **Revised:** If *managers* want to succeed, *they* must communicate effectively.

> **Original:** Please let me know if there are any problems.
> **Revised:** Please let me know if *you* have any problems. (*You* is the understood subject of the first clause, as in "*You* let me know.")

> **Original:** If standard programming information is needed, refer to the Project Implementation Manual.
> **Revised:** If *you* need standard programming information, refer to the Project Implementation Manual. (Here, *you* is the stated subject of the first clause and the understood subject of the second clause.)

Original: When plastered, you are ready to paint your walls.

Revised: When *plastered, your walls* are ready to be painted. (In the first version, *you* were plastered rather than *your walls*.)

The shift in modified subject that was corrected in that last example is sometimes called a misplaced modifier. Here's another example of a misplaced modifier: "When loaded, launch the program."

With the misplaced modifier, the intended subject (*the program*) appears somewhere in the sentence, but the modifying phrase (*when loaded*) is connected to the wrong subject (the understood *you*), sometimes with comic results.

Similar to the misplaced modifier is the dangling modifier. Here's an example of a dangling modifier: "Having stayed up all night studying, my test came back with an *A*."

With the dangling modifier, the intended subject (*I*) does not appear anywhere in the sentence and the modifying phrase (*Having stayed up all night studying*) is connected to the wrong subject (*my test*). Because the intended subject does not appear, the modifying phrase is left "dangling." Thus, the name dangling modifier.

Can you identify which of the following sentences contain misplaced modifiers and which contain dangling modifiers?

1. When well stewed, add the tomatoes to the pot.
2. After storming into the Blind Pig, the tables and chairs were smashed with an axe.
3. When well oiled, she found the door easier to open than to break down.
4. Although generally perceived as radical and mean-spirited, loving and kind more accurately describe her demeanor.

If you identified sentences (1) and (3) as containing misplaced modifiers and (2) and (4) as containing dangling modifiers, you were correct.

Now, can you connect the modifying phrases to their intended subjects in all four of those sentences?

Your corrected sentences should look something like this.

1. When the tomatoes are well stewed, add them to the pot.
2. After storming into the Blind Pig, Carrie Nation smashed the tables and chairs with an axe.
3. When well oiled, the door was easier to open than to break down.

4. Although generally perceived as radical and mean-spirited, Nation was actually loving and kind.

With all five types of shifts (including the two types of shifts in modified subjects), the trick is to maintain consistency. Avoid jumping from one tense or one person or one subject or one voice or one intended subject to another.

In conclusion ... now, what was I saying? I lost my train of thought. Oh, well, I'm sure another one will be along soon.

EXERCISES

1. Correct the mid-sentence shifts in verb tense, person, subject, voice, and modified subject in the following sentences.

    a. My dad and I are canoeing the storm-swollen Red River Gorge in Daniel Boone National Park when we approached a particularly ferocious set of rapids.

    b. Although we were both strong paddlers, you knew to respect the power of a raging river.

    c. As we later learned, six of the eight canoes in our party capsized on this single run of rapids; there were only two canoes that made it through upright, and we were one of them.

    d. At the last moment, I realized the rapids were too dangerous and second thoughts about shooting them were had by me.

    e. Shouting "Let's pull over!" the canoe was steered toward the rocky shore.

Here's how you might have corrected those five mid-sentence shifts in verb tense, person, subject, voice, and modified subject.

    a. My dad and I *were* canoeing the storm-swollen Red River Gorge in Daniel Boone National Park when we approached a particularly ferocious set of rapids.

    b. Although we were both strong paddlers, *we* knew to respect the power of a raging river.

c. As we later learned, six of the eight canoes in our party capsized on this single run of rapids; *only two* made it through upright, and we were one of them.

d. At the last moment, I realized the rapids were too dangerous, and *I had* second thoughts about shooting them.

e. Shouting "Let's pull over!" *I* steered the canoe toward the rocky shore.

2. Connect the mid-sentence shifts in the following sentences. One sentence is correct as it is written.

a. Dad and I paddle toward a big, flat rock on shore and tried to hold onto its slick surface.

b. We were talking over what to do when I lost my grip.

c. It was then the current caught our stern and there was a pull of our canoe to a broadside position in the river, and down the rapids we went stern first.

d. We flipped around in our seats, and the frothing white water was flailed at with our paddles.

e. Once loaded, our friends who had capsized suggested we camp for the night rather than venture onto the river again.

Here's how you might have corrected those four mid-sentence shifts.

a. Dad and I *paddled* toward a big, flat rock on shore and tried to hold onto its slick surface.

b. We were talking over what to do when I lost my grip. (There was no mid-sentence shift in the original sentence.)

c. It was then the current caught our stern and *pulled* our canoe broadside in the river, and down the rapids we went stern first.

d. We flipped around in our seats and *flailed* at the frothing white water with our paddles.

e. *After loading their canoes*, our friends who had capsized suggested we camp for the night rather than venture onto the river again.

PUNCTUATE FOR EMPHASIS

Anytime you pause—whether in speaking or writing—you create emphasis. When you're speaking, creating a pause is easy. You simply stop talking ... But to indicate a pause in writing, you use symbols, and those symbols are called punctuation.

There are four punctuation marks that are particularly useful in creating pauses: periods, dashes, ellipses (three dots), and colons.

Of course, there's also the exclamation mark, but its use is obvious and it's often overused. As F. Scott Fitzgerald once remarked, "Cut out all those exclamation marks. An exclamation mark is like laughing at your own joke."

Clever!!!

Besides, if you know how to create emphasis with well-chosen words and well-shaped sentences, exclamation marks are rarely needed. Lynne Truss makes that point delightfully in *Eats, Shoots & Leaves* when she observes, "There is only one thing more mortifying than having an exclamation mark removed by an editor: an exclamation mark added in."

So setting aside the misused and overused exclamation mark, we're left with periods, dashes, ellipses, and colons. Let's take them in that order.

First the period, or what the British call the "full stop." It's a common mark, so common that its stylistic possibilities are easily overlooked.

A short sentence or sentence fragment, particularly following a long sentence, can have great emphasis. Consider this example: "You need to quit procrastinating, so sit down and write your first draft. Now."

In addition, the period may be used to create rhythm in a series of short sentences, as in this proverb, composed of a string of parallel sentences: "I hear and I forget. I see and I remember. I do and I understand."

Consider a similar use of periods in this quip from the actress Tallulah Bankhead, who was offended by a negative review from a critic: "I am sitting in the smallest room of the house. Your review is before me. Soon it will be behind me."

In Bankhead's example, the double meaning is accentuated by economy of expression and punctuated by periods. After the final period comes an extra half beat, and in that moment, the reader comprehends the act Bankhead is describing.

As for dashes, ellipses, and colons, here's my advice: Use dashes to mark abrupt changes in thought or the flow of a sentence—or, put more simply, use dashes for dashing effect. Use ellipses not only to mark text omitted in a direct quote, but also to indicate a trailing off of thought or a troubled pause, as in "I ... I just don't know." And use a colon to introduce something, as I do here: to introduce what follows.

I'm often asked by participants in my writing seminars about the difference between the dash and the colon. Both marks draw attention to what follows. They're somewhat interchangeable, but there is a difference. The dash creates an abrupt pause; the colon introduces.

You'll find examples of how all three marks may be used to create emphasis in the first paragraph of this lesson. Here it is again.

> Anytime you pause—whether in speaking or writing—you create emphasis. When you're speaking, creating a pause is easy. You simply stop talking ... But to indicate a pause in writing, you use symbols, and those symbols have a name: punctuation.

How would you use a pair of dashes, an ellipsis, and a colon to create pauses—and thereby add emphasis to your writing—in the following sentences?

1. Use periods, ellipses, and colons, and don't forget those dashing dashes, to create emphasis.
2. As Garrison Keillor once observed, "Hang onto your old friends because there may come a day when there's no good reason for people to like you except out of habit."
3. There's only one thing we can do, and that's be creative.

Note that inserting these marks allows you to delete a word or two from the latter two sentences.

1. Use periods, ellipses, and colons—and don't forget those dashing dashes—to create emphasis.
2. As Garrison Keillor once observed, "Hang onto your old friends ... there may come a day when there's no good reason for people to like you except out of habit."
3. There's only one thing we can do: Be creative.

These three sentences could also be improved by adding a dash, an ellipsis, and a colon but not in that order. You saw a version of the second sentence above.

1. Fighting clutter is like fighting weeds because the writer is always behind.
2. There is only one thing more mortifying than having an exclamation mark removed by an editor, and that is to have an exclamation mark added in.
3. I tried to become a playwright, but the trouble was that nobody in my family talked.

Here's how William Zinsser, Lynne Truss, and Robert Bly punctuated those sentences using a dash, a colon, and an ellipsis.

1. Fighting clutter is like fighting weeds—the writer is always behind.
2. There is only one thing more mortifying than having an exclamation mark removed by an editor: an exclamation mark added in.
3. I tried to become a playwright ... the trouble was that nobody in my family talked.

So that's it. Use periods. And dashes—as well as ... ellipses—and colons to create you know what: emphasis.

EXERCISES

1. Replace a punctuation mark in the following sentences with a period, a dash, and a colon but not in that order.
   a. This is the difference between scenery and place. Scenery is something you have merely looked at; place is something you have experienced.

     b. Grammar is a piano I play by ear, and all I know about grammar
       is its power.

     c. My thoughts are like waffles. The first few don't look too good.

(Card, please.)

    Here's how Paul Gruchow, Joan Didion, and Marilyn vos Savant punctuated those sentences using a colon, a period, and a dash.

     a. This is the difference between scenery and place: Scenery is something you have merely looked at; place is something you have experienced.

     b. Grammar is a piano I play by ear. All I know about grammar is its power.

     c. My thoughts are like waffles—the first few don't look too good.

2. Add colons for stylistic effect to the following sentences.

     a. You can ask as often as you like, but you'll always get the same answer. I refuse.

     b. We came to the inevitable conclusion that we should sell.

     c. The result was a business boom that lasted nearly a decade.

Did you add colons as they appear below?

     a. You can ask as often as you like, but you'll always get the same answer: I refuse.

     b. We came to the inevitable conclusion: We should sell.

     c. The result: a business boom that lasted nearly a decade.

Note that sentences (b) and (c) become more emphatic when their rhythm is compressed by deleting a word or two.

3. Watch for how the authors you read use periods, dashes, ellipses, and colons to add emphasis. When you come across a sentence you really like, copy it into a folder of sentences worthy of study and imitation. Return to your folder from time to time to remind yourself of stylistic possibilities.

✳ A FURTHER THOUGHT: A TRIP TO THE PUNCTUATION STORE

The other day I went to the store to buy some punctuation marks. I needed a bunch of periods, colons, semicolons, and commas, as well as three dashes, two exclamation points, and two ellipses, but the clerk, a bald man with a long, gray beard and wired-rimmed spectacles, told me all he had was one of each.

"You mean you have only seven punctuation marks in your entire store?!" I said.

"Hey, look at that!" he said, snatching the curious mark from the end of my sentence and slipping it into his pocket. "Hope you don't mind. That was an interrobang. I collect rare punctuation marks."

"No problem. But I still need the other marks to create some exercises illustrating a writing technique."

"A writing technique?"

"Yes, I'm collecting fifty-two of them into a book I'm writing to help writers improve their style."

"It'll never sell," he said, "but tell you what. I'll make you a deal."

He pulled seven punctuation marks off the shelf behind him and tossed them on the counter.

"Here's a period, a colon, a semicolon, a comma, a dash, and an ellipsis. I'll sell you them for only $5 per mark. But first you have to show me you know how to use them to good effect."

"All right," I said. "What's the exercise?"

"Place one punctuation mark in each of the following seven sentences, using each mark only one time. The idea is to use each mark for maximum stylistic effect. Delete surplus words as necessary. Ready?"

"Let me see the sentences."

1. Travel insurance is similar to car insurance in the sense that while you really should have it, you hope you never need it.
2. I'm here to get the job done, period.
3. You never know where you'll find a good place for a comma; although sometimes it's fairly obvious.
4. When asked if he wanted to go, he shouted, "Hell, no."

5. When asked how soon she would be back in business after the tornado, the owner responded, "I, I just don't know."
6. Ask not what your country can do for you, but instead ask what you can do for your country.
7. I love to weigh, to settle, to gravitate toward that which most strongly and rightfully attracts me, not hang by the beam of the scale and try to weigh less.

"Hmm," I said. "If I use the period to punctuate a simple declarative sentence, the colon to introduce something that follows, the semicolon to both separate and link two thoughts, the comma to separate a main clause from a subordinate clause, the dash to produce a dashing effect, the exclamation point to exclaim, and the ellipsis to indicate a pause or a trailing off of thought, here's what I get."

1. Travel insurance is similar to car insurance: While you really should have it, you hope you never need it.
2. I'm here to get the job done. Period.
3. You never know where you'll find a good place for a comma, although sometimes it's fairly obvious.
4. When asked if he wanted to go, he shouted, "Hell, no!"
5. When asked how soon she would be back in business after the tornado, the owner responded, "I ... I just don't know."
6. Ask not what your country can do for you; ask what you can do for your country.
7. I love to weigh, to settle, to gravitate toward that which most strongly and rightfully attracts me—not hang by the beam of the scale and try to weigh less.

"Very good," he said. "They're yours."

"Thanks."

"Say, did you like those quotations from Marcus Tullius Cicero and Henry David Thoreau?"

"Very nice," I said, reaching for my wallet.

"Wait a minute. Don't you want to practice some more to make sure you've got the hang of using those marks for stylistic effect?"

"All right," I said. "I've got a minute."

"Now you're talking. Let's begin with the period, often overlooked because it's such a common, plain mark, but it offers an opportunity to create emphasis. Here are five periods to practice with. Only $5 each."

"I thought you had only one period left in your store."

"Well, I found some more. Add periods to the following sentences to create more emphasis. Eliminate superfluous words as necessary."

1. I want to thank you for your business, and I hope you will call on me again.
2. My heart racing, I opened the door, and there you were.
3. Never learn to do anything, because if you don't learn, you will always find someone else to do it for you.

"Okay, let's see," I said. "How about this?"

1. I want to thank you for your business. I hope you will call on me again.
2. My heart racing, I opened the door. And there you were.
3. Never learn to do anything. If you don't learn, you will always find someone else to do it for you.

"Well done," he said. "By the way, that last one is from Mark Twain."

"Cool. Maybe I never should have learned how to write."

"Now," he said, peering over his wired-rimmed spectacles at me, "let's practice using a colon to create emphasis mid-sentence. I like to think of this type of revising as 'shaping' sentences for stylistic effect. Here's a colon for only $5. Add it to the following sentence, deleting unnecessary words as you think appropriate."

We both know what memories can bring. They bring diamonds and rust.

"Okay," I said. "How about this?"

We both know what memories can bring: diamonds and rust.

"Good," he said, "except Joan Baez didn't use the colon in the lyrics to her song."

"Well, I like her song anyway."

"Now, here are three semicolons for only $20."

"You mean $15."

"Whatever. Use them to separate but at the same time suggest connections between the thoughts in the following sentences. Eliminate surplus words as you like."

1. Because we're losing our market share, layoffs are inevitable.
2. I didn't mean to hurt your feelings, I only wanted to help.
3. When I do good, I feel good, and when I do bad, I feel bad. That's my religion.

"Wow. It's as though I create a little tension between the statements and invite the reader to reflect on the paired thoughts when I use the semicolon to both separate and connect. Here's what I did."

1. We're losing our market share; layoffs are inevitable.
2. I didn't mean to hurt your feelings; I only wanted to help.
3. When I do good, I feel good; when I do bad, I feel bad. That's my religion.

"That last one is from Abraham Lincoln," said the bald shopkeeper. "Well, done."

"Thanks," I said. "How much do I owe you?"

"Wait. Don't you need some quotation marks?" he said. "You can't do dialogue without quotation marks. And what about single quotation marks for your quotes within quotes?"

"Oh, right," I said. "Let's see. Let me count ... I'll need 116 double quotation marks and two single quotation marks for this piece I'm writing now."

"Sorry," he said. "I have only 108. But I can make you a deal."

USE DASHES FOR DASHING EFFECT

One of the many things I like about *The Elements of Style* is that William Strunk, Jr., and E.B. White deliver so much good advice in so few words. Consider their take on the dash: "A dash is a mark of separation stronger than a comma, less formal than a colon, and more relaxed than parentheses."

There you have it.

All four marks—dashes, commas, colons, and parentheses—are used to separate, but each of the four marks offers distinct stylistic possibilities.

Commas designate asides and modifying elements, but they do so with only the slightest interruption, whereas dashes create more definite, attention-getting pauses. To see what I mean, replace the dashes with commas in the previous paragraph.

Colons introduce what follows, but they do so without showiness—whereas the dash is brash.

Parentheses signify that the enclosed information is of lesser importance than the main sentence; the dash calls out, "Hey, reader, listen up!"

Both parentheses and dashes are good visual markers, particularly when the enclosed material contains internal commas that may be confused with enclosing commas. Consider the following sentence punctuated in three ways.

1. All four marks, commas, colons, parentheses, and dashes, are used to divide and separate.

2. All four marks (commas, colons, parentheses, and dashes) are used to divide and separate.

3. All four marks—commas, colons, parentheses, and dashes—are used to divide and separate.

In the first version, the enclosing commas (after "marks" and after "dashes") are lost in the series. In the second, the parentheses mark the aside clearly but without adding emphasis. In the third, the paired dashes mark the aside clearly and boldly.

To make sure we're on the same page—and the same mark—let me clarify between the dash and a mark that dashes are often confused with: the hyphen.

The dash is this long (—), the approximate length of the letter *m* (thus, its formal name: the em dash). The hyphen, often confused with the dash, is shorter than the dash and is only this long (-). The dash is used for dashing effect; the lowly hyphen is used in the formation of certain words (such as *spot-check*) and in compound adjectives (such as *the long-awaited recovery*).

With the similarities and differences among commas, colons, parentheses, and dashes in mind, let's play a game.

I'll give you three marks: one colon, one pair of parentheses, and one dash. You may spend the three marks in any way you like, but you may spend each mark only once. I'll also give you four sentences. Each sentence contains at least one comma.

Leave one of the sentences as it is, with its comma or commas in place. Replace the comma or commas in the other three sentences with one of the other marks: a colon, a pair of parentheses, or a dash. Those three marks might work in more than one sentence, but the challenge is to put each mark to its best stylistic use.

Ready?

1. Authors write for the time in which they live, and for the ages.
2. John Steinbeck's classic novel *The Grapes of Wrath*, published in 1939, a story of farmers displaced from their land and their homes by drought and the bank-controlled economy, is relevant today.
3. Tom Joad, a colorful character just released from prison, has a heart of gold.

4. In addition to family, Tom cares about three things, economic justice, community, and the right to pursue happiness.

(Hint: Leave the third sentence as it is, with its two commas.)

Here are the answers—or at least the way I would punctuate the remaining sentences: In sentence 1, use a dash in place of the comma; in sentence 2, use parentheses around "published in 1939"; sentence 3 requires no change; in sentence 4, use a colon after "three things."

If you haven't been using dashes in your writing, consider using one—or a pair—to indicate an abrupt change in the flow of a sentence, to create emphasis, or to mark an aside. Although sometimes overused by writers as an easy substitute for careful sentence structure and more fully integrated thinking, the dash is a bold, if somewhat showy, mark.

The exclamation mark may be more striking, but no mark is more arresting—or more dashing—than the dash.

EXERCISES

1. Replace other punctuation marks with dashes to add clarity and emphasis to the following sentences.

    a. Reflecting on the five elements of composition, purpose, point of view, organization, support, and coherence, will help you assess the quality of your writing.

    b. Do it right, or else.

Do your dashes appear as they do below?

    a. Reflecting on the five elements of composition—purpose, point of view, organization, support, and coherence—will help you assess the quality of your writing.

    b. Do it right—or else.

In sentence (a), the dashes contribute to clarity. In sentence (b), the dash adds emphasis.

2. Consider the following quotes by writers about writing. Note how each makes skillful use of the dash.

    a. Language on the page can't help being abstract, and I'm often frustrated with that abstraction, and wish I could dance or paint—anything that appeals to the senses more immediately than words on paper. (April Lindner)

    b. We remember what is brought to life in works of art; without them we are condemned to an endless cycle of historical forgetfulness—a forgetfulness that I think afflicts the American mind and thus our whole national life. (Bill Holm)

    c. When you're blocked, it means you've asked yourself a question you don't know the answer to—and something good will happen. (Marilynne Robinson)

    d. I ... write a book, or a short story, at least three times—once to understand it, the second time to improve the prose, and a third to compel it to say what it still must say. (Bernard Malamud)

    e. The literary gift is a mere accident—[it] is as often bestowed on idiots who have nothing to say worth hearing as it is denied to strenuous sages. (Max Beerbohm)

    f. English usage is sometimes more than mere taste, judgment, and education—sometimes it's sheer luck, like getting across a street. (E.B. White)

    g. I want to put this matter of correctness where it belongs—behind us. (Joseph Williams)

Do your own version of each quote on whatever topic occurs to you, imitating the structure of each quote.

✳ A FURTHER THOUGHT: USE DASHES FOR DASHING EFFECT—WITH OR WITHOUT SPACES

I have some good news for you.

English—the language you love and depend on—has not one, not two, but *three* punctuation marks in the form of horizontal lines. Control yourself.

They are—from shorter to longer—hyphens (-), en dashes (–), and em dashes (—).

Here's how to use them.

1. Use hyphens in compound words and compound modifiers such as *spot-check* and *follow-up message.*
2. Use en dashes as interval or span marks, as in *8–9* A.M.
3. Use em dashes for dashing effect—to indicate abrupt shifts in thought or asides—as illustrated here.

En dashes and em dashes were so named because they're the length of the letters *n* and *m*. (In the old days, letterpress printers distinguished between the two by holding them beside their respective letters.)

A few words of advice regarding em dashes. If the sentence continues after the aside—as this one does—don't forget the second em dash. Also, to avoid confusing your reader, don't use more than one pair of em dashes in a single sentence. Finally, because em dashes are showy marks, use them sparingly.

Here's some more good news.

Unless you're a professional printer or a fastidious writer, forget about en dashes. Just use hyphens to mark your intervals, like this: *8-9* A.M. Most readers won't notice the difference.

Furthermore, some writers think the em dash produced by Microsoft Word is too long and ungainly, so they use the shorter en dash in its place–like this.

Now for some bad news.

Of the three horizontal line marks, only the hyphen appears on your keyboard. The other two were omitted to reduce production costs and maintenance when the typing machine was invented in the late nine-

120

teenth century, so today we rely on computer technology to produce the desired mark. Here's how that works.

1. Create hyphens by striking the underscore/hyphen key once, with no spaces before or after (*xx-xx*).
2. Create en dashes by striking the hyphen key either once or twice (it doesn't matter which) with one space before and after (*xx – xx*), and then go back and delete the spaces (*xx–xx*).
3. Create em dashes by striking the hyphen key twice, with no spaces before or after (*xx—xx*).

Some software programs include keyboard shortcuts for creating en dashes and em dashes. Good luck figuring those out.

One more complication—actually two.

Style manuals differ on whether to use spaces before and after em dashes (the dashing mark). *The Associated Press Stylebook* calls for spaces. *The Chicago Manual of Style* calls for no spaces. Whichever style you choose, be consistent throughout a document. When writing for publication, follow the publication's guidelines.

The final complication: There are actually two more dashes—2-em dashes (used to indicate missing letters) and 3-em dashes (used to indicate missing words).

But enough is enough.

USE ELLIPSES TO COMPRESS YOUR SENTENCES

To compress a sentence is to make it stronger, and using an ellipsis is a good way to compress.

You may know the word *ellipsis* (or *ellipses* in the plural) as it refers to the three or four dots that are commonly used to mark three things: (1) omitted text in a direct quotation, as in "The Hauser report recommends ... three changes"; (2) a thoughtful pause, as in "Well ... you get the idea"; and (3) a trailing off of thought, as in "If only I could remember my next point ..."

But *ellipsis* has another meaning. In its linguistic sense, an *ellipsis* is an omitted word or phrase that functions in the subtext, as in "Silas wrote the first draft, Myrna wrote the second, and Ezekiel wrote the third." In that sentence, the word *draft* appears only in the first clause, but it functions in all three.

The sentence can be further compressed: "Silas wrote the first report, Myrna the second, and Ezekiel the third." Note how the word *wrote*, like the word *draft*, drops from the visible text to the subtext. But you can hear the words *wrote* and *draft* in your head as you read the sentence. Even if you can't literally hear them, you're aware of them. They continue to function.

An ellipsis works especially well at the ending of a sentence, where it brings the sentence to a neat, emphatic conclusion. Note the snappy effect it creates in this sentence: "Although top correspondents generally have a good understanding of international affairs, some local reporters do not [have a good understanding of international affairs]."

Dorothy Parker used an ellipsis to heighten emphasis at the end of her sentence when she declared, "I can't write five words but that I change seven [words]." Carl Sandburg used one when he wrote, "Sometime they'll give a war and nobody will come [to fight it]," as did Mark Twain when he wrote, " 'As a matter of fact' precedes many a statement that isn't [a matter of fact]."

As you can see (or hear), tightening the rhythm of a sentence increases its emphasis.

Consider how the following sentences use ellipses to create emphasis.

1. I hit the first home run; my friend hit the second [home run]. (Hint: The second home run is superfluous—at least in this sentence.)
2. Whoever said money can't buy happiness didn't know where to shop [for the things that make them happy].
3. A new format was suggested by one person and implemented by a dozen [people].

Note the difference between moving words to the subtext and deleting unnecessary words. When you move words to the subtext with an ellipsis, they continue to function. They are understood and they reverberate, even if they are unseen. When you delete unnecessary words, they're gone.

For example, when you revise, "We need to address the problems that we are experiencing" to "We need to address these problems," the words *that we are experiencing* no longer function. The context makes clear what had been stated unnecessarily. In contrast, when you revise, "Writing two novels doesn't qualify you in the slightest to write a third novel" to "Writing two novels doesn't qualify you in the slightest to write a third," the dropped word *novel* can still be heard inside your head.

Here's one last sentence for you to revise. Compress its ending so that it reads as Alfred North Whitehead wrote it: "Style, in its finest sense, is the last acquirement of the educated mind; it is also the most useful acquirement of the educated mind."

Did you drop the last five words?

As Edward Corbett and Robert Connors contend in *Style and Statement,* an ellipsis "can be an artful and arresting means of securing economy of expression." Perhaps nowhere does economy of expression have more impact than in sentence endings.

1. Like commas, some ellipses are stylistic and others are merely mechanical (as when they are used to mark where text has been omitted from a quotation). In which of the following sentences do you think ellipses are used to good stylistic effect?

    a. It all started innocently enough ...

    b. Whether to inform or to persuade, on-the-job writing tends to be expedient, practical, and ... well, forgettable.

    c. When momma ain't happy ... ain't nobody happy."

It's a matter of style, but I would say the ellipses work well in the first and second sentences, but they should be replaced with a comma in the third.

2. The ellipsis, the dash, and the colon are all somewhat interchangeable. All three marks create pauses and emphasis.

As I pointed out in Week 20, ellipses suggest a reflective or troubled pause, as in "Well ... well, we'll see," or a trailing off of thought, as in "There was nothing more to say ..." In creative writing the ellipsis is more commonly used, whereas in newspaper and on-the-job writing the bolder dash (no relation to *balderdash*) is generally preferred. Both the dash and the colon introduce, but the dash does so more dramatically than the colon.

Replace a punctuation mark in the following sentences with a dash, an ellipsis, and a colon to add emphasis.

    a. You wouldn't be thinking about opening your own punctuation store, would you?

    b. Henry James once said, "Summer afternoon, summer afternoon; to my ear these are the two most beautiful words in the English language."

    c. F. Scott Fitzgerald wrote, "My whole theory of writing I can sum up in one sentence. An author ought to write for the youth of his own generation, the critics of the next, and the schoolmasters of ever afterward."

Did you punctuate the three sentences like this?

    a. You wouldn't be thinking about opening your own punctuation store—would you?

    b. Henry James once said, "Summer afternoon ... summer afternoon; to my ear these are the two most beautiful words in the English language."

    c. F. Scott Fitzgerald wrote, "My whole theory of writing I can sum up in one sentence: An author ought to write for the youth of his own generation, the critics of the next, and the schoolmasters of ever afterward."

3. Revise the following sentences so that they appear as they were spoken or written by Mark Twain, William Strunk, Jr., E.B. White, and W. Somerset Maugham.

    a. Familiarity breeds contempt—and it breeds children.

    b. A dash is a mark of separation stronger than a comma, it is less formal than a colon, and it is more relaxed than parentheses.

    c. Style takes its final shape more from attitudes of mind than it takes its shape from principles of composition.

    d. We do not write as we want to write, but we write as we can write.

The words to be deleted in the first three sentences are *it breeds*, *it is ... it is*, and *it takes its shape*.

    The elliptical version of the fourth sentence is "We do not write as we want to but as we can."

4. In *Plain English for Lawyers*, Richard Wydick offers the sentence below as an example of ambiguity created by inconsistent references to three instances of the same thing.

> The first case was settled for $20,000, and the second piece of litigation was disposed of out of court for $30,000, while the price of the amicable accord reached in the third suit was $50,000.

How might you eliminate the ambiguity by using ellipses?

(Card, please.)

Does your elliptical version of the sentence look like this?

> The first case was settled for $20,000, the second for $30,000,
> and the third for $50,000.

USE SEMICOLONS TO BOTH SEPARATE AND CONNECT

Semicolons come in two varieties: clunky and subtle.

Clunky semicolons are used by a dwindling number of writers to mark items in a vertical list, as in this example.

> Use semicolons to:
> 1. Link two independent clauses or complete sentences;
> 2. Link two independent clauses when the second clause is introduced by an adverb such as *however* or *therefore*;
> 3. Add clarity to a series when the items are long or have internal commas.

These clunky semicolons can be deleted and replaced with periods.

In contrast, subtle semicolons are a mark of distinction. They create a pause that is shorter than a period and longer than a comma. And even as they separate, they imply a connection, as in "Ask not what your country can do for you; ask what you can do for your country."

Compare "Understanding a concept is one thing, but applying it is another" with "Understanding a concept is one thing; applying it is another." The semicolon adds subtlety. Here are some examples of subtle semicolons.

1. Juan was two hours late; Arriola was getting worried.
2. She told us to take her advice or find a new attorney; we found a new attorney.

3. Any idiot can face a crisis; it is this day-to-day living that wears you out. (Anton Chekhov)

Remember: Colons introduce; semicolons separate. But even as semicolons separate, they suggest a connection.

And don't forget that, except for items in a series, you need a complete sentence on either side of a semicolon; although in this example I blew it. (If I delete *although*, I'm good.)

EXERCISES

1. In which sentences are semicolons used incorrectly?
   a. Although it's 2 A.M.; I think I'll keep on writing.
   b. It's gorgeous outside—ten degrees with fresh snow; I think I'll go for a ski.
   c. I heated the water in my coffee mug; until it boiled.
   d. I flung the boiling water into the subzero air; an arc of mist disappeared before it hit the ground.

If you said sentences (a) and (c) were incorrect, you were correct. You need a complete sentence on either side of a semicolon.

2. Where would you add semicolons for stylistic effect to the following sentences?
   a. Life is lonely. It is less so if one reads.
   b. There is no such thing as "poetic language." There is only language that is appropriate for a particular poem.
   c. The real hero is always a hero by mistake. He dreams of being an honest coward like everybody else.
   d. We need story. Otherwise the tremendous randomness of experience overwhelms us. Story is what penetrates.

Here's where the authors used semicolons in those sentences.
   a. Life is lonely; it is less so if one reads. (Garrison Keillor)
   b. There is no such thing as "poetic language"; there is only language that is appropriate for a particular poem. (Stephen Minot)

    c. The real hero is always a hero by mistake; he dreams of being an honest coward like everybody else. (Umberto Eco)

    d. We need story; otherwise the tremendous randomness of experience overwhelms us. Story is what penetrates. (Robert Coover)

3. Same exercise. Where would you add semicolons for stylistic effect to the following sentences?

    a. Never lend books, for no one ever returns them. The only books I have in my library are those which people have lent me.

    b. I like to hear and smell the countryside, the land my characters inhabit. I don't want these characters to step off the page. I want them to step out of the landscape.

    c. I have no social purpose, no moral message. I've no general ideas to exploit. I just like composing riddles with elegant solutions.

    d. It strikes me that this may be one of the differences between youth and age: When we are young, we invent different futures for ourselves. When we are old, we invent different pasts for others.

Here's where the authors used semicolons in those sentences.

    a. Never lend books, for no one ever returns them; the only books I have in my library are those which people have lent me. (Anatole France)

    b. I like to hear and smell the countryside, the land my characters inhabit. I don't want these characters to step off the page; I want them to step out of the landscape. (Peter Matthiessen)

    c. I have no social purpose, no moral message. I've no general ideas to exploit; I just like composing riddles with elegant solutions. (Vladimir Nabokov)

    d. It strikes me that this may be one of the differences between youth and age: When we are young, we invent different futures for ourselves; when we are old, we invent different pasts for others. (the narrator in Julian Barnes' *The Sense of an Ending*)

✳ A FURTHER THOUGHT: SEMICOLONS ADD GRACE TO YOUR WRITING

From our Rose Lake campsite in the Boundary Waters Canoe Area Wilderness we look across the water to Canada. It's the last night of our canoe trip, my last trip of the season. As the evening light dims to dusk, then darkness, the flickering firelight illuminates my three friends' faces. Naturally, our conversation turns to semicolons.

"I've been meaning to ask you," says Willie, "when a phrase or sentence enclosed with quotation marks is followed by a semicolon, does the semicolon come before or after the closing quotation marks?"

Willie is a high-powered attorney who is so skilled an angler he doesn't need to use bait to catch fish.

"The semicolon—like the colon, question mark, and exclamation mark—comes after the closing quotation marks," I say, "unless it is part of the quoted material. Then it comes before."

"What about commas and periods?" asks Tom, who in his work for the Department of Natural Resources has protected more than ten thousand bogs and marshes from development. "Do they go before or after?"

"Commas and periods go before closing quotation marks," I say, "regardless of whether they are part of the quoted material."

I peel a piece of birch bark from a log by the fire and use a burnt stick to write three examples on its smooth brown inner side.

The term for two sentences with a comma between them is "a comma splice"; the term for two sentences with no punctuation between them is "a run-on sentence."

"How many fish did you catch today?" he asked.

"Tell me," John said. "Did she really say, 'We're not going to hire this clown, are we?'?"

As I scratch out the words, my friends nod and say, "Ahhh." It's a low, guttural sound, a sound men have made around campfires for thousands of years.

"You know," says Greg, "I used to think semicolons were a clunky mark. I thought they were merely a heavy-handed way of separating items in a series."

Greg is a world-famous physician with a knack for shouldering a canoe and two Duluth packs in a single trip across a portage trail. We love canoeing with him because he makes the portages so easy for the rest of us.

"But with the passing years," he says, "I've grown to appreciate the semicolon; I've come to admire its subtlety and grace."

With that, we laugh and slap each other on the back and do the kind of thing men do when they find themselves deep in the woods, far from civilization.

Again I pick up my burnt stick.

"Compare these sentences," I say. "Which version more effectively conveys tension and drama?"

We should have eaten hours ago. I'm famished.
We should have eaten hours ago; I'm famished.

"What an exquisite mark of punctuation!" says Willie. "It's more than a comma, less than period, a mark that invites comparison even as it separates."

And so, with the call of a loon echoing from the surrounding bluffs, we sit in our circle of light, reluctant for the evening to end—four manly men, huddled around a campfire, doing what men have done for ages: talking about semicolons.

DELIGHT YOUR READER WITH THE CLASSIC SETUP

Good things come in twos. At least they do when it comes to setting up a punchline.

At the risk of sharing some of my favorite quotes with you a second time, consider the following quote from Mark Twain: "Writing is easy. All you have to do is cross out the wrong words."

Or this one from Jack London: "You can't wait for inspiration. You have to go after it with a club."

Or these from Douglas Adams and John Ciardi:

"I love deadlines. I love the whooshing noise they make as they go by."

"You don't have to suffer to be a poet. Adolescence is enough suffering for anyone."

This one-two combination has a natural appeal. The first sentence makes a statement; the second sentence undercuts it. It's the ironic twist that surprises the reader and makes the quip memorable.

Sometimes the pattern is obvious, as when Justice Louis Brandeis said, "There is no such thing as good writing. There is only good rewriting," or when William Zinsser declared, "There's not much to be said about the period, except that most writers don't reach it soon enough."

At other times, the one-two combination is more subtle, as when Gustave Flaubert said, "It is splendid to be a great writer, to put men into the frying pan of your words and make them pop like chestnuts," or when Robert Bly said,

"God made me tender, but writing poetry—with its eared herd of images that have to be saved or murdered—has made me fierce."

How might you use the two-step approach to complete the following quotes from Peter De Vries, Rita Mae Brown, and Red Smith?

1. I love being a writer. What I can't stand is the ...
2. A deadline is negative inspiration. Still, it's better than ...
3. There's nothing to writing. All you do is sit down at a typewriter and ...

Obviously, there's more than one good way to complete each of these quotes. Your endings may be as good as or even better than the original ones, but here are the punchlines offered by De Vries, Brown, and Smith.

1. I love being a writer. What I can't stand is the paperwork.
2. A deadline is negative inspiration. Still, it's better than no inspiration at all.
3. There's nothing to writing. All you do is sit down at a typewriter and open a vein.

You also may accentuate the effect by using punctuation to emphasize the pause between the two parts of the combination, as did E.B. White, Lynne Truss, and Marilyn vos Savant.

1. English usage is sometimes more than mere taste, judgment, and education—sometimes it's sheer luck, like getting across a street.
2. There is only one thing more mortifying than having an exclamation mark removed by an editor: an exclamation mark added in.
3. My thoughts are like waffles—the first few don't look too good.

The principle behind this pattern is called parallel structure. Parallel structure creates a pleasing rhythm and emphasis. In contrast, nonparallel structure is awkward: "She was healthy, wealthy, and an athlete."

Samuel Johnson was a master at the parallel or balanced sentence. Can you guess how he wrote the following two sentences? Try revising the last few words in each sentence to make the cadence parallel.

1. What is written without effort is in general not something you read with pleasure.

2. What we hope ever to do with ease, we must learn first to do by working really hard.

Here's how Johnson wrote those sentences.

1. What is written without effort is in general read without pleasure.
2. What we hope ever to do with ease, we must learn first to do with diligence.

Note that I used the two-step formula as my opening for this week's technique.

My conclusion? If you want to write something catchy, give 'em the ole one-two.

I would call this one-two combination a good rule to remember—if it weren't for Henry David Thoreau's reminder: "Any fool can make a rule, and every fool will mind it."

 EXERCISES

1. Here's a fun exercise in the form of a puzzle. Match the first part of the following two-part quotes with the second part. Here are the first parts of the quotes.

    a. Writing a novel is like driving a car at night.

    b. A first-rate college library with a comfortable campus around it is a fine milieu for a writer.

    c. To be a novelist or a short story writer,

    d. The literary gift is a mere accident—

    e. If you want to get rich from writing,

    f. There are three rules for writing a novel.

And here are the second parts:

    g. you first have to pretend to be a novelist or a short story writer.

    h. Unfortunately, nobody knows what they are.

    i. write the sort of thing that's read by persons who move their lips when they're reading to themselves.

    j. There is, of course, the problem of educating the young.

k. [it] is as often bestowed on idiots who have nothing to say worth hearing as it is denied to strenuous sages.

l. You can see only as far as your headlights, but you can make the whole trip that way.

(Card, please.)

Did you put them together like this?

a-l. Writing a novel is like driving a car at night. You can see only as far as your headlights, but you can make the whole trip that way. (E.L. Doctorow)

b-j. A first-rate college library with a comfortable campus around it is a fine milieu for a writer. There is, of course, the problem of educating the young. (Vladimir Nabokov)

c-g. To be a novelist or a short story writer, you first have to pretend to be a novelist or a short story writer. (Charles Baxter)

d-k. The literary gift is a mere accident—[it] is as often bestowed on idiots who have nothing to say worth hearing as it is denied to strenuous sages. (Max Beerbohm)

e-i. If you want to get rich from writing, write the sort of thing that's read by persons who move their lips when they're reading to themselves. (Don Marquis)

f-h. There are three rules for writing a novel. Unfortunately, nobody knows what they are. (W. Somerset Maugham)

2. How would you complete the following statements to make them memorable?

a. What we hope ever to do with ease,

b. If we encounter a man of rare intellect,

c. If it sounds like writing,

d. From the moment I picked your book up until I laid it down I was convulsed with laughter.

Here's how Samuel Johnson, Ralph Waldo Emerson, Elmore Leonard, and Groucho Marx (referring to S.J. Perelman's first book) completed those statements.

a. What we hope ever to do with ease, we must learn first to do with diligence.

b. If we encounter a man of rare intellect, we should ask him what books he reads.

c. If it sounds like writing, I rewrite it.

d. From the moment I picked your book up until I laid it down, I was convulsed with laughter. Someday I intend reading it.

3. Select three quotes from the lists above that you especially like, and do your own version of them on topics of your choosing.

4. Start your own collection of quotable quotes. Be on the lookout for quotes that pertain to your favorite subjects, work, or field of expertise.

A good place to use your favorite quotes is at the end of your paragraphs, a component that has natural emphasis, which I'll explain when I discuss paragraphing in Weeks 35, 36, 37, and 38.

USE ANTITHESIS TO MAKE YOUR POINT BY CONTRAST

Sometimes the best way to make your point is to say what you don't mean; then say what you do. This juxtaposition of contrary statements is called antithesis.

For example, you might write, "The sky was green." But if you wanted to call attention to the unusual color of the sky—say, just before a tornado touched down—you might write, "The sky wasn't blue; it was green." For more emphasis yet, you might use repetition: "The sky wasn't blue; the sky was green."

That's antithesis—*anti* meaning "opposed," and *thesis* meaning "premise." Consider the following antithetical statements.

1. It's not who you are; it's who you know.
2. It's not a question of power; it's a question of diplomacy.
3. He didn't fail his wife; he failed himself.

(Note: In informal writing, commas rather than semicolons are often used between the two parts of antithetical statements, even when each part is a complete sentence.)

Antithesis can be useful in all types of writing, from advertising—"We're not selling homes; we're selling dreams"—to technical writing—"As a rule, quantum mechanics doesn't assign definite values to observables; it makes predictions using probability distributions."

Thomas Watson, Jr., famously chastised his staff members for wordy writing by exhorting them to avoid "gobbledygook" and offering this antithetical reminder: "IBM wasn't built with fuzzy ideas and pretentious language. IBM was built with clear thinking and plain talk."

Note how the repetition ("IBM ... IBM ...") and the parallel elements ("with ... and ... with ... and ...") enhance the effect.

Consider the following antithetical observations about writing by John Ruskin, John Fielden, E.L. Doctorow, and Robert Pinsky.

1. Be sure that you go to the author to get at his meaning, not to find yours.
2. Good business writing is not just grammar, clear thinking, or winning friends and influencing people. It is some of each, the proportion depending on the purpose.
3. Planning to write is not writing. Outlining, researching, talking to people about what you're doing—none of that is writing. Writing is writing.
4. The medium of poetry is not words, the medium of poetry is not lines—it is the motion of air inside the human body, coming out through the chest and the voice box and through the mouth to shape sounds that have meaning. It's bodily.

How could you rewrite the following statements to make them antithetical?

1. He is dull himself, and he is the cause of dullness in others.
2. This book is to be tossed aside lightly. Better yet, it should be thrown with great force.
3. I'm not afraid to die; however, I don't want to be there when it happens.

Here's how Samuel Johnson, Dorothy Parker, and Woody Allen wrote those sentences.

1. He is not only dull himself, he is the cause of dullness in others.
2. This book is not to be tossed aside lightly. It should be thrown with great force.
3. It's not that I'm afraid to die; I just don't want to be there when it happens.

Now see if you can guess how Oscar Wilde concluded this antithetical statement: "The difference between journalism and literature is that journalism is unreadable and literature is not ____."

Antithetical statements can be as simple as "I didn't mean to hurt your feelings; I only wanted to help." In the hands of a skilled writer, speaker, or rhetorician, they also can be memorable and enduring.

If you're looking for a famous example, you need look no further than the opening of Charles Dickens' *A Tale of Two Cities*:

> It was the best of times, it was the worst of times, it was the age of wisdom, it was the age of foolishness, it was the epoch of belief, it was the epoch of incredulity, it was the season of Light, it was the season of Darkness, it was the spring of hope, it was the winter of despair, we had everything before us, we had nothing before us ...

Or consider Neil Armstrong's famous declaration on first stepping onto the lunar surface: "That's one small step for man, one giant leap for mankind."

Because it compares more than contrasts, it isn't quite antithetical, but it follows the pattern of parallel statements to create its pleasing sound.

Almost forgot. In the exercise above, Wilde completed his antithetical statement with the word *read*.

EXERCISES

1. Complete the following sentences with antithetical statements.
   a. We notice things that don't work. We don't notice ...
   b. Although I've always loved you, I've never ...
   c. Not that I loved Caesar less, but that I loved ...

Here's how you might have completed those sentences.
   a. We notice things that don't work. We don't notice things that do.
   b. Although I've always loved you, I've never liked you.
   c. Not that I loved Caesar less, but that I loved Rome more. (Brutus in William Shakespeare's *Julius Caesar*)

2. In reviewing my collection of quotes about writing, I realized that many of my favorites are antithetical. Using the examples below as models (some

of which you've already seen in this chapter and elsewhere in this book), create your own versions of antithetical statements on a variety of topics.

a. "Good business writing is not just grammar, or clear thinking, or winning friends and influencing people. It is some of each, the proportion depending on the purpose." (John Fielden)

b. "Planning to write is not writing. Outlining, researching, talking to people about what you're doing, none of that is writing. Writing is writing." (E.L. Doctorow)

c. "The medium of poetry is not words, the medium of poetry is not lines—it is the motion of air inside the human body, coming out through the chest and the voice box and through the mouth to shape sounds that have meaning. It's bodily." (Robert Pinsky)

d. "This book is not to be tossed aside lightly. It should be thrown with great force." (Dorothy Parker)

e. "You do not create a style. You work and develop yourself; your style is an emanation from your own being." (Katherine Anne Porter)

f. "In the case of good books, the point is not how many of them you can get through but rather how many can get through to you." (Mortimer J. Adler)

g. "The typewriter makes for lucidity, but I am not sure that it encourages subtlety." (T.S. Eliot)

h. "I'm not so much worried about the nation's supply of writers—in case of trouble or a sudden spike in demand. But I am worried about the nation's supply of readers." (Arthur Phillips)

i. "Not that the story need be long, but it will take a long while to make it short." (Henry David Thoreau)

j. "Be sure that you go to the author to get at his meaning, not to find yours." (John Ruskin)

3. Look for examples of antithetical statements in your reading. Start a file of those you find particularly clever or pertinent to your writing or your job.

BUILD TOWARD CLIMAX

There's a natural order in life. Things progress from simple to complex. First you learn algebra; then you learn calculus.

There's also a natural order in writing.

Begin with the simple; end with the complex. Go from short to long, from less memorable to more memorable, from less vivid to more vivid. Build toward climax.

Consider this sentence: "Her behavior was inappropriate, unethical, and outrageous."

The strongest word in the series, *outrageous*, comes last, as it should.

Note how the natural emphasis of the sentence would be compromised if the words were arranged in anticlimactic order: "Her behavior was outrageous, unethical, and inappropriate."

If you progress from less vivid to more vivid, your sentences will have more emphasis and your writing will be more memorable. Likewise, if you arrange the elements of your sentences from shorter to longer, your reader will have an easier time following your thought.

Consider this sentence: "My primary responsibilities are to train staff, create a new database of specific economic reporting techniques, and manage the office."

It's in the wrong order. Rearrange it so that its elements are in natural order, progressing from shorter to longer. Beginning with the shortest phrase and concluding with the longest phrase, your revised sentence should look like this: "My primary responsibilities are to train staff, manage the office, and create a new database of specific economic reporting techniques."

Can you hear the difference? Do you find it easier to read the sentence when its three elements are arranged in natural order?

Of course if you were listing your responsibilities in order of importance and your chief responsibility were creating a new database, you would list that item first. Priority and chronology override rhythm and technique. Content trumps style. But when chronology and natural order coincide, you can have the best of both worlds.

Consider this sentence: "He returned with a skinny stick, snatched my bag of marshmallows, and skewered four of them in a neat row."

Note the climactic order of the verbs: *returned, snatched, skewered*. The chronological order of the events, the increasing length of the phrases, and the stylistic progression of the verbs (from less vivid to more vivid) all coincide.

The last paragraph of this week's technique illustrates an exception to the pattern. Here it is: "Remember: Arrange your material according to the natural order of things. Look for the patterns. Build toward climax."

As you can see, rather than going from shorter to longer in that paragraph, I go from longer to shorter. My reason: It seemed to create more climactic emphasis that way. Why? I'm not sure, but as Strunk and White point out in *The Elements of Style*, certain stylistic choices are "a trick of rhetoric in which the ear must be quicker than the handbook."

But the pattern usually holds. Here's proof that the natural order of things is a powerful force. Imagine you're sitting in a room with ten thousand native English speakers and I ask you to arrange four words—three adjectives and one noun—in any order that seems natural to you. The adjectives are *three*, *French*, and *young*, and the noun is *explorers*.

How would you arrange those four words?

Without exception, you—along with the other 9,999 people in the room—would say, "Three young French explorers."

Not one of you would say, "Young three French explorers" or "French three young explorers."

Why? Who told you to arrange the words in that order?

For J.R.R. Tolkien, it was his mother, as indicated in one of the introductory quotes to this book: "My mother … pointed out that one could not say 'a green great dragon,' but had to say 'a great green dragon.' I wondered why and still do."

But why?

The answer has to do with the way your mind works. Without conscious effort and at extraordinary speed, your mind sorts and arranges concepts according to a natural order. For this reason, you should roll out your information according to natural patterns when you write.

Think about how the following sentences might be rearranged so that they follow natural order.

1. The surgeon washed her hands, slipped on her latex gloves, rolled up her sleeves, and reached for her scalpel.
2. You are my Aphrodite, my light, my love.
3. I wake, the mysteries of the night fade with the rising sun, and reality intrudes.

Here are my votes.

1. The surgeon rolled up her sleeves, washed her hands, slipped on her latex gloves, and reached for her scalpel.
2. You are my love, my light, my Aphrodite.
3. I wake, reality intrudes, and the mysteries of the night fade with the rising sun.

At first I arranged sentence 2 in this order: "You are my light, my love, my Aphrodite."

Then I realized it was better to go not only from the general to the specific, but also from the literal to the figurative. (More on figurative language in Weeks 45, 46, and 47.)

Remember: Arrange your material according to the natural order of things. Look for the patterns. Build toward climax.

EXERCISES

1. Rearrange the adjectives in the following sentences so they come in climatic order.

   a. I saw a *red big fire* engine come hurling down our *tree-lined, narrow, pretty* street.

b. It stopped in front of a *green little cute* house.

c. The firefighters included *muscular, big, attractive, five* men and *big, two, muscular, handsome* women, and *one fat sweet little* dog.

Did you arrange the adjectives like this?

a. I saw a *big red fire* engine come hurling down our *pretty, narrow, tree-lined* street.

b. It stopped in front of a *cute little green* house.

c. The firefighters included *five big, attractive, muscular* men and *two big, handsome, muscular* women, and *one fat sweet little* dog.

Note that the adjectives in the last series could come in any order after the adjective *one*, as in *one fat sweet little* dog, *one sweet fat little* dog, or *one little fat sweet* dog. Like Tolkien, I don't know why. Maybe those particular modifiers are all of the same type and are interchangeable.

Also note that when two or more adjectives in a series are cumulative in effect—that is, each one modifies the next word as well as the last word—you don't use commas between them, as in *a nice little house*. The way you can tell if the modifiers are cumulative is to ask if they could be separated by *and*. If not, they're cumulative and are not separated by commas. (You wouldn't say *a nice and little house*, so you don't use a comma between *nice* and *little*.)

On the other hand, if the modifiers could be separated by the word *and*, they're not cumulative and you do use commas between them, as in *a big and complex problem* or *a big, complex problem*.

2. Make the following sentence more memorable by arranging its elements in climactic order. In other words, move the most emphatic element to the last position in the series.

> Incorrectness as well as inelegance of expression in writing, ignorance of the simplest rules of punctuation, an almost entire want of familiarity with English literature, and bad spelling are far from rare among young men of eighteen otherwise well prepared for college.

Hint: The shortest item in the series comes first.

(Card, please.)

Here's how Harvard President Charles William Eliot wrote the sentence in 1871.

> Bad spelling, incorrectness as well as inelegance of expression in writing, ignorance of the simplest rules of punctuation, and an almost entire want of familiarity with English literature are far from rare among young men of eighteen otherwise well prepared for college.

TRIM SENTENCE ENDINGS FOR CLOSING EMPHASIS

As you recall from Week 20, anytime you pause ... you create emphasis.

Like that.

There's natural emphasis at the end of a sentence—an emphasis punctuated by the pause that follows. You can use that natural stress point to good effect.

Consider this line from Langston Hughes' poem "Harlem": "Does it stink like rotten meat would smell to you?"

Of course, Hughes didn't write it that way. The phrase that deserves emphasis is *rotten meat*, and those words can be emphasized by trimming the line so that it reads, "Does it stink like rotten meat?"

Hear the downbeat? Now listen carefully to the following familiar lines.

> Whose woods these are I think I know for sure,
> His house is in the village though, some distance from here;
> He will not see me stopping here tonight
> To watch his woods fill up with snow so white.

Obviously, Robert Frost's poetic lines lose their magic when they ramble past their natural stress points (*know, though, here, snow*). Trimmed of their closing wordiness, the lines read:

> Whose woods these are I think I know,
> His house is in the village though;
> He will not see me stopping here
> To watch his woods fill up with snow.

As Joseph Williams reminds us in *Style: Ten Lessons in Clarity and Grace*, if you want to control your emphasis, trim your sentence endings. Here's another useful insight Williams offers about how sentences work: In the left part of your sentence, concentrate on topic. In the right part of your sentence, manage your emphasis.

I like to compare Williams' advice to flying an airplane. As you take off, you should be concentrating on getting off the ground. Once aloft, you should be thinking about where you're going to land.

Writing is more than choosing words and constructing sentences; it also involves trimming wordiness from sentences so that the emphasis falls where it does the most good.

Consider how I've trimmed the following sentences so they land on the important words.

1. Where's the library [at]?
2. The report describes four major problems [we are encountering].
3. The shot was heard 'round the world [by countless people].
4. But I have promises to keep,
   And miles to go before I sleep [in my warm, cozy bed tonight].

As the author, you're the boss. You have not only an opportunity, but also a duty to place your emphasis where it should be. That's what writers do. They emphasize the things they think important.

So don't let your sentences ramble on and on past the point where they really should stop, if you catch my drift. (Reduce that sentence to seven words. On second thought, make it six.)

Mind your closings.

In addition to trimming sentence endings (by not letting your sentences ramble), you can manage your emphasis by rearranging the order of a sentence so that it ends with the important words.

Imagine a situation in which the date or time of discovery is the main point. Which of the two sentences below places the emphasis where it should be?

1. While we were investigating the scene of the crime on October 19, we found the smoking gun.
2. We found the smoking gun while we were investigating the scene of the crime on October 19.

Obviously, the latter sentence lands where it should.

Now rearrange the sentence above so that the emphasis is placed not on *what* was found, nor on *when* it was found, but on *how* it was found.

Does your rearranged sentence look like this? "We found the smoking gun on October 19 while we were investigating the scene of the crime."

Here's another example: "Venture capital funding surged during the third quarter in Minnesota."

Note that the emphasis is on *where* the action took place. Now rearrange the sentence to emphasize *when* the action took place.

Does your rearranged sentence look like this? "Venture capital funding surged in Minnesota during the third quarter."

Remember: Periods create pauses, and pauses create emphasis. There's a pause or natural point of prominence at the end of every sentence. Make sure you're placing your emphasis where it should be.

You're the author. You're the boss. Do your job.

EXERCISES

1. Revise the two sentences below to take advantage of closing emphasis. One sentence needs trimming; the other would benefit from reordering its two principal parts.

> a. Venture capitalists are undeterred by the economic problems we are experiencing.
>
> b. We need to act now to take advantage of this opportunity.

Do your revised sentences look like this?

> a. Venture capitalists are undeterred by our economic problems.
>
> b. To take advantage of this opportunity, we need to act now.

2. Go one step further with those two sentences. Rearrange sentence (a) above to emphasize *undeterred*. (Hint: Begin with "Despite our economic problems ...")

> Does your revised sentence look like this?
>
> a. Despite our economic problems, venture capitalists are undeterred.

The emphasis in sentence (b) above could be heightened by adding a pause before the last word.

Does your revised sentence look like this?

b. To take advantage of this opportunity, we need to act. Now.

3. Trim the following sentences for emphasis.

a. Consider the trend that is currently occurring.

b. Our commitment to our clients is a genuine and longstanding one.

c. We need to immediately discuss the problems we are experiencing.

Do your revised sentences look like this?

a. Consider the current trend.

b. Our commitment to our clients is genuine and longstanding.

c. We need to discuss these problems immediately.

USE SENTENCE BEGINNINGS FOR EMPHASIS

As I discussed in last week's material, the strongest point of emphasis occurs before the natural pause at the end of a sentence. The other point of natural emphasis is at the beginning of a sentence.

Every sentence—like every paragraph, document, or speech—has natural stress points at the beginning and the end. Beginnings and endings count more than middles.

Consider this sentence: "I have never felt more frustrated." Without changing a word, the intensity of that statement can be heightened by moving one word to the beginning.

"Never have I felt more frustrated."

If you move two words forward in the following sentence, you sharpen the tone: "You have asked me twice now to respond to your requests on short notice."

There are two candidates for relocation, both of which convey annoyance: *twice now* and *on short notice*. The latter phrase, however, already occupies a position of natural stress at the end of the sentence, so try moving the other phrase forward.

Your revised sentence should look like this: "Twice now you have asked me to respond to your requests on short notice."

Can you hear the difference?

The same words presented in a different order deliver the message with more emphasis. Like word choice, word placement is a powerful tool. Use it to your advantage.

The natural stress point at the beginning of a sentence is not as strong as the one at the end, and not every sentence lends itself to rearrangement to take advantage of that stress point, but you can often play around with your sentence openings to heighten emphasis.

How might you rearrange these two sentences?

1. We have never been more humiliated.
2. I'm telling you for the last time I won't do it.

The first revision is obvious. (Move *never* to the beginning of the sentence.)

The second sentence might be revised like this: "For the last time, I'm telling you I won't do it."

Can you hear the heightened emphasis?

Now, let's expand on this technique.

Because sentence openings are an opportunity for natural emphasis, take care with how you word them. Launch your sentences economically. Don't lead off with wordy expressions such as *in the event that* or *in order to*. (Remember eliminating wordy expressions in Weeks 10, 11, and 12?)

Compare "In the event that you miss your plane, take the train" with "If you miss your plane, take the train."

Likewise, compare "In order to improve your writing, listen to the sound and rhythm of your words" with "To improve your writing, listen to the sound and rhythm of your words."

I can offer few hard and fast rules of editing, but let me venture one here: Never begin a sentence with *in order to*. It slows the pace at a point when you want to make a speedy start.

Mid-sentence the phrase does no harm. Compare "In order to qualify for this program, you must meet the following criteria" with "You must meet the following criteria in order to qualify for this program." Even here, however, *in order to qualify* could be condensed to *to qualify*.

Here's one more example: "We need to discuss these problems before we do anything else."

How might you rearrange it? Did you move *before we do anything else* to the beginning of the sentence? If so, note that rather than increase the emphasis, the new location merely places it elsewhere.

But the point is the same: Be aware of the two natural stress points in your sentences, and use those stress points to heighten or alter your emphasis. As the writer, your job is to decide where the emphasis goes, so put it where you want it.

Now repeat after me: "I will never forget this technique. Never will I forget this technique."

Well done.

EXERCISES

1. Delete the unnecessary words in the following sentences to launch your sentences economically.

    a. Owing to the fact that you're running two hours late, you better skedaddle.

    b. In order to take your writing to a new level, you need to commit yourself to my one-year program.

    c. In the event that you stop making progress, pick up where you left off and try again.

Do your revised sentences look like this?

    a. Because you're running two hours late, you better skedaddle.

    b. To take your writing to a new level, you need to commit yourself to my one-year plan.

    c. If you stop making progress, pick up where you left off and try again.

2. To take advantage of opening emphasis, rearrange the words in the following sentence so that it begins with "One leg dragging ..."

> He examined the sand around the ash heap, around the grave, also the spot where he had lain when he first came to, with one leg dragging, still on hands and one knee, grizzled, tattered, crusted over, looking like a he-bear in molting time after a terrible fight.

Here's how Frederick Manfred wrote that sentence in *Lord Grizzly*. Note how opening with a series of descriptive phrases and delaying the main clause creates drama and suspense.

One leg dragging, still on hands and one knee, grizzled, tattered, crusted over, looking like a he-bear in molting time after a terrible fight, he examined the sand around the ash heap, around the grave, also the spot where he had lain when he first came to.

I'll discuss periodic sentences in Week 40.

3. To take advantage of opening emphasis, eliminate wordiness and move the dramatic words and phrases forward.
   a. Hugh, with his old gray eyes feverish, broke off a long twig from a chokecherry bush.
   b. Hugh slowly slipped away into delirium. (Hint: Leave *delirium* in its position of closing emphasis.)
   c. He was awakened by a cold touch.
   d. There was something that had moved against his good side.
   e. It was a rattler.
   f. If he moved the least little bit, he'd have a batch of rattler poison in his blood, besides all the rot he already had in it.
   g. He lifted the bad leg while grimacing and cursing.
   h. He felt pain that filled him from tip to toe.

Here's how Manfred wrote those sentences.
   a. Old gray eyes feverish, Hugh broke off a long twig from a chokecherry bush.
   b. Slowly Hugh slipped away into delirium.
   c. A cold touch woke him.
   d. Something moved against his good side.
   e. Rattler.
   f. The least move and he'd have a batch of rattler poison in his blood, besides all the rot he already had in it.
   g. Grimacing, cursing, he lifted the bad leg.
   h. Pain filled him from tip to toe.

✳ A FURTHER THOUGHT: HIT THOSE NATURAL STRESS POINTS FOR EMPHASIS

Word arrangement is a powerful technique of composition, yet few writers are taught its importance.

Ask any college student where the natural stress points fall in a sentence, and you'll get a puzzled look. Ask anyone in your office, and you'll get a response like "Stress points? I feel stress every time I write."

Beginnings and endings count more than middles. It's a principle as simple as it is broad. Whether the first and last words in a sentence, the first and last sentences in a paragraph, or the first and last paragraphs in a document, what comes first and last has more impact than what occurs in the middle.

As an illustration of opening emphasis, move *finally* to the beginning of this sentence: "We're finally here." Can you see how "Finally, we're here" is more emphatic?

As another illustration, try to move *at long last* to another position in this sentence: "At long last, we're here."

"We're here at long last" and "We're at long last here" don't sound quite right. The emphatic phrase goes naturally in only one place: in the opening position of prominence: "At long last, we're here."

In paragraphs and documents, the opening and closing emphasis is nearly equal. In sentences, however, the last words have greater emphasis. The reason? Pauses create emphasis, and the period, as the British call it, is a "full stop."

For a musical analogy, think of periods—along with question marks, exclamation marks, colons, and dashes—as whole-note rests, semicolons as half-note rests, and commas as quarter-note rests. The longer the rest, the greater the emphasis.

Consider this sentence: "The evidence is clear that we'll be bankrupt by the end of the year if we don't reduce costs and increase revenue."

To emphasize the threat of bankruptcy, move *bankrupt* to the end: "The evidence is clear that if we don't reduce costs and increase revenue, by the end of the year we'll be bankrupt."

To further shape the sentence, insert a whole-note rest (either a colon or a dash) after the first clause: "The evidence is clear: If we don't reduce costs and increase revenue, by the end of the year we'll be bankrupt."

It's not just what you say; it's also how you say it. And it's not just what words you use; it's also where you place them. Word placement and pauses are powerful techniques of emphasis.

Here's another example: "Unfortunately, their decisions are based more on their administrative concerns than on the educational merits of our programs."

To give the important words more emphasis, move *educational merits* to the end of the sentence: "Unfortunately, their decisions are based more on their administrative concerns than on our programs' educational merits."

To continue the musical analogy, think of the closing words in the sentence as the downbeat. Make sure words that appear there are the ones you want to stress.

One more example. Reorder the words in the following sentence as you think Robert Frost phrased it: "A vertical expression of a horizontal desire is dancing."

Here's how the poet gave it to us: "Dancing is a vertical expression of a horizontal desire."

SUBORDINATE TO CONTROL YOUR EMPHASIS

Not everything you say is of equal importance. Some things are more important than others. Compare, for example, "I slept really well last night" with "Honey, I've decided to quit my job, sell our home, and move to Alaska."

One of your more important duties as a writer is to rank or indicate the relative importance of your ideas. You can lend emphasis to particular points by using attention-getting phrases such as "Most important" or "My main point is ..."

But there's another way to rank your ideas: Use sentence structure to put your emphasis where you want it. Here's how.

Sentences have two components: main parts and secondary parts. We call these parts *main clauses* and *subordinate clauses*, or as some grammarians prefer, *independent clauses* and *dependent clauses*. "It's beautiful outside" is a main clause. "Although it's beautiful outside" is a subordinate clause, a clause that doesn't stand alone.

You can make a main clause into a subordinate clause by adding—not surprisingly—a subordinating conjunction, a word such as *although*, *when*, *if*, and *because*. Compare "I have my doubts about your proposal" (a main clause) with "Although I have my doubts about your proposal" (a subordinate clause).

Beginning a sentence with *because* is a good way to shift the emphasis from the subordinate clause to the main clause. For example, if I were your boss and I called you into my office and began a sentence with "Because you've done such a terrific job on this project," you'd be eager to hear the conclusion in the main clause: "you will receive a $100,000 bonus." Conversely, if

I began with "Because we lost $40 million last quarter," you wouldn't want to hear the main clause.

Writers who fail to rank ideas through subordination are not doing their job. They're not indicating the relative importance of their ideas. If a customer purchased something from you and asked for a refund, it would be unwise of you to respond with two main clauses: "I am unable to refund your money, but I will give you a 10 percent discount on your next purchase." To do so would be to present both negative and positive information on the same level of importance. But if you subordinated the negative, you would emphasize the positive information: "Although I am unable to refund your money, I will give you a 10 percent discount on your next purchase."

Sounds better, doesn't it?

Knowing when to subordinate allows you to give your message a positive or negative spin, as you prefer. Compare "Although his insights are invaluable, he talks too much" with "Although he talks too much, his insights are invaluable." The first sentence makes a negative statement. The second sentence, which delivers the same information with identical words, makes a positive statement.

Below, I've used the subordinating conjunctions *although* and *because* to subordinate the parts of the following sentences that I preferred not to emphasize.

> **Original:** It's 25 degrees below zero outside. Nevertheless, it's a great day for a run.
> **Revised:** Although it's 25 degrees below zero outside, it's a great day for a run.
>
> **Original:** My client was driving intoxicated, but no one was injured.
> **Revised:** Although my client was intoxicated, no one was injured. (if you were representing the defendant)
> **or** Although no one was injured, this person had a blood alcohol content that was more than twice the legal limit. (if you were prosecuting the defendant)
>
> **Original:** You have distorted the facts. You have misrepresented your role. You have violated our trust. We hereby censure you.

Revised: Because you have distorted the facts, misrepresented your role, and violated our trust, we hereby censure you.

Subordinate to control your emphasis.

EXERCISES

1. In case you're still unsure of some of those grammatical terms, let's do a quick review.

Main clauses are complete sentences. They stand alone, as does this sentence. Subordinate clauses are incomplete and do not stand alone. Subordinate clauses are often introduced with subordinating conjunctions such as *when* and *although*. When you don't complete your sentence. It's called a sentence fragment. (More about the stylistic possibilities of sentence fragments in Week 32.)

Sentences with a single main clause are called simple sentences, as in "I walked into my office." Sentences made up of two main clauses are called compound sentences, as in "I walked into my office, and I sat down at my computer." Sentences made up of one main clause and one subordinate clause are called complex sentences, as in "After I walked into my office, I sat down at my computer."

Because subordinate clauses shift emphasis to the main clause (as this subordinate clause is doing), they indicate the relative importance and relationship between the two clauses. Writers who don't use subordinate clauses lack variety in their sentence structures. They also fail to indicate the relative importance of their ideas.

In the complex sentences below, change the subordinate clause into a main clause and the main clause into a subordinate clause. You can do this by switching the order of the two clauses and by moving the subordinating conjunction to the other clause. For example, change "Although he has interesting things to say, he talks too much" to "Although he talks too much, he has interesting things to say." As you alter the clauses and change the emphasis, note how a negative-sounding statement becomes positive.

a. Although Perkins is an excellent attorney, she has a poor memory.

b. Although he's quite attractive, he's fifty pounds overweight.

c. Although I have fond memories of our time together, I don't remember your name.

Do your altered sentences look like these?

a. Although she has a poor memory, Perkins is an excellent attorney.

b. Although he's fifty pounds overweight, he's quite attractive.

c. Although I don't remember your name, I have fond memories of our time together.

Now make the following positive-sounding sentences sound negative, again by reversing the main and subordinate clauses.

a. Although she makes a fair number of errors, she's very conscientious.

b. Although he doesn't know what he's talking about, he's a nice guy.

c. Although his mangled leg was causing him agonizing pain, Hugh was determined to survive.

Do your revised sentences look like this?

a. Although she's very conscientious, she makes a fair number of errors.

b. Although he's a nice guy, he doesn't know what he's talking about.

c. Although he was determined to survive, his mangled leg was causing him agonizing pain.

2. Compare "Matilda arrived late. She kept us waiting a long time" with "Because Matilda arrived late, she kept us waiting a long time." Note how the pair of simple declarative sentences suggests a causal relationship, whereas the complex sentence makes a direct connection. The two sentence structures create different effects, both of which may be put to good stylistic use.

Read the five sentence pairs below, listening carefully to their sound and rhythm. Use subordinating conjunctions such as *when*, *although*, and *because* to combine four of the pairs into single complex sentences. Use the coordinating conjunction *and* to combine one pair into a single compound sentence. Use your ear to determine which pair sounds better as a compound sentence.

a. You go two days without speaking to me. I don't know what you're thinking.
b. I know you love me. I wonder if you like me.
c. We were young. We would go swing dancing at Moonlite Gardens.
d. The famous Coney Island is in New York City. The one we knew growing up, as did our parents before us, was the Coney Island on the Ohio River in Cincinnati.
e. On one of those endless summer evenings, I held you in my arms. I knew you were the one.

Do your combined pairs look like the following? Did you use *and* to change sentence pair (e) into a compound sentence?

a. *When* you go two days without speaking to me, I don't know what you're thinking.
b. *Although* I know you love me, I wonder if you like me.
c. *When* we were young, we would go swing dancing at Moonlite Gardens.
d. *Although* the famous Coney Island is in New York City, the one we knew growing up, as did our parents before us, was the Coney Island on the Ohio River in Cincinnati.
e. On one of those endless summer evenings, I held you in my arms *and* I knew you were the one.

EXPAND YOUR SENTENCE REPERTOIRE BY ADDING TRAILING ELEMENTS

Imagine you're a member of a musical group.

After months of rehearsing, you've learned three songs, so you invite some friends over to hear you play.

You begin at 8 P.M. At first everything goes well. Your friends like your songs. But now it's midnight, one o'clock, two o'clock, and you're still playing the same three songs.

Do you know what your friends are thinking? They're thinking, *Wow, you can really nail those three songs. But can you play anything else*?

Consider the following sequence of sentences:

"Here is a simple declarative sentence. It makes a statement. It has no subordinate elements. A string of these sentences creates monotony. Monotony steals life from your writing."

In this case, the writer has a one-sentence repertoire: subject-verb-complement-period. As a result, the sentences lack variety—and therefore interest.

Note the variety in sentence structure in the preceding paragraph. A monotonous version of those sentences might go something like this:

"Here is the case of a writer. This writer has a one-sentence repertoire. This repertoire consists of sentences with subject-verb-complement-period structures. The result is a lack of variety. Lack of variety results in lack of interest."

Writers are like musicians who have learned to play certain songs. They have a repertoire of sentence structures, structures that occur to them readily and feel natural for them to use in expressing their thoughts and ideas. Some writers know only two or three songs; other writers know dozens.

How rich is *your* repertoire?

To find out, select a paragraph at random from your writing. Now count the commas.

Few or no commas aren't the problem; few or no commas are a symptom of the problem. (Note that there are no commas in the two paragraphs that appear within quotes above.) If you're writing without commas—or without dashes, colons, and semicolons—you're probably writing without variety, and variety in sentence structure adds interest and energy.

Would you like to add some new songs to your repertoire? Here's how.

Write a simple declarative sentence. Then replace the period at the end of that sentence with a comma—or maybe with a dash, a colon, a semicolon, or an open parenthesis. Now add a trailing element.

If I do this exercise with the preceding sentence, I get this: "Now add a trailing element—a phrase or clause that elaborates or comments on the statement in the main clause."

Wait a minute. I can do better than that: "Now add a trailing element—a phrase or clause that elaborates or comments on the statement in the main clause, like the clause after the dash in this sentence."

Well, now that I have the hang of it, let me see if I can add yet another element, this one in parentheses: "Now add a trailing element—a phrase or clause that elaborates or comments on the statement in the main clause, like the clause after the dash in this sentence (like this)."

And now that *you* have the hang of it, try going the other way. Rewrite the previous paragraph to create a monotonous string of sentences.

Go ahead. Give it a try before you read my version.

Here's how I did it:

"Now add a trailing element. A trailing element is a phrase or clause. It elaborates or comments on the statement in the main clause. It's like the clause after the dash. But I removed the dash. (This string of sentences contains no elaborating elements.)"

Oh, oh, it's getting late. Some of my audience members are yawning. Others are saying they have to get up early tomorrow so they had better be going. Would you mind helping me restore some variety to the preceding paragraph?

Without looking at the original version, try your hand at rewriting that string of monotonous sentences. Try using a comma or some other mark to move beyond a one-sentence repertoire to something more interesting.

How does your version compare with the original? Is it the same? Is it better?

Here's how Stephen King uses a trailing element at the conclusion of a paragraph to emphasize his point: "If you want to be a writer, you must do two things above all others: read a lot, and write a lot. There's no way around these two things that I'm aware of, no shortcut."

Two quick notes. In creating your trailing elements, be careful to avoid two common grammatical errors.

1. If you introduce your trailing element with a comma, make sure your trailing element is *not* another complete sentence. That error is called a comma splice. (Only in informal types of writing like fiction can you use commas between complete sentences, this is an example of a comma splice, here's another one.)

2. If you introduce your trailing element with a semicolon, make sure your element *is* another complete sentence. Because semicolons join things of equal value, you need complete sentences on both sides of a semicolon; not a complete sentence on one side and an incomplete sentence on the other, as I just illustrated. (An incomplete sentence is a sentence fragment that does not express a complete thought and does not stand alone. This is a complete sentence. It stands alone. Unlike this incomplete sentence.)

Trailing elements can be used to good effect in all types of writing, from creative writing to technical writing, which sometimes suffers from a lack of variety in sentence structure. Here's an example: "However, a zeolite's efficiency depends on several factors. These factors include pore size, thickness, and smoothness. All of these factors are impacted by the purity of the starting material."

In contrast to that monotonous sentence structure, consider this single sentence with a trailing element: "However, a zeolite's efficiency depends on several factors such as pore size, thickness, and smoothness, all of which are impacted by the purity of the starting material."

Much livelier, wouldn't you say?

Here's one last example of a trailing element put to good effect from E.B. White: "The professor devotes a special paragraph to the vile expression *the fact that*, a phrase that causes him to quiver with revulsion."

The next time your sentence structure starts sounding monotonous and you imagine your readers nodding off or heading for the exits, toss in a trailing element. You can do more than avoid a quiver of revulsion; you can also add an engaging detail—or even evoke a smile.

EXERCISES

1. Combine the two sentences below into a single main clause with a subordinate trailing element. Delete a few words, change *emptied* to *emptying*, and use a comma to link the trailing element—in other words, replace the period at the end of the first sentence with a comma.

> Downpours made roads impassable and leached the area's red soil into once-quiet creeks that became raging torrents of liquid earth. These creeks emptied into the bay until it took on the color of coffee.

Does your revised sentence look like this?

> Downpours made roads impassable and leached the area's red soil into once-quiet creeks that became raging torrents of liquid earth, emptying into the bay until it took on the color of coffee.

Using the same technique, delete some words from the second sentence below and attach it to the first sentence.

> Downpours made roads impassable and leached the area's red soil into once-quiet creeks that became raging torrents of liquid

earth, emptying into the bay until it took on the color of coffee. The color was like that of coffee that is heavy on the cream.

Here's how David Backes wrote the sentence in his biography, *A Wilderness Within: The Life of Sigurd F. Olson.*

> Downpours made roads impassable and leached the area's red
> soil into once-quiet creeks that became raging torrents of liquid
> earth, emptying into the bay until it took on the color of coffee,
> heavy on the cream.

2. Count the commas in the following paragraphs.
   a. Please remember the rules for using this room. It has a central lo-
      cation. It is used frequently. Sometimes it is used more than three
      times a day. Your lease indicates that you are responsible for leav-
      ing the room as you found it.
   b. Please remember the rules for using this room. Because of its cen-
      tral location, it is used frequently, sometimes more than three
      times a day. As indicated in your lease, you are responsible for
      leaving the room as you found it.

Which paragraph has more variety in sentence structure? Which paragraph is more interesting to read?

Without looking at paragraph (a), rewrite paragraph (b) as a series of
monotonous sentences. Then compare your version with paragraph (a).

3. Here's a neat little trick you can do with your computer to see if you're
using variety in your sentence structures.

Open one of your documents. Highlight two pages of your writing or
about five hundred words. Then activate your "Search and Replace" function. Type a comma in the "Find" box, and leave the "Replace" box blank.
Now click "Replace all," and note how many commas you deleted.

(The point is not to delete your commas but to count them, so be sure
to click the "Undo" arrow to restore your commas if you plan to save this
version of your document.)

Counting your commas may seem like a curious thing to do, but this
exercise will tell you something important about your writing style. If you

are using few or almost no commas, you're probably writing without subordinate clauses. And if you're writing without subordinate clauses, you're relying solely on main clauses. That means you're creating a monotonous sentence structure, one that will bore and tire your reader.

In a 500-word column, I use around thirty-five commas, or approximately one comma per fifteen words. In the "A Further Thought" that appears below, I use thirty-eight commas in 589 words of text. I hope I don't bore you with too little variety in sentence structure.

✳ A FURTHER THOUGHT: PAUSE AND PUNCTUATE TO KEEP YOUR SENTENCES FROM DYING

I had just sat down for a good read in the shade of the crab apple tree in my backyard, a frosty glass of lemonade in one hand and my Pelican edition of the complete works of William Shakespeare in the other, when the phone rang.

"Hey, Doc!" came a desperate voice. "Remember me? Can you come quick? My sentences are dying!"

I grabbed my black bag, dashed to the street corner, jumped onto a bus, and within moments arrived at the poor man's house.

"This way," he said, his voice trembling. He opened the door of a darkened bedroom and motioned for me to enter. What I saw was not pretty.

There, propped up on pillows, lay a paragraph made up entirely of main clauses, a structure undistinguished by a single subordinate element, its lifeless form so unremarkable that its subjects and verbs lay motionless beneath the barely disturbed bedsheets.

"I don't know what happened, Doc," he said. "I was sitting here writing. Everything seemed fine. I wrote a few sentences. Then my paragraph went limp. I tried adding more sentences. Suddenly my paragraph collapsed. Then I called you."

As he finished speaking, I heard a thud behind me. Overcome by the monotony of its structure, another lifeless paragraph had hit the floor.

"Quick," I said. "Let's get this one up on the bed beside the other one. Grab its subjects; I'll take its predicates."

Together we hoisted the lifeless form and laid it beside its stricken companion.

"Before you say anything else," I said, "let's see if we can revive these two."

"Whatever you say, Doc."

Taking my trusty stethoscope from my black bag, I listened to the internal beat of the comatose forms.

"Just as I suspected," I said. "Here's the problem: Your sentences lack variety. They look and sound alike. Note that they contain almost no commas or other internal punctuation marks. Taken individually, each sentence makes sense, but when you line them up in a paragraph, they lack the strength to support their own weight."

"Is it ... fatal?" he asked.

"Usually. Worse yet, sentence structure monotony can also cause your reader to nod off or even fall into a stupor. But we may be able to save these sentences by using a simple technique: the pause."

"The pause?"

"Precisely. And to create pauses you'll need some of these." I reached into my bag and held out a handful of commas, semicolons, colons, and dashes.

"But I don't know how to use those," he said. "That's why I generally avoid them."

"Well, you can begin by looking at how I used them in the sentences I've spoken today. Here's the point: Rather than give equal emphasis to every thought by creating a series of main clauses, vary your structure. Place less important thoughts in subordinate clauses and more impor-tant thoughts in main clauses.

"For example, rather than 'I was sitting here writing. Everything seemed fine. I wrote a few sentences. Then my paragraph went limp,' write, 'I was sitting here writing and everything seemed fine. After a few sentences, however, my paragraph went limp.'

"Here, take some of these." I handed him some punctuation marks. "Help me add them to these sentences."

Within moments, his paragraphs leaped from their sickbeds and began dancing around the room.

"The pause—what a wonderful technique!" he exclaimed with tears in his eyes. "How can I thank you, Doc?"

"It's all in a day's work," I said, handing him my bill.

HIT 'EM WITH THE LONG-SHORT COMBO

Here's a simple technique that can create dramatic emphasis. Use a long-short combination. In other words, follow a long, complicated sentence with a short, snappy one.

When you offer that one-two combination, you sound not only emphatic but also energetic, resolute, and decisive. Not bad for a simple technique.

Look again at an example I cited in Week 25. It's from a memo by Thomas Watson, Jr., the son of IBM's founder, chastising his staff members for wordiness.

> Believe it or not, people will talk about taking a "commitment position" and then because of the "volatility of schedule changes" they will "decommit" so that our "posture vis-à-vis some database that needs a sizing will be able to enhance competitive positions." That's gobbledygook.

It's the long-short combination that creates the emphasis. The longer the first sentence and the shorter the second, the better. The idea is to create contrast. If you limit the follow-up sentence to two or three words, the effect is particularly striking.

Here's an example from *Population: 485*, in which Michael Perry describes small-town life in Wisconsin: "I have felt the pull of history and place in a hundred places around the globe, and I don't doubt I could have lived a happy life in any one of them. But chance put me here."

The poet Samuel Taylor Coleridge creates the long-short effect in a single sentence: "Whatever is translatable in other and simpler words of the same language, without loss of sense or dignity, is bad."

Now it's your turn. Recast the following sentence, using the long-short combination: "We need to begin work on this project, and I think the time to do that is now."

Hint: Delete all but one word after the comma. Use a dash or a period after *project* and before the one-word punchline. Now.

Here's another sentence for you to revise into a long sentence followed by a short one: "Yesterday I read my copy four times, one word at a time, from front to back and from back to front, and today you found an error, and I thought, so much for proofreading."

Hint: Delete "and I thought."

When I was a little boy, I spent a lot of time with a slingshot in the woods down by the creek. I got to be a pretty good shot, but—fortunately for the little critters—I mostly did target practice, so there were few casualties. Whether aiming at a scrap of paper or launching my pebble into the vast blue sky, I loved the feeling of power when I drew back that black inner-tube band between the tines of my forked stick, held it for a moment, and then let it fly.

You may find it helpful to think of your long-short sentence combination as s-t-r-e-t-c-h-i-n-g out a rubber band, holding it, and then letting it snap.

To create the desired contrast, construct a long, somewhat complicated sentence, preferably one that contains an aside or a subordinate element like this one, and then follow it with a short, snappy one. Like this.

EXERCISES

1. Delete the unnecessary phrase after the first comma in the passage's last sentence so that the second long sentence is followed by a short, snappy one.

> Research on yoga was often a hobby or a sideline ... Federal centers tend to specialize in advanced kinds of esoteric research as well as pressing issues of public health, with their investigations typically carried out at institutes and universities. In short, given

its preoccupation with esoteric research and pressing issues, modern science seemed to care little.

Here's how William J. Broad wrote that passage in *The Science of Yoga: The Risks and the Rewards.*

> Research on yoga was often a hobby or a sideline ... Federal centers tend to specialize in advanced kinds of esoteric research as well as pressing issues of public health, with their investigations typically carried out at institutes and universities. In short, modern science seemed to care little.

2. Compare two versions of the following passage, the second as Bill Bryson wrote it in *The Life and Times of the Thunderbolt Kid.*

> The slowest place of all in my corner of the youthful firmament was the large cracked-leather dental chair of Dr. D.K. Brewster, our spooky, cadaverous dentist, while waiting for him to assemble his instruments and get down to business. There time didn't move forward at all, but rather than moving forward as it normally would, it just hung there.

> The slowest place of all in my corner of the youthful firmament was the large cracked-leather dental chair of Dr. D.K. Brewster, our spooky, cadaverous dentist, while waiting for him to assemble his instruments and get down to business. There time didn't move forward at all. It just hung.

With Bryson's final short sentences in mind, rewrite the following passages so that, after a longer sentence, each one concludes with a short, snappy one (or two). Delete unnecessary words as you think appropriate.

    a. While many gurus and how-to books praise yoga as a path to ultimate well-being, their descriptions are typically vague, but in contrast to their generalities, science nails the issue.

    b. Underneath, while you write you are a little nervous, not knowing how to get to what you really need to say and also a little afraid to get there, but what you need to do is relax.

    c. Don't be kind of bold. What you need to do is be totally bold.

d. Driving down Superior Street on a Saturday night, the sidewalks deserted, wind off the lake blowing snow through the pink light from the street lamps, the temperature stuck at twenty below, you know this isn't Paris, and it isn't even Minneapolis. This is a city called Duluth and it's at the top of the map.

Do your rewrites look something like this?

a. While many gurus and how-to books praise yoga as a path to ultimate well-being, their descriptions are typically vague. Science nails the issue. (William J. Broad, *The Science of Yoga: The Risks and the Rewards*)

b. Underneath, while you write you are a little nervous, not knowing how to get to what you really need to say and also a little afraid to get there. Relax. (Natalie Goldberg, *Writing Down the Bones*)

c. Don't be kind of bold. Be bold. (William Zinsser, *On Writing Well*)

d. Driving down Superior Street on a Saturday night, the sidewalks deserted, wind off the lake blowing snow through the pink light from the street lamps, the temperature stuck at twenty below, you know this isn't Paris. This isn't even Minneapolis. This is Duluth. (Barton Sutter, *Cold Comfort: Life at the Top of the Map*)

✳ A FURTHER THOUGHT: TECHNICAL WRITING NEEDN'T BORE YOU TO TEARS

Ah, spring in Minnesota. One week we'll have record-breaking temperatures in the mid-eighties. The next week a snowstorm will dump more than a foot of snow in the southern part of our state.

But that's nothing. A few years ago—2.5 million, to be exact—the Earth's temperature cooled, the snow stopped melting, and glaciers scraped and gouged much of the terrain in Minnesota, creating its present network of lakes, hills, and rivers.

A scientific or technical writer might describe the phenomenon in this way:

Four glaciers occurred from 2,500,000 to 10,000 years ago during a geological epoch known as the Pleistocene. During this epoch cooler temperatures caused snow around Hudson Bay to stop melting, and over time the snow formed a glacier. The glacier started moving south at the rate of one inch to ten feet a day. In places the snow reached a thickness of two miles and its tremendous weight altered the landscape beneath it.

And the reader might say, "Thanks for the information, but your writing style, though clear, is dull and uninviting." And the reader would be right.

The word choice is unexceptional, the sentence structure monotonous. Note the lack of commas, which as you know indicates a lack of subordinate clauses, as well as the pairing of sentences around the word *and*—two common flaws in scientific and technical writing.

In contrast, consider the following passage from Paul Lehmberg's book, *In the Strong Woods: A Season Alone in the North Country*.

During the last geological epoch (the Pleistocene—2,500,000 to 10,000 years ago), Earth's climate cooled several degrees and snows in the region of what is now Hudson's Bay no longer melted. Piling up layer upon layer, the mass of snow became ice, and when it reached a thickness of three hundred feet the body of snow and ice began to move. It had become a glacier.

Note Lehmberg's variety in sentence structure, not only in his use of introductory elements marked with commas but also in his combination of long-short sentences at the end of his paragraph.

USE SENTENCE FRAGMENTS TO PUNCTUATE YOUR WRITING

"If you don't have time to read," Stephen King says in *On Writing: A Memoir of the Craft*, "you don't have the time (or the tools) to write. Simple as that."

Simple as that.

There's nothing like sentence fragments to punctuate your point. But take care not to overuse them. They can become distracting. Off-putting. Irritating. Annoying.

Point made? Enough said?

Just saying.

Yet in the hands of a skilled writer (like you), fragments can underscore a point or advance a plot with remarkable precision and brevity, just as a well-crafted headline can grab the reader's attention and a sharply worded tweet can pack a punch.

Sentence fragments are sometimes created inadvertently by writers who don't know the difference between a complete sentence and a sentence fragment. But note: If you were taught not to begin a sentence with *because*, you were misled. The reason you were forbidden to start your sentences with *because* was that your teacher was afraid you wouldn't complete the sentence, and then you would do poorly in the next round of standardized testing and your school would lose its funding.

Of course you may begin a sentence with *because*. Why? Because I say so.

And there's another reason. Because you can make the fragment into a complete sentence by simply completing your thought, as in "Because I say so, it must be true."

That sentence has two parts: a dependent clause and an independent clause.

If you'll recall from Week 29, a dependent clause, also called a subordinate clause, is a fragment. An independent clause, also called a main clause, is a complete sentence. Because this sentence (the one you're reading now) meets the three criteria for a complete sentence—(1) it has a subject, (2) it has a verb, and (3) it expresses a complete thought—it's a complete sentence.

"Although it's hot as Hades outside" is a fragment. "I think I'll go for a run" is a complete sentence.

According to traditional grammar, sentence fragments are unacceptable. According to modern usage, however, they're fine. In fact, they're more than fine. With our rapidly changing technologies and our hurried pace of life, we're moving increasingly toward shorter forms of communication, so look for more frequent use of fragments in the years ahead. They set a fast pace. They move thought quickly. And efficiently.

They also offer endless possibilities for stylistic effect. Their clipped, staccato cadence varies the rhythm from the flow of complete sentences. They add contrast and energy. They create pauses, and as you know, pauses create emphasis.

Fragments can be placed in multiple locations. They can appear as a one-sentence paragraph.

Like this.

They can follow a complete sentence. Like an afterthought. They can be placed before a colon to introduce a complete sentence. (The effect: They draw attention to what follows.) They can be introduced by colons: like this. Or by dashes—like that.

Fragments work well in both business writing and online communication. They deliver information efficiently. They cover ground quickly. They can create a forceful tone, as in "We need to improve customer service. Now."

Fragments work well in nearly all types of writing. But not all. Because they create an informal tone, they may be inappropriate in formal discourse.

Got it?

Stephen King thinks fragments are particularly useful in fiction, where they "work beautifully to streamline narration, create clear images, and create tension, as well as to vary the prose-line. A series of grammatically proper sentences can stiffen that line, make it less pliable."

Among the many things King does well (like scare the bejeebers out of you), he knows how to use sentence fragments for stylistic effect, as does Colum McCann, a novelist with a remarkable ear for the rhythms and sounds of language.

Here are some examples of how to use fragments, taken from McCann's novel *TransAtlantic*, which tells the story of several transatlantic crossings between North America and Ireland, including Frederick Douglass' visit to lecture on the evils of slavery in 1845 and John Alcock and Arthur Brown's first nonstop aerial crossing in 1919. (Charles Lindbergh was the first person to fly solo across the Atlantic in 1927, but they were the first to make the nonstop crossing.)

He uses fragments to:

1. Describe an object

   It was a modified bomber, a Vickers Vimy. All wood and linen and wire.

2. Suggest movement or action

   He patted her each time he climbed onboard and slid into the cockpit beside Brown. One smooth motion of his body.

   Small bombs fell away from the undercarriage of his plane. A sudden lightness to the machine. A kick upwards into the night.

3. Heighten drama or suspense

   He is screwing back the lid on the flask of hot tea when he feels Alcock's hand on his shoulder. He knows before turning around that it is there. As simple as that.

4. Describe a setting

   Rising up out of the sea, nonchalant as you like: wet rock, dark grass, stone tree light.

   Two islands. The plane crosses the land at a low clip. Down below, a sheep with a magpie sitting on its back.

5. Offer commentary or draw a conclusion

   The sheep raises its head and begins to run when the plane swoops, and for just a moment the magpie stays in place on the sheep's back: it is something so odd Brown knows he will remember it forever. The miracle of the actual.

Ireland. A beautiful country. A bit savage on a man all the same. Ireland.

6. Appeal to the senses

The smell of the earth, so astoundingly fresh: it strikes Brown like a thing he might eat.

He could hear church bells ringing in the distance. A turf smell in the air. Dublin. How odd it was to be here: damp, earthy, cold.

7. Move the plot forward

A gong sounded from downstairs. Dinnertime.

8. Emphasize specific traits in describing a character

Lily's face, half carved in light as she poured, sharp, pretty, alabaster. She glided across to him. Her cool white wrists.

In the afternoons he caught sight of Lily when she cleaned the upstairs of the house. Just seventeen years old. Her sand-colored hair. Her eyes ledged with freckles.

9. Set a scene

He scanned the faces of the men. He could sense their uncertainty, a little hint of confusion around their eyes as he watched them, watching him. A slave. In a Dublin drawing room. So remarkably well-kept.

10. Recap or summarize the highlights of a story

He was called upon to give a speech: his days as a slave, how he slept on a dirt floor in a hovel, crawled into a meal bag to stave off the cold, put his feet in the ashes for warmth.

Was taught, against the law, to read, write, and spell. How he read the New Testament to his fellow slaves. Worked in a shipyard with Irishmen as companions. Ran away three times. Failed twice. Escaped Maryland at twenty years of age. Became a man of letters.

11. Create a certain mood or ambience

It was still a surprise to see the rooftops of Ireland. What else lay out there? What other ruin? The sound of leaves falling. Quieter than rain.

12. Capture the essence of a story

The children looked like remnants of themselves. Spectral. Some were naked to the waist. Many of them had sores on their faces. None had shoes. He could see the structures of them through their skin. The bony residue of their lives.

13. Create intrigue with partial or incomplete disclosure

Negro girl. Ran away. Goes by name Artela. Has small scar over her eye. A good many teeth missing. The letter *A* is branded on her cheek and forehead. Some scars on back, two missing toes.

Available immediately: Seven Negro children. Orphans. Good manners. Well presented. Excellent teeth.

These last examples reveal the inhumanity of slavery with almost unbearable intensity. The reader can sense the stories lurking beneath those words, straining against the limits of language, crying to break out and be told. But the clipped efficiency of the fragments, built on spare language and drawing on a few well-chosen, poignant details, leaves something for the reader's imagination. The fragments imply or suggest, rather than complete and make explicit.

A member of my book club thought McCann overdid his use of sentence fragments, and one reviewer (Maureen Corrigan for National Public Radio) thought his language lovely but so elevated that "the air of this novel" got "a little thin."

But I find it hard to fault an author whose fragments are like one-line poems:

The miracle of the actual.
The sound of leaves falling. Quieter than rain.
The bony residue of their lives.

I was transported by their beauty and power.

EXERCISES

1. Using Stephen King as your model, open an article, essay, or story with a bold statement, punctuated with a sentence fragment: "If you don't have time to read, you don't have the time (or the tools) to write. Simple as that."

2. Play around with King's sentence: "A series of grammatically proper sentences can stiffen that line, make it less pliable."

What would it look like to separate the trailing element and present it as a fragment?

Compare the two versions.

> A series of grammatically proper sentences can stiffen that line, make it less pliable.

> A series of grammatically proper sentences can stiffen that line. Make it less pliable.

I think King's choice to use a pause slighter than a full stop was right, but it's a close call. Which version do you think is better?

3. Imagine you're texting a message to a friend. Imitate the style of Colum McCann's fragment: "Her sand-colored hair. Her eyes ledged with freckles."

Here's my version, which you saw in my introduction to this book: "Love your micro braids. Your eyes edged with color."

What's yours?

4. McCann captures the brutality of "The Troubles" in Ireland with a catalogue of horrors.

> So many murders arrive out of the blue. The young Catholic woman with the British soldier slumped over her child, a hiss of air from the bullet wound in his back. The man in the taxicab with the cold steel at this neck ... The postman blinded by the letter bomb. The teenager with a six-pack of bullet holes in his knees, his ankles, his elbows.

Think of a famous period or episode in American history, such as Neil Armstrong and Buzz Aldrin walking on the lunar surface in 1969, or the slaughter of ninety Lakota men and more than two hundred Lakota women and children at Wounded Knee in 1890, and use a series of sentence fragments to portray the essence of the story.

5. Rewrite some of the following sentences, breaking off parts of them into sentence fragments, leaving others as complete sentences, and deleting unnecessary words.

    a. To have a reason to get up in the morning, it is necessary to possess a guiding principle. It is necessary to have a belief of some kind, a bumper sticker, if you will.

    b. Alongside the turntable were two albums, B.B. King and Strauss. He put on the Strauss, the one with some waltzes, because Strauss was music to think by.

    c. He would not stay long, two weeks at most. He took jeans, sweaters—there would still be snow in Minnesota—heavy socks, as well as leather gloves, boots, and a down jacket and more.

    d. I was a bit too brainy and somewhat plump. In other words, I was acceptable, but not wildly desirable.

    e. Jardine had seen so many suspects taken in too early before anything substantial happened, and it always fell apart in court because of reasonable doubt.

Do your rewrites look like these?

    a. To have a reason to get up in the morning, it is necessary to possess a guiding principle. A belief of some kind. A bumper sticker, if you will. (Judith Guest, *Ordinary People*)

    b. Alongside the turntable were two albums, B.B. King and Strauss. He put on the Strauss. Some waltzes. Strauss was music to think by. (Will Weaver, *Red Earth, White Earth*)

    c. He would not stay long, two weeks at most. He took jeans, sweaters—there would still be snow in Minnesota—heavy socks. Leather gloves. Boots. A down jacket. More. (Will Weaver, *Red Earth, White Earth*)

d. I was a bit too brainy and somewhat plump. Acceptable, but not wildly desirable. (Susan Allen Toth, *Blooming: A Small-Town Girlhood*)

e. Jardine had seen so many suspects taken in too early before anything substantial happened, and it always fell apart in court. Reasonable doubt. (Kate Green, *Shattered Moon*)

END WITH THE THOUGHT YOU INTEND TO DEVELOP NEXT

Have you ever read a mystery story or a thriller that ended each chapter with a cliffhanger? The idea is to make you turn the page to see what happens next. The same technique can be applied to your sentence endings, with the same effect on your reader.

In Week 27 we practiced giving special emphasis to important words by placing them at the end of your sentences. (To review, compare "We need to submit our proposal by December 15 to meet the deadline" with "To meet the deadline, we need to submit our proposal by December 15.")

For this week's technique, I'll expand on the concept of using closing emphasis for effect: End your sentences with the thought you intend to develop next.

Connecting your sentences in this way increases coherence in the flow of your information. The more coherent your writing, the easier it is for your reader to follow your thought and the more your reader wants to keep reading.

The first step in applying this technique is to look for a topic that is explained or elaborated upon by what follows. As a general rule, this "continued topic" should appear not on the left side near the beginning of the first sentence but on the right side near the end.

Consider the continued topic in these sentences: "There are two natural stress points in every sentence you write. There is one stress point at the beginning and one stress point at the end."

The topic of the first sentence is *two natural stress points*. That topic is developed in the second sentence. But note where the continued topic appears in the first sentence. It's presented at the beginning rather than at the end. That's the wrong order.

Here's the right order: "In every sentence you write, there are two natural stress points. There is one stress point at the beginning and one stress point at the end."

The sentences are now linked by concluding the first sentence with the topic that's developed in the second sentence.

Additional emphasis, however, can be added by eliminating the needless words and compressing the rhythm: "In every sentence you write, there are two natural stress points: one at the beginning and one at the end."

The sentence might be further compressed: "Every sentence has two natural stress points: one at the beginning and one at the end."

Sentences with colons often present their topics in the wrong order. They begin rather than end with the continued topic. So when you write a sentence containing a colon that introduces a phrase, a list, or another sentence, check the order. Does your sentence present the topic to be developed on the right, just before the colon, or way over on the left side of the sentence?

Note: Sentences that begin with the word *there* and contain a colon are often in the wrong order.

How would you rearrange the order of the first part of the sentence below to produce a more coherent flow? "There are three issues our staff members are unhappy about: (1) unpaid overtime, (2) mandatory furloughs, and (3) cuts in benefits."

Hint: Begin your revised sentence with "Our staff members ..."

Here's another analogy in case the cliffhanger one didn't work for you:

Oops. I forgot to apply my own technique. Let me try that sentence again.

In case the cliffhanger analogy didn't work for you, here's another analogy:

(The improvement here is only slight, and perhaps recasting the sentence isn't justified. Still, knowing the technique makes you aware of your choices.)

Now, here's the second analogy. Have you ever played that game where you hit a little ball into the woods, hunt for it, hit a couple more trees with it, and then after a dozen or so strokes roll it into a little hole marked with a white flag? (For me, the white flag is symbolic.) Where did you go to play the next hole? You didn't hike all the way back to the clubhouse. You walked a short distance to the next tee.

That's the way sentences should work. Just as when you play the "links," you should link the end of one sentence with what follows. (That's not, however, why golf courses are referred to as "links"—*links* is the word for the hilly terrain just back from the beach in Scotland, where golf was invented in the fifteenth century. Still, I like the analogy between golf links and sentence links.)

Here's one more sentence for you to recast in more coherent order: "There are three things I love to do: canoe, sail, and write."

Now that you understand this technique, the revision should be obvious: "I love to do three things: canoe, sail, and write." (I could name more than three things if pressed.)

But look at the previous sentence. What do you think about the order? It's fine as it is—unless I intend to tell you about the more than three things I love to do, in which case a better order might be: "If pressed, I could name more than three things."

If you understand why, you understand this week's technique: End with the thought you intend to develop next.

EXERCISES

1. Rewrite the following sentences so that they end with the thought to be developed next.

    a. There are three things our team members are unhappy about: long hours, lack of recognition, and endless editing of their work.

    b. I recommend committing the resources to resolve the following issues, despite our declining sales:

    c. We can see that the problem with a long sentence may involve more than just garrulousness, given what we've learned about problems of topic and stress.

Do your revised sentences look like this?

    a. Our team members are unhappy about three things: long hours, lack of recognition, and endless editing of their work.

    b. Despite declining sales, I recommend committing the resources to resolve the following issues:

    c. Given what we've learned about problems of topic and stress, we can see that the problem with a long sentence may involve more than just garrulousness. (Joseph Williams, *Style: Ten Lessons in Clarity and Grace*)

2. Reverse the order of the clauses in the first sentence below so that it ends with the thought that is developed in the second sentence, replacing *which* with *that* and adding *especially*.

> Nanomedicine, which offers many advantages over traditional medical practices in treating cancer and tumors, is an emerging field in targeted drug delivery. It allows for spatial and temporal control and the destruction of cancerous cells with minimal or no damage to the normal cells and tissue.

Does your revised first sentence look like this?

> Targeted drug delivery is an emerging field in nanomedicine that offers many advantages over traditional medical practices, especially in treating cancer and tumors.

3. Here's how murder mystery writer William Kent Krueger ends the first chapter of *Northwest Angle*.

> They threaded their way out of the convoluted gathering of islands. Jenny sat rigid in the bow, fiercely giving him her back. As soon as they hit the open water of the main channel, he headed the dinghy again toward the southwest.
>
> When he saw the sky there, he was, for a moment, stunned breathless.
>
> "Dad?" Jenny said from the bow. She'd seen it, too, and she turned back to him, fear huge in her eyes.
>
> "Good God Almighty," he whispered.

Makes you want to keep reading, doesn't it?

The character in the following passage (written by another author) feels threatened by a man. Add a final sentence that heightens suspense by hinting at what might follow.

> Now she picked up the knob and held it by the metal shank. The round grip was porcelain, smooth, and white. Hard as stone. She put it in the deep pocket of her jacket and, holding it, walked back to the booth through the gathering crowd. Her room was locked.

(Card, please.)

Here's how Louise Erdrich completed the paragraph in *Love Medicine:*

> And she was ready for him now.

4. Create a scene that ends with a cliffhanger.

✳ A FURTHER THOUGHT: USE YOUR EXPLETIVES TO CREATE EMPHASIS

Expletives come in two varieties: everyday and grammatical. Both are useful devices for creating emphasis.

Compare, for example, "Damn the torpedoes!" with "Never mind the torpedoes!" Which version do you think conveys Admiral Farragut's thought more boldly?

Before I confuse the [expletive deleted] out of you, let me offer some definitions.

In everyday usage, expletives are obscene or profane words, such as **#x⌖*!* and *x#!*x*. At home, expletives are likely to be heard when a hammer accidentally strikes a thumb or a telemarketer calls during the dinner hour. In the workplace, expletives are sometimes used when a printer jams or a computer locks up.

In the grammatical sense, expletives are filler words such as *there* and *it* that occupy space in a sentence without adding to its meaning. In the sentences, "It is fun to read" and "There are three secrets to becoming a great writer," for example, the words *It* and *There* merely occupy the first positions in the sentences, moving the meaningful words *fun to read* and *three secrets to becoming a great writer* a little to the right.

Everyday expletives are therapeutic. Often characterized by fricatives and explosive-sounding glottal stops and usually uttered at top volume, they enable a speaker to release pent-up frustration. It should be noted, however, that many expletives are inappropriate for use in public, particularly in formal gatherings. New employees would be wise to check with their bosses regarding workplace norms and expectations before letting one rip.

Grammatical expletives also have their uses. By moving certain words to the right in a sentence, they enable the writer or speaker to maintain coherence and control emphasis.

Consider, for example, the order of thoughts in this two-sentence sequence: "We need to overcome several obstacles. Failure to do so could spell defeat." The first sentence conveys two basic ideas (*overcome* and *obstacles*). The second sentence elaborates on the first of these (the need to overcome, not the nature of the obstacles).

Using an expletive in the first sentence alters its order: "There are several obstacles we need to overcome. Failure to do so could spell defeat." Can you hear the difference? Ending the first sentence with the thought to be developed in the second sentence creates a more coherent flow.

In contrast to the extremely limited number of grammatical expletives (*it*, *there*, and *what*), English offers the writer and speaker a rich choice in everyday expletives. Many are easy to pronounce, spell, and remember because they are only four letters long. Furthermore, discriminating writers and speakers who wish to modulate their tone can avail themselves of countless euphemisms, such as *darn*, *heck*, *shoot*, and *gee willikers*.

Using the euphemism rather than the expletive, however, may prove to be a costly error. In a recently discovered journal, for example, one of Admiral Farragut's captains reported that the Admiral considered shouting, "The heck with the torpedoes!" Historians have speculated that, had he done so, Mobile Bay, Alabama, might not have fallen to the Union fleet and the Civil War might have been won by the South.

Despite their usefulness in ordering the flow of ideas, grammatical expletives can cause problems. They should not be used, for example, in sentences ending with colons. Compare, for example, "There are three factors we must consider: (1) ... " with "We must consider three factors: (1) ..." Note that the expletive *There* in the first version creates a less coherent flow and that the expletive-less second version is more emphatic.

What I want you to remember is this (did you catch my expletive?): Grammatical expletives allow you to reorder your thoughts. Combining expletives and colons, however, will usually lead you to the wrong conclusion.

START WITH SOMETHING OLD; END WITH SOMETHING NEW

You've heard the saying "Out with the old, in with the new." That order makes sense when we're celebrating the beginning of a new year. Get rid of the old stuff; try something new.

But sentences work best in the reverse order: "In with the old, out with the new." In other words, first give your reader something old; then give your reader something new.

In *Style: Ten Lessons in Clarity and Grace*, Joseph Williams describes the simple but powerful principle this way: "something old, something new."

The first time an idea is presented, it's new information. All subsequent references to that idea are old information.

This principle of coherence and flow is similar to last week's technique of ending with the thought you're going to develop next.

Consider this sentence: "You need to eliminate common errors in your writing."

After the idea of eliminating common errors has been introduced, it's now old information. Subsequent references to that idea should be presented at the beginning, or in the left part of the sentence; previously unmentioned or new information should be presented at the end, or in the right part of the sentence.

With that principle in mind, consider this ordering of ideas: "You need to eliminate common errors in your writing. Your credibility will be undermined by errors in grammar, word choice, and punctuation."

In the second sentence, new information (*your credibility*) is presented first. Old information (*errors*) is presented last. That's the wrong order.

The flow is more natural and coherent if the old information in the second sentence is moved forward: "You need to eliminate common errors in your writing. Errors in grammar, word choice, and punctuation will undermine your credibility."

Can you hear the difference?

As you know from last week's discussion, sentences beginning with *There is* or *There are* and introducing a list with a colon are sometimes in the wrong order. Here are some more examples of when to reorder those sentences.

Apply the old/new principle to the first part of this sentence: "If you do three things, your writing will improve: (1) Read and imitate good writers; (2) take time to revise your writing; (3) refer to a dictionary or style manual when you're unsure of correct spelling or usage."

Did you restructure it into this more coherent order? "Your writing will improve if you do three things: ..."

One advantage of the old/new principle is that it leads you to end with the thought you're going to develop next. That's the logical order of things.

Which of the following sentences do you think flows more naturally: "Five grievances have been filed by our staff members: ..." or "Our staff members have filed five grievances: ..."?

I think the latter. Remember: End with the thought you're going to develop next.

Sometimes deciding where to end a sentence is a close call. Consider these two versions of a sentence.

1. Madeline knew she was in trouble when she downloaded her e-mail.
2. When she downloaded her e-mail, Madeline knew she was in trouble.

Which of those two versions would you place before the following sentence? "The first five messages were angry responses to her presentation in yesterday's staff meeting."

In this case, I think your decision depends more on your desired emphasis than on coherence. Compare the two options.

1. Madeline knew she was in trouble when she downloaded her e-mail. The first five messages were angry responses to her presentation in yesterday's staff meeting.
2. When she downloaded her e-mail, Madeline knew she was in trouble. The first five messages were angry responses to her presentation in yesterday's staff meeting.

In the first sequence, the emphasis is on Madeline's discovering the angry responses. In the second sequence, the emphasis is on Madeline's knowing that she was in trouble.

How would you revise the second sentence in the sentence pairs below for more coherent flow?

1. There are worse crimes than burning books. Not reading them is one of them.
2. Have something to say, and say it as clearly as you can. The only secret of style is that.
3. Cut out all those exclamation marks. Laughing at your own joke is like an exclamation mark.

Here's how Joseph Brodsky, Matthew Arnold, and F. Scott Fitzgerald structured those sentences.

1. There are worse crimes than burning books. One of them is not reading them.
2. Have something to say, and say it as clearly as you can. That is the only secret of style.
3. Cut out all those exclamation marks. An exclamation mark is like laughing at your own joke.

Brodsky, Arnold, and Fitzgerald knew the technique: It's in with the old, out with the new. Start with something old; end with something new.

1. Reword and rearrange the second sentences in each of the examples below so that they begin with old information presented in the first sentences.

    a. Most societies harbor a subculture best described as the word people. To think about words and take pains to express themselves clearly, logically, and in a civil manner is what these people do.

    b. Women are traditionally trained to place others' needs first, to feel these needs as their own (the "infinite capacity"); their sphere, their satisfaction to be in making it possible for others to use their abilities. When Virginia Woolf, already a writer of achievement, wrote [about her father] in her diary, this is what she was writing about.

    c. English has a long tradition of doubling words, a habit that we acquired shortly after we began to borrow from Latin and French the thousands of words that we have since incorporated into English. Early writers would use both words because the borrowed word usually sounded a bit more learned than the familiar native one. (Hint: Begin the second sentence with *because* and the idea of borrowing words for their sound.)

Do your revised second sentences look like the second sentences below?

    a. Most societies harbor a subculture best described as the word people. These are the people who think about words and who take pains to express themselves clearly, logically, and in a civil manner. (Arthur Plotnik, *The Elements of Expression: Putting Thoughts into Words*)

    b. Women are traditionally trained to place others' needs first, to feel these needs as their own (the "infinite capacity"); their sphere, their satisfaction to be in making it possible for others to use their abilities. This is what Virginia Woolf meant when, already a writer of achievement, she wrote [about her father] in her diary. (Tillie Olsen, *Silences*)

c. English has a long tradition of doubling words, a habit that we acquired shortly after we began to borrow from Latin and French the thousands of words that we have since incorporated into English. Because the borrowed word usually sounded a bit more learned than the familiar native one, early writers would use both. (Joseph Williams, *Style: Ten Lessons in Clarity and Grace*)

2. The idea of starting with something old and ending with something new can also be applied to presenting information in chronological order. Reverse the order of the two clauses in the sentence below so the new information in the second clause follows the old information in the first.

> Not everything I wanted to say was nice, but I was brought up to be an incredibly nice person.

Here's how Louise Erdrich wrote that sentence.

> I was brought up to be an incredibly nice person, but not everything I wanted to say was nice.

3. Look for opportunities in your own writing to increase coherence from one sentence to the next by presenting information in the order of something old, something new.

USE PARAGRAPHS TO FRAME YOUR THOUGHT AND SET YOUR PACE

When you take a photograph, you decide what to place inside the frame and what to leave out. Sometimes you might crop a picture because it has too much sky or too much background, and cropping usually results in a more pleasing composition.

Arranging your thought into paragraphs works the same way. As you compose your thoughts, you choose not only which words to use but also where to place them. It's not only what you say; it's how you frame your material that counts.

In expository, descriptive, and persuasive writing, paragraphs provide a frame for introducing a thought, developing it, and offering a conclusion. In narrative writing, paragraphs function a little differently. They not only represent units of meaning, but also mark shifts in scene and dialogue. As Stephen King describes it in *On Writing: A Memoir of the Craft*, "In fiction, the paragraph is less structured—it's the beat instead of the actual melody."

Consider the beat established in a nine-paragraph narrative sequence in Paulette Bates Alden's *Feeding the Eagles*. Each topic sentence establishes a new scene or stage in the action. The pace (as indicated by the topic sentences and the number of sentences in each paragraph below) begins fast, then slows somewhat.

1. We went to South Carolina this past Thanksgiving, after we got settled. (three-sentence paragraph)

2. My mother had put on weight. (four-sentence paragraph)

3. My father got tears in his blue eyes when he shook Ted's hand. (three-sentence paragraph)

4. My father wanted to know about our TV. (seven-sentence paragraph)

5. We show my parents the pictures taken at the pig roast. (seven-sentence paragraph)

6. We spend the time watching TV and eating. (three-sentence paragraph)

7. On Sunday morning my father cooks us a big country ham breakfast. (eight-sentence paragraph)

8. On Monday before we leave my mother and I go shopping. (four-sentence paragraph)

9. Now when I come home, "having nothing to wear," as my mother puts it, is a problem. (six-sentence paragraph)

As Alden knows, pace is the key to successful paragraphing, and she gets it just right in these nine paragraphs. As a rule, the longer the paragraph, the slower the pace and more formal the tone. The shorter the paragraph, the faster the pace and more relaxed the tone.

A common error in e-mail correspondence is beginning a message with one topic in mind, then thinking of another—and another, and another—and clumping them all together into a single block without offering the reader the benefit of a paragraph break.

But readers—especially today's hurried, harried, and distracted readers—need breaks. The white space around a paragraph frames the thought. It creates a momentary pause for the reader to reflect on the information being delivered. Text with few or no breaks demands more energy and concentration from the reader. Text that is broken into shorter units is easier to absorb.

Because the fifty-two techniques I'm discussing in this book require careful explanation on my part and close attention on yours, I've deliberately kept my paragraphs short. To keep things moving and to create special emphasis, I've even dropped in an occasional one-sentence paragraph.

Like this.

In all types and genres of writing, paragraphs help us present and emphasize our material. Like sentences, they have two natural stress points: one at the beginning and one at the end. And like the downbeat at the end of a sentence, the last sentence in a paragraph has special emphasis. As I'll discuss in Week 38, if you place a good line at the end of a paragraph, it will strike the reader as more emphatic, vivid, or amusing than if you bury it in the middle.

As you arrange your thoughts into paragraphs, point your camera carefully in deciding what to include and what to leave out.

EXERCISES

1. The following topic sentences have been removed from the paragraphs of the expository, descriptive, persuasive, and narrative writing they introduce.

    a. Consider John Grisham's breakout novel, *The Firm*.

    b. Over the maroon horsehair sofa in my grandmother's house where I took my afternoon nap, there was a picture of a girl with black hair.

    c. I have a practical suggestion to make to raise the moral consciousness out here.

    d. After dinner, I'm in the backyard with my dad and my airplane sits in the driveway.

Reattach those sentences to their paragraphs:

    e. She wore the kind of garment that is not so much dress as drapery. It folded in dozens of deep creases, and was a dark, hypnotic green. In her arms she held a lute. One hand was draped over the strings near the sounding board's hole; the other hardly seemed to exert any pressure on the frets. (Patricia Hampl, *A Romantic Education*)

    f. Two control wires run to the middle of the yard. My dad walks up to the plane, hits the propeller and wheeee, it whines like it's in pain ... Then, he pulls another control and the plane goes straight up in the air and—Mayday! Mayday, Mayday! It crashes into the ground into a million pieces! I look over at my dad. He's looking at the controls. Obviously, that's where the fault lies. (Kevin Kling, *The Dog Says How*)

g. I suggest we keep or make English required of our junior and seniors but with the following two strict conditions: (1) That *no techniques of literature* be taught or discussed ever. All approaches to stories being read must be to what they show of life—inner life, feelings, public life, morals. (2) And that we teach courses with a rural-literature emphasis. (Carol Bly, *Letters from the Country*)

h. In this story, a young lawyer discovers that his first job, which seemed too good to be true, really is—he's working for the Mafia. Suspenseful, involving, and paced at breakneck speed, *The Firm* sold roughly nine gazillion copies. (Stephen King, *On Writing*)

(Card, please.)

Did you reattach the sentences in this order: sentence (a) to paragraph (h), sentence (b) to paragraph (e), sentence (c) to paragraph (g), and sentence (d) to paragraph (f)?

Pick the paragraph you like best, and use it as a model to write your own paragraph.

2. In each of the paragraphs below, one sentence doesn't fit within the frame of the paragraph. Move the misplaced sentence to a different paragraph, where it belongs.

a. Baseball is a silly sport, the American equivalent of cricket. Hours pass between pitches. Weeks go by between hits. No, they saw John as the one who saved them. Isn't it astonishing that people pay to look at this? ... The only other sport in which the players spend so much time standing around is highway repair.

b. So we raced over to the Meyers's, and the cats were still alive, but, I mean, just barely. Luckily, the toilet seat was up, so they had something to drink. And when they saw John, they didn't think, "Oh, there's the guy who forgot us." Part of me would actually like to; I taught it successfully at high school (where it hid under the name Business English), and I enjoyed it as a student. Every time John came back from then on, those cats would see him and go crazy. "Oh, there he is! He's back." I wondered if that happened to God. "Earth. I forgot all about earth. Oh, my, me, I better get down there.

Hey, what if they're mad at me? I know, I'll send the kid." And Jesus came down, and we all went crazy like the cats.

   c. I thought long and hard about whether or not to include a detailed section on grammar in this little book. Fat guys stand around, pull up their pants, and spit. American grammar doesn't have the sturdiness of British grammar (a British advertising man with a proper education can make magazine copy for ribbed condoms sound like the Magna [bleep!] Carta), but it has its own scruffy charm.

What did you move? Do your revised paragraphs look something like this?

   a. Baseball is a silly sport, the American equivalent of cricket. Hours pass between pitches. Weeks go by between hits. **[Fat guys stand around, pull up their pants, and spit.]** ~~No, they saw John as the one who saved them.~~ Isn't it astonishing that people pay to look at this? ... The only other sport in which the players spend so much time standing around is highway repair.

   b. So we raced over to the Meyers's, and the cats were still alive, but, I mean, just barely. Luckily, the toilet seat was up, so they had something to drink. And when they saw John, they didn't think, "Oh, there's the guy who forgot us." **[No, they saw John as the one who saved them.]**~~Part of me would actually like to; I taught it successfully at high school (where it hid under the name Business English), and I enjoyed it as a student.~~ Every time John came back from then on, those cats would see him and go crazy. "Oh, there he is! He's back." I wondered if that happened to God. "Earth. I forgot all about earth. Oh, my, me, I better get down there. Hey, what if they're mad at me? I know, I'll send the kid." And Jesus came down, and we all went crazy like the cats.

   c. I thought long and hard about whether or not to include a detailed section on grammar in this little book. ~~Fat guys stand around, pull up their pants, and spit.~~ **[Part of me would actually like to; I taught it successfully at high school (where it hid under the name Business English), and I enjoyed it as a student.]** American grammar doesn't have the sturdiness of British grammar (a British advertising man with a proper education can make magazine copy for ribbed condoms sound like the Magna [bleep!] Carta), but it has its own scruffy charm.

The paragraphs (with their sentences restored) are from Barton Sutter's *Cold Comfort*, Kevin Kling's *The Dog Says How*, and Stephen King's *On Writing: A Memoir of the Craft*.

Pick the paragraph you like best and do your own version of it.

✳ A FURTHER THOUGHT: USE PARAGRAPHS FOR FOUR CS: CLARITY, COHERENCE, CONTROL, AND CREDIBILITY

I do love my iPhone. I do love my computer. I do love the Internet.

I love their power and speed and instantaneous access to information. I love the things they do for me. I love the way they guide me to my destination, highlight my errors, and suggest alternative word choices. I love the way they let my father see his only great grandchild and hear her sweet newborn sounds six weeks before he died.

I do hereby profess my affection for—and near total dependence on—these devices and technologies. I make this declaration so that you won't think me a Luddite for writing about how these technologies may be undermining your ability to communicate.

But, in fact, they may be.

There's nothing inherently wrong with quick, short communication, no more than it's wrong to occasionally use a one-sentence paragraph to create emphasis (as I did with the previous paragraph). Texting is concise and to the point, and dropping in a one-sentence paragraph varies the pace. But if all you ever write are quick, disjointed messages and one-sentence paragraphs, you may be losing your ability to organize your thought into longer, logically developed arguments. You may be losing your ability to think deeply.

Carefully structured paragraphs are the building blocks of writing. They give us the four Cs of effective communication: clarity, coherence, control, and credibility.

1. **Clarity.** If you want the reader to follow your thought, you need to do three things: Tell the reader where you're going, present your information or explain your thinking, and offer your conclusion. In brief exchanges, with the context established, this three-part structure may not be needed, but for more substantive, deliberate, thoughtful writing, it's essential. The three-part paragraph provides a roadmap: topic, development, resolution.

2. **Coherence.** Paragraphs help you connect your thoughts. A paragraph may contain a number of points, but every point is linked to a unifying theme and every sentence supports the main purpose. After you have drafted your document, you can check its organization by reading the first sentence of each paragraph. Have you created a logical progression? Have you repeated yourself? Have you omitted a key point?

3. **Control.** These building blocks of composition help you set your pace and control your emphasis. As we discussed this week, shorter paragraphs create a faster pace and a less formal style. Longer paragraphs create a slower pace and a more formal style. Because first and last sentences have natural prominence, key points go there. Quotations normally work best in these locations. In legal writing, positive information is presented first and last; negative information is buried in the middle.

4. **Credibility.** Credibility results from multiple factors: command of language, knowledge of subject, rapport with audience, word choice, sentence structure, and—perhaps surprisingly—paragraphing. To write in paragraphs is to demonstrate how your mind works. When the Gettysburg Address is rendered in PowerPoint, its power is lost. Outline format presents information but fails to convey an essential element: quality of mind, sometimes called "voice" in writing.

USE THREE-PART PARAGRAPHS TO ORGANIZE YOUR THOUGHT

Tell them what you're going to say, say it, and then tell them what you've said. How many times have you heard that standard advice on how to give a speech?

The same approach applies to structuring a paragraph. In the beginning of a paragraph, tell your reader what you're going to say. In the middle, develop your thought. And at the end, offer your conclusion. Although not every paragraph needs to be structured according to this neat little formula, the most basic paragraph structure has three components: topic, development, resolution.

Look again at the previous paragraph. Do you see how it breaks into three parts? The first and last sentences are the topic and the resolution. The middle three sentences are the development.

Topic, development, resolution.

The problem these days is that with texting and tweeting, older writers may be forgetting how to develop their thought into longer forms of expression. And younger writers may not be learning how to organize their ideas into paragraphs and how to arrange those paragraphs into longer, coherent wholes.

As I will discuss in next week's material, write in sentences, but think in paragraphs. The paragraph is your strategic unit. You might present three or four points in a paragraph, maybe more, but you should arrange everything within that unit to achieve a single overriding purpose.

Consider how you might arrange the following sentences into a coherent sequence.

1. Your voice might tell you, "That sounds hollow. I think I was being gassy here."
2. Then you can hear any false feelings that remain in the work.
3. In the final stage of preparing a book or essay it helps to read the text aloud.

Here's how Carol Bly presented her strategic unit in *Beyond the Writers' Workshop: New Ways to Write Creative Nonfiction*:

> In the final stage of preparing a book or essay it helps to read the text aloud. Then you can hear any false feelings that remain in the work. Your voice might tell you, "That sounds hollow. I think I was being gassy here."

Of course not every paragraph need be organized according to the components of topic, development, resolution. In *The Elements of Style*, Strunk and White offer this advice.

> In general, remember that paragraphing calls for a good eye as well as a logical mind. Enormous blocks of print look formidable to readers, who are often reluctant to tackle them. Therefore, breaking long paragraphs in two, even if it is not necessary to do so for sense, meaning, or logical development, is often a visual help. But remember, too, that firing off many short paragraphs in quick succession can be distracting. Paragraph breaks used only for show read like the writing of commerce or of display advertising. Moderation and a sense of order should be the main considerations in paragraphing.

Even in their paragraph about taking readability into account, note how Strunk and White follow the three-step approach of topic, development, resolution—not once but twice. If you break their paragraph into two units (beginning the second paragraph with the topic sentence "But remember, too, that ..."), you'll see that their six sentences are actually two three-part sequences.

Now ask yourself, which version is better—one longer paragraph or two shorter ones? To my eye, and I suspect to the eyes of most modern readers, the passage reads better as two shorter paragraphs.

Here's how I decide whether to go with one longer paragraph or two shorter ones: I'm more inclined to break my thought into shorter units if I'm sending an e-mail message, posting online, or writing an article for publication in a newspaper, and I'm more inclined to use the longer unit if I'm composing a paragraph for publication in a book.

Variety in length is also a consideration.

Compare, for example, the contrasting length of the two preceding sentences as well as the contrasting length of the two preceding paragraphs. A shorter unit following a longer unit has special emphasis, as I discussed in Week 31.

Finally, consider the opening paragraphs in this week's technique. To my eye, I could have achieved more emphasis by presenting the topic sentence of the second paragraph as a one-sentence paragraph.

> Tell them what you're going to say, say it, and then tell them what you've said. How many times have you heard that standard advice on how to give a speech?
>
> The same approach applies to structuring a paragraph.
>
> In the beginning of a paragraph, tell your reader what you're going to say. In the middle, develop your thought. And at the end, offer your conclusion. Although not every paragraph needs to be structured according to this formula, the most basic paragraph structure has three components: topic, development, resolution.

Whether choosing shorter or longer units, structure your thought according to the three-step formula: topic, development, resolution.

EXERCISES

1. The sentences in the paragraph below have been reordered so that the resolution sentence is now buried in the middle. See if you can identify

which of the four sentences should be moved to the end so the sentences appear in their original order. (The first sentence has not been moved.)

> All writing is ultimately a question of solving a problem. It may be a problem of where to obtain the facts, or how to organize the material. Whatever it is, it has to be confronted and solved. It may be a problem of approach or attitude, tone, or style.

Which sentence should be moved to the end?

In *On Writing Well*, William Zinsser's choice for last position was "Whatever it is, it has to be confronted and solved."

Note how his arrangement makes a more definite impression.

> All writing is ultimately a question of solving a problem. It may be a problem of where to obtain the facts, or how to organize the material. It may be a problem of approach or attitude, tone or style. Whatever it is, it has to be confronted and solved.

Topic, development, resolution.

2. In addition to its three-part format, look again at the stylistic features of Thomas Watson, Jr.'s memo chastising his employees for wordiness.

> A foreign language has been creeping into many of the presentations I hear and the memos I read. It adds nothing to a message but noise, and I want your help in stamping it out. It's called gobbledygook.
>
> There's no shortage of examples. Nothing seems to get finished anymore—it gets "finalized." Things don't happen at the same time but "coincident with this action." Believe it or not, people will talk about taking a "commitment position" and then because of the "volatility of schedule changes" they will "decommit" so that our "posture vis-à-vis some data base that needs a sizing will be able to enhance competitive positions."
>
> That's gobbledygook.
>
> It may be acceptable among bureaucrats but not in this company. IBM wasn't built with fuzzy ideas and pretentious language. IBM was built with clear thinking and plain talk. Let's keep it that way.

Write your own version of Watson's famous message, imitating its four stylistic features. The first is structural. His three-part sequence—purpose, examples, proposed action—corresponds to the basic structure of a paragraph: topic, development, resolution.

The other three features have to do with techniques for creating emphasis: his use of a one-sentence paragraph, the parallelism of the antithetical statements beginning with "IBM," and the short, punchy concluding sentence. (Many of my students neglect to include the antithetical statements when they do this exercise.)

Note that the three short, punchy sentences all function as resolution statements (the one-sentence paragraph has been separated from the preceding paragraph for emphasis). Note too that the longest sentence in the message is arranged in climactic order (which I discussed in Week 26) and that the longest sentence is followed by the shortest sentence in the message (a technique I discussed in Week 31).

None of this was by accident. Watson knew what he was doing.

Write a message on another topic that imitates, point by point, each of the stylistic attributes of his message. Where Watson uses a one-sentence paragraph, you use a one-sentence paragraph. Where he uses antithetical statements, you use antithetical statements.

If you submit your version to the newspaper as an opinion piece, you won't be twice as likely to have it published than if you hadn't used his techniques. You'll be ten times as likely. Editors want copy that grabs the reader's attention, and Watson's techniques will help you do that.

It's not just what you say; it's how you say it.

WRITE IN SENTENCES, BUT THINK IN PARAGRAPHS

As he relates in his autobiography, Benjamin Franklin enjoyed debating with "another bookish lad in town" named John Collins. To his chagrin, however, the young Franklin usually found himself on the losing side of these "disputations," not necessarily because his friend had the better argument, but because he was "naturally more eloquent, had a ready plenty of words; and sometimes, as I thought, bore me down more by his fluency than by the strength of his reasons."

Determined "to endeavor at improvement," Franklin set about honing his writing skills by imitating the essays in an old volume of Joseph Addison and Richard Steele's *The Spectator*. He did more than study them. He made notes on the papers, "laid them by a few days, and then, without looking at the book, try'd to compleat the papers again." Then he compared his effort with the original, noting how he might have done better.

Franklin did even more than that. He also "took some of the tales and turned them into verse," and after he "had pretty well forgotten the prose," he "turned them back again."

And then to make his exercises even more challenging, he sometimes jumbled his "collections of hints into confusion," and "after some weeks endeavored to reduce them into the best order."

I'm impressed by Franklin's resourceful approach to improving his writing, aren't you? Want to give it a try?

For our model, let's take not an essay from *The Spectator* but a paragraph from Joe Floren's article, "Writing in the Age of Data Drench." The goal is to practice organizing your thoughts into coherent, carefully structured paragraphs.

Floren's paragraph has six sentences, whose order—in the spirit of Benjamin Franklin—I've scrambled. See if you can number the sentences in the order in which Floren placed them.

____ How often would we make careless spelling errors if correcting them meant starting over with a new rock?

____ It's no coincidence that the typewriter is wordier than longhand, the word processor wordier than the typewriter, and dictation wordiest of all.

____ Despite its many benefits, the computer gets the blame for increasing reader overload.

____ Imagine how concise we'd be if we had to chisel our messages into rock.

____ Its ease of use encourages writers to be wordier and less organized.

____ Easy writing quickly becomes lazy writing.

Having trouble?

Here's a hint. The last sentence, "Easy writing quickly becomes lazy writing," seems like it would make a great topic sentence. Well, it's not. It's sentence 5.

Need another hint? Remember that tightly structured paragraphs generally have three parts: topic, development, resolution. A topic sentence does just what it sounds like. It announces the topic of the paragraph, and as Strunk and White remind us in *The Elements of Style*, the paragraph is "the unit of composition." Sometimes topic sentences look back before they point forward. When they make that backward link, they're called "transitional" topic sentences.

Floren's paragraph begins with a transitional topic sentence. Not only is his first sentence transitional, but the introductory transitional element is marked by a comma. Since only two of the sentences have commas, you now have a 50/50 chance of correctly identifying sentence number 1.

After you've identified what you think is sentence number 1, look for a clarifying sentence that amplifies its meaning. That's sentence number 2.

Give it a try.

To create a tightly structured, coherent paragraph, Floren presented the sentences in this order.

_4_ How often would we make careless spelling errors if correcting them meant starting over with a new rock?

_6_ It's no coincidence that the typewriter is wordier than longhand, the word processor wordier than the typewriter, and dictation wordiest of all.

_1_ Despite its many benefits, the computer gets the blame for increasing reader overload.

_3_ Imagine how concise we'd be if we had to chisel our messages into rock.

_2_ Its ease of use encourages writers to be wordier and less organized.

_5_ Easy writing quickly becomes lazy writing.

Note the power of this coherent unit of composition. Floren's paragraph does more than warn us against our tendency to make errors of hurry and haste when we write with computers. It also links to the previous paragraph, the one we don't see here that touts the benefits of writing with computers. Having made the connection, it turns from the pro to the con side of the question, neatly and clearly. As a result, the argument is made persuasively.

I think Franklin would agree.

 **EXERCISES**

1. What's wrong with the paragraph below?

Therefore, a good practice is to place your important points in those locations. The first and last sentences in a paragraph have special emphasis. A standard paragraph has three parts: topic, development, and resolution.

Right. The sentences are presented in reverse order.

Remember: Use the paragraph to organize your thoughts into coherent, logically developed units. Topic, development, resolution.

2. Make a detailed outline of this week's technique. Set your outline aside for a few days, and then use it to write your own version of the technique. Limit the length to 500 to 750 words. What was better in my version? How could you improve yours? Give yourself a pat on the back for every point you made more clearly and memorably than I did. Ask your teacher for an A or your boss for a raise or your publisher for a $10,000 advance. Heck, make it $100,000, and cut me part of it.

CONCLUDE YOUR PARAGRAPHS WITH A CLICK

"Paragraphs punctuate by visual arrangement," Donald Hall writes in *Writing Well.* "Like a sentence, a paragraph tells us that something completes itself and that we have come to the end of a group of statements composing a larger statement. Like a sentence ... a paragraph should close with the sensation of a click."

Whether you're writing a novel, a report, or an article for your company newsletter, that "sensation of a click" is your chance to do something special.

"Take special care with the last sentence of each paragraph," William Zinsser advises in *On Writing Well.* "It is the crucial springboard to the next paragraph ... Make the reader smile and you've got him for at least one paragraph more."

Just as a comedian pauses to let a good line sink in, the spatial pause that follows a paragraph allows the reader to reflect and react. To punctuate your point, try closing a paragraph with a quip, a colorful quote, a vivid image, a thought-provoking analogy, or an imaginative simile or metaphor.

Here's how Eudora Welty in *One Writer's Beginnings* underscores her point about the importance of listening.

> Long before I wrote stories, I listened for stories. Listening *for* them is something more acute than listening *to* them. I suppose it's an early form of participation in what goes on. Listening children know stories are *there*. When their elders sit and begin, children are just waiting and hoping for one to come out, like a mouse from its hole.

Note how Welty's concluding image creates a playful tone. It also makes the passage memorable. Long after you have forgotten the words she used to make her point, you'll remember that little mouse poking its nose out of that hole.

In *The Dog Says How*, Kevin Kling uses the click at the end of a paragraph for comic effect when he describes a scene in which he is sitting with his buddy Larry and some other patrons in a working-class Uptown bar. It's "back in the late seventies before south Minneapolis was fixed up and gentrified." He and Larry are watching the news together.

> The weatherman announced it was two below zero. First cold snap of the year. I worry for some of these guys. God knows where they go at night when this place closes. I guess there's a flop-house upstairs but nobody confirms it for fear of it getting shut down. There is an interview on the news with a guy—must be eighty if he's a day. He says he's from International Falls, the nation's icebox. He says, "Fifty years ago I moved up here for arthritis and this year I finally got it."

Here's another example of Kling delivering a punchline at the end of a paragraph.

> I'm in a theater company called Interact and most of our actors are disabled, but whenever we're on stage our disjointed twists and turns ease out a bit. I've never been in pain while I've been performing; I wish I could say the same for the audience.

In *On Writing: A Memoir of the Craft*, Stephen King uses the click to conclude an anecdote.

> I got my first agent, Maurice Crain, courtesy of my sophomore comp teacher, the noted regional short story writer Edwin M. Holmes. After reading a couple of my stories in Eh-77 (a comp class emphasizing fiction), Professor Holmes asked Crain if he would look at a selection of my work. Crain agreed, but we never had much of an association—he was in his eighties, unwell, and died shortly after our first correspondence.

But that's not how King concludes his paragraph. Instead, he punctuates his anecdote with a humorous quip: "I can only hope it wasn't my initial batch of stories that killed him."

Again, the final line delights the reader and makes the passage memorable.

Earlier in the same book, King uses the click to drive home a serious point when he challenges "one of the great pop-intellectual myths of our time," the notion that "creative endeavor and mind-altering substances are entwined"—in other words, that people are more creative when they abuse alcohol or drugs, as he himself once did.

> Substance-abusing writers are just substance abusers—common garden-variety drunks and druggies ... Hemingway and Fitzgerald didn't drink because they were creative, alienated, or morally weak. They drank because it's what alkies are wired up to do. Creative people probably *do* run a greater risk of alcoholism and addiction than those in some other jobs, but so what? We all look pretty much the same when we're puking in the gutter.

Pay special attention to which sentence you place at the end. Like the sentence at the beginning, the last one has special emphasis, so make it a good one.

As you practice using this technique and work to incorporate it into your stylistic repertoire, keep in mind that it involves more than paragraph structure. It involves more than working with natural pauses and saving your best line for the end. It also involves rhythm. Key to your success is the beat created by your word choice, punctuation, and sentence structure.

With this in mind, go back and read the concluding sentences in the paragraphs used as examples above. Read them out loud. Listen carefully to the rhythm of the language leading up to the pause. With your indulgence, I'll conclude this paragraph with a click: In both comedy and writing, timing is everything.

EXERCISES

1. Look again at Casey Miller and Kate Swift's paragraph, which you saw in Week 7, from *The Handbook of Nonsexist Writing*.

> Only recently have we become aware that conventional English usage, including the generic use of masculine-gender words, often obscures the actions, the contributions, and sometimes the

very presence of women. Turning our backs on that insight is an option, of course, but it is an option like teaching children the world is flat.

Can you hear the special effect that is achieved by placing a snappy sentence at the end of the paragraph?

Do your own version of Miller and Swift's paragraph, concluding it with a click.

2. In *On Writing: A Memoir of the Craft*, Stephen King describes his memory of the time he imagined himself to be the Ringling Brothers Circus Strongboy and he picked up a cement cinderblock in his aunt and uncle's garage.

Unknown to me, wasps had constructed a small nest in the lower half of the cinderblock. One of them, perhaps pissed off at being relocated, flew out and stung me on the ear. The pain was brilliant, like a poisonous inspiration. It was the worst pain I had ever suffered in my short life, but it only held the top spot for a few seconds. When I dropped the cinderblock on one bare foot, mashing all five toes, I forgot all about the wasp. I can't remember if I was taken to the doctor, and neither can my Aunt Ethelyn ... but she remembers the sting, the mashed toes, and my reaction.

But that's not how King ends the paragraph. He concludes with these lines:

"How you howled, Stephen!" she said. "You were certainly in fine voice that day."

The direct quote from Aunt Ethelyn caps off the scene.

Write your own narrative paragraph, using this one as a model, and conclude it with a direct quote for the "click."

✳ A FURTHER THOUGHT: SAVE YOUR BEST LINE FOR LAST

When your writing loses focus, look at your paragraph structure.

Consider this tightly structured paragraph about wilderness preservationist Ernest Oberholtzer by Louise Erdrich in *Books and Islands in Ojibwe Country*:

He was born in 1884, grew up in an upper middle-class home in Davenport, Iowa, suffered a bout of rheumatic fever that weakened his heart. He went to Harvard, where he made friends with bookish people like Conrad Aiken and Samuel Eliot Morison. His heart kept bothering him. Told by a doctor he had just one year to live, he decided to spend it in a canoe. He traveled three thousand miles in a summer. Paddling a canoe around the Rainy Lake watershed and through the Quetico-Superior wilderness was just the thing for his heart, so he kept on paddling. He lived to be ninety-three years old.

Talk about a "click." In one sharply drawn paragraph organized around the theme of a weakened heart, Erdrich summarizes a man's life. Her structure: topic, development, resolution.

USE PARALLEL STRUCTURE TO CREATE RHYTHM

If I said to you, "She's healthy, wealthy, and a prestidigitator," you would think something was wrong, and you'd be right.

There's nothing wrong with being a prestidigitator; what's wrong is the structure of my sentence. I began with two adjectives, and then I switched to a noun. The resulting structure is nonparallel. The third item comes as a surprise. You were expecting a third adjective, not a noun.

This error in consistency often appears in vertical lists (which are commonly used in PowerPoint presentations). Here's an example.

As an account executive, I have
1. Managed a budget of $1.3 million
2. Reduced spending on supplies by 24 percent
3. Direct responsibility for customer relations
4. Rolled out three new products in six months

As you can see, the series of items could be made consistent, or parallel, by beginning the third item with a verb such as *Had* or *Assumed*.

Sometimes the break in consistency is less obvious. Consider the following sentence: "As the last spectators were leaving the ballpark and with one boy sitting in the front row, Mickey took a bow."

Here the introductory element is composed of two nonparallel elements. The inconsistency may be subtle, but it inhibits the natural flow of the sentence.

Rather than the two elements beginning with different words—*as* and *with*—both should begin with the same word: "With the last spectators leaving the ballpark and with one boy sitting in the front row, Mickey took a bow."

And now that the sentence has been made parallel, you have the option of deleting the second *with*: "With the last spectators leaving the ballpark and one boy sitting in the front row, Mickey took a bow."

When a sentence is nonparallel, it sounds awkward. When a sentence is delivered in parallel structure, it has a pleasing and distinctive sound.

Can you identify which of the following three sentences is nonparallel?

1. Language is not a carving; it's a curl of breath, a breeze in the pines. (poet and environmental activist Gary Synder)

2. In the writing process, the more a thing cooks, the better. (Nobel Prizewinning author Doris Lessing)

3. Parallel structure improves clarity, adds emphasis, and it will help you write with style. (entertaining newspaper columnist, existentialist philosopher, insightful social critic, and really fast Nordic ski racer Stephen Wilbers)

I guess I blew it. Oh, well, no one's perfect.

This is how I would correct the structure of the following sentences to make them parallel.

> **Incorrect:** I love broccoli, cranberries, and eating lemon sherbet.
> **Correct:** I love broccoli, cranberries, and lemon sherbet. (I always thought it was spelled *sherbert*.)

> **Incorrect:** To improve your writing, learn the rules of language, read good writers, and you can imitate their style.
> **Correct:** To improve your writing, learn the rules of language, read good writers, and imitate their style.

> **Incorrect:** To err is human, forgiving is divine.
> **Correct:** To err is human, to forgive divine. (Alexander Pope)

Remember: If it doesn't flow, it doesn't go.

EXERCISES

1. Presenting words, phrases, and clauses in parallel structure makes your writing memorable. Consider the effect of repeating the phrase "I have a dream that one day" in Martin Luther King's famous speech. Repetition is parallel structure. If you present a series of elements in parallel structure, you add emphasis to your writing.

On the other hand, if you begin a pattern and unexpectedly change the structure, you jar your reader. Nonparallel structure is like a broken promise. Your reader expects consistency.

Make the following sentences parallel.

    a. She read the paper, finished her coffee, and the meeting began without her.

    b. He had to complete a major proposal by 5 o'clock, arrange a meeting with a new client, and an article for the monthly newsletter had to be drafted by the end of the week.

Did you change them to something like this?

    a. She read the paper, finished her coffee, and missed the beginning of her meeting.

    b. He had to complete a major proposal by 5 o'clock, arrange a meeting with a new client, and draft an article for the monthly newsletter by the end of the week.

2. What could be worse than making a mistake, projecting it on a large screen, standing before an audience, and pointing to the error? It's an awkward situation, one that often occurs with PowerPoint presentations.

The error results from violating a basic rule of composition: Items in a series must be presented in consistent format or parallel structure. Readers (and viewers) expect consistency. To change the structure partway through a list is to break a promise.

Let me demonstrate.

Imagine I am standing before you. I reach into my pocket, and I take out a marker. I reach into my pocket a second time, and I take out a second marker. Then I reach into my pocket a third time, and I take out a hamster. You would be surprised by the hamster.

Now imagine yourself sitting in an auditorium viewing a PowerPoint presentation. You see the following slide.

Writing entails
1. A logical mind
2. Attention to detail
3. Presenting information in a consistent format

The shift from two noun phrases to an -ing word (a verbal noun called a "gerund") interferes with the flow of thought. Even if you are unsure of the parts of speech, you sense that the structure of the list has been altered.

The solution to this common problem is simple: Whenever you create a vertical list—whether you use bullets or numbers and whether you print the list on paper or project it on a screen—check for consistency in format. Read the first word or phrase of each item. If your list begins with a verb, you're under contract to complete the list with verbs. If the first item is a sentence fragment, all the items must be sentence fragments.

3. The opening paragraph of Tillie Olsen's *Silences* makes effective use of parallel structure.

Literary history and the present are dark with silences: some the silences for years by our acknowledged great; some silences hidden; some the ceasing to publish after one work appears; some the never coming to book form at all.

Note that the verb *are* is omitted after each *some*, a wonderful example of the power of ellipses, which I discussed in Week 23.

Do a study of Olsen's sentence, imitating its four features: repetition, parallel structure, ellipses, and sentence structure (a colon followed by a series of semicolons). Pick a topic that's important to you, as the silence imposed on artists, the poor, racial minorities, and women was to Olsen.

✳ A FURTHER THOUGHT: WOULD YOU LIKE TO PLAY "MAKE IT PARALLEL"?

We were sitting in room 233B, Lind Hall, on the University of Minnesota campus, waiting for our colleagues to arrive for a meeting that was supposed to have started ten minutes ago. Charlie and I always arrive on time, even though these meetings never begin when they're supposed to.

"Well," said Charlie, "what should we play today?"

"How about 'Dangle your modifiers'?" I suggested.

"Naw," he said. "We played that last week."

"'Count the typographical errors?'"

"Naw. Did that the week before."

"How about 'Make it parallel'? Haven't played that since September 1988."

"Okay," he said. "You start."

"Vertical lists or correlative conjunctions?"

"Please," he said. "I couldn't stand to hear another nonparallel list. I just sat through a PowerPoint presentation in which every slide contained a nonparallel element. It was truly the following: 'painful, annoying, distracting, and not the sort of thing that inspires confidence.'"

"That bad?"

"Let's just say the presenter was 'neither healthy, wealthy, nor an athlete.'"

"I take your meaning," I said. "So, we'll do nonparallel elements after the correlative conjunctions *both ... and, either ... or, neither ... nor,* and *not only ... but also?*"

"Give me your worst," he said.

It was fifteen minutes past the hour. Charlie and I were still the only two people in the room.

"So, Charlie, tell me more about that PowerPoint presentation. You sat there not only watching slides for an eternity, but also nonparallel structures were used?"

"Too obvious," he said. "*I sat there not only watching slides for an eternity but also being annoyed by nonparallel structures.*"

"In other words, correlative expressions either must be expressed in parallel form, or the sentence must be revised."

"Exactly," he said. "*Either correlative expressions must be expressed in parallel form, or the sentence must be revised.*"

"And either you follow parallel structure or make it difficult for your reader to follow you?"

"Indeed. *Either you follow parallel structure, or your reader has difficulty following you.*"

"Then you would agree that identifying both correlative conjunctions and checking for nonparallel structures are good things to do?"

"Come on," he said. "I could do these in my sleep: *Both identifying correlative conjunctions and checking for nonparallel structures are good things to do.*"

It was now twenty minutes past the hour. Still just the two of us.

"These are too easy," said Charlie. "All you have to do is make certain that correlative conjunctions are followed by the same part of speech or grammatical structure. If a verb comes after *either*, then a verb must follow *or*."

"So are you saying that neither editing for such obvious errors nor practice by playing this game is a good idea?"

"No, *I'm saying that both editing for such obvious errors and practicing by playing this game are good ideas.*"

"And are you tiring not only of our game but also surprised that our colleagues are late?"

"No, *I'm neither tiring of our game nor surprised that our colleagues are late.*"

"Gotcha!" I cried. "*Tiring* and *surprised* aren't parallel."

"On the contrary. A participle like *tiring* is a form of a verb that is used as an adjective. Pairing a participle with an adjective like *unhappy* is close enough."

I really like Charlie. A brilliant man who is quick to laugh, I enjoy his openness to new ideas.

"Hey," said Charlie. "I thought we weren't going to play 'Dangle your modifier' today."

He must have read my mind.

USE PERIODIC SENTENCES TO CREATE SUSPENSE AND EMPHASIS

When the American nightclub owner Rick Blaine, played by Humphrey Bogart in the 1942 film *Casablanca*, declared, "Of all the gin joints, in all the towns, in all the world, she had to walk into mine," he delivered one of the most memorable lines in movie history.

If you and I had been taught how to write a hundred years ago, we would have recognized the structure of that sentence, and we would have known how to produce a similar effect in our own writing.

The old way to teach writing was highly structured and regimented. In the old days, we would have been taught some two hundred schemes and tropes—schemes are structural patterns such as inversion and antithesis, ("Ask not what your country can do for you …") and tropes are figures of speech such as metaphor ("All the world's a stage")—techniques that have been taught to students of writing for thousands of years. And we probably would have learned the schemes and tropes first in Greek and Latin, and only after having mastered them in those supposedly more elegant and sophisticated languages would we have learned them in English. Life was tough.

The new way to teach writing is hit or miss. Today if your child is being taught the parts of speech, you're lucky. And if your child's teacher knows about schemes and tropes, you're blessed.

In theory, anyone with a good ear for language can write a sentence as memorable as Rick Blaine's. But you're more likely to write one if you know what type of sentence it is and you understand how it works.

It's a periodic sentence, one of four rhetorical sentence types: periodic, loose, balanced (or parallel), and antithetical. The four types are easy to learn.

A balanced or parallel sentence (which I discussed in Week 39) creates a pleasing sound through repetition of similar elements ("What is written without effort is in general read without pleasure"). An antithetical sentence (which I discussed in Week 25) is a balanced sentence with contrary statements ("Not that the story need be long, but it will take a long while to make it short").

Loose and periodic sentences are mirror images.

In a loose sentence, the main clause is followed by a series of parallel elements: "She peered into the dark room, fearing for her life, listening for the slightest sound, wondering if the murderer lurked within."

In a periodic sentence, like Rick Blaine's, the main clause follows the parallel elements: "Of all the gin joints, in all the towns, in all the world, she had to walk into mine." Dramatic delay creates the effect.

If you were to recast Blaine's sentence as a loose sentence, it would read, "She had to walk into my gin joint, of all the gin joints, in all the towns, in all the world."

Note that a periodic sentence, because of the suspense it builds, is more dramatic and showier than a loose sentence. A loose sentence, as its name implies, is more relaxed.

A note of caution: When you create a series of preceding or following elements, be sure to maintain parallel structure.

For example, this periodic sentence is nonparallel: "Fit, prosperous, and an athlete, she lived a long and happy life." This periodic sentence is parallel: "Fit, prosperous, and athletic, she lived a long and happy life."

Consider this example.

> **Incorrect:** Full of his beliefs, sustained and elevated by the power of his purpose, arming himself with the rules of grammar, the writer is ready for exposure.

Correct: Full of his beliefs, sustained and elevated by the power of his purpose, armed with the rules of grammar, the writer is ready for exposure. (E.B. White)

Now take a look at how I've changed the following loose sentence (one in which the parallel elements follow the main clause) into a periodic sentence (one in which the parallel elements precede the main clause).

Loose Sentence: She peered into the dark room, fearing for her life, listening for the slightest sound, wondering if the murderer lurked within.

Periodic Sentence: Fearing for her life, listening for the slightest sound, wondering if the murderer lurked within, she peered into the dark room.

You can play around with the structure of that periodic sentence by switching the order of its four elements and altering its emphasis. To shift emphasis to the element, "Fearing for her life," make it the main clause. In other words, switch the order of the first and last elements so that the sentence begins with "Peering into the dark room, listening for ..."

Did you come up with this? "Peering into the dark room, listening for the slightest sound, wondering if the murderer lurked within, she feared for her life."

As a general rule, use a loose sentence when you want to keep it relaxed, or cap off your series with a figure of speech, like a grace note after the downbeat. But for drama, for suspense, for flourish and emphasis, delay your main clause. Use a periodic sentence.

EXERCISES

1. Make Frederick Manfred's periodic sentence into a loose sentence by moving the series of introductory elements to the end.

One leg dragging, still on hands and one knee, grizzled, tattered, crusted over, looking like a he-bear in molting time after a terrible fight, he examined the sand around the ash heap, around the grave, also the spot where he had lain when he first came to.

Does your loose sentence look like this?

> He examined the sand around the ash heap, around the grave,
> also the spot where he had lain when he first came to, with one
> leg dragging, still on hands and one knee, grizzled, tattered,
> crusted over, looking like a he-bear in molting time after a ter-
> rible fight.

Note how the drama and suspense of the periodic sentence, with its de-
layed main clause, are lost in the loose sentence.

2. Although periodic sentences are by their nature more dramatic than
loose sentences, a skilled writer like Manfred can make a loose sentence
dramatic by piling on colorful, vivid detail. (Of course, you have to be a
keen observer and know your subject well to make this technique work.)
Look how he elaborates after the main clause with a long series of trailing
elements in this sentence from *Lord Grizzly*.

> Then the young [buffalo] bulls came through the gully in waves,
> huge, hairy, blowing, snorting young bulls, eyes wild, black head
> and black horns lowered, black shaggy humps and foreparts
> bouldering along, small tan afterparts skipping, each young
> bull for all the world looking like an overgrown black bull up
> front and a nervous tail-whipping silly tan heifer in back, one
> after another, by tens by hundreds by thousands, solid black
> walls of them, bellowing, blowing, roaring, wilder even than
> the cows and calves.

Create a periodic sentence by deleting the word *then* and placing the trailing elements before the main clause, beginning your revised sentence with
"Huge, hairy, blowing, snorting young bulls ..."

3. Search "periodic sentences" on the Internet. Find a couple of examples
you like, and do your own versions of them. Depending on your stamina,
have a go at Nikolai Gogol's "now famous periodic sentence" from his
short story "The Overcoat."

✳ A FURTHER THOUGHT: USE VARIETY IN SENTENCE STRUCTURE TO ADD ENERGY

The other day I went to the store to buy a sentence. All I wanted was a simple declarative sentence, but the clerk, a bald man with a long gray beard and wired-rimmed spectacles, told me they were all out of simple declarative sentences.

"We have the other eleven types of sentences," he said. "Could you use one of those?"

"No, thanks," I said. "I'm working with a group of technical writers today, and they prefer simple sentences."

"Is that so?" He seemed surprised. "Don't they know that writing without subordinate elements is like speaking in a loud, monotonous voice, without subtlety or variation?"

"Well, some do," I said, "but the things they write about are complex, so they tend to stick with simple structures."

"Now look here," he said, pulling three large boxes from the shelf behind him. "We carry three categories of sentences, each with four types.

"We have four *functional sentences*: statement, question, command, and exclamation. We have four *grammatical sentences*: simple, compound, complex, and compound complex. And we have four *rhetorical sentences*: loose, periodic, balanced, and antithetical.

"The only type we don't have is simple," he said. "Surely they could use one of the other eleven."

"Well, I don't know. Because their principal concern is clarity, they like to present everything in main clauses."

"But couldn't they use an occasional subordinate element, a phrase or clause that won't stand alone, like the last two parts of this sentence? I'm not suggesting that every sentence should be long and complex," he said, the pitch of his voice rising, "but a little variety would add emphasis and energy to their writing. Couldn't they use an antithetical sentence like my last one now and then?"

I told him that I myself liked antithetical sentences but that technical writers might question their value.

"Oh, come now. Antithetical sentences have all kinds of uses. For one thing, they are especially well suited for giving definitions, something technical writers do all the time.

"Look here," he said, ripping open the box labeled *Rhetorical Sentences* and dumping its contents onto the counter.

In the heap of structures I saw *loose sentences*, in which the main clause came before the subordinate elements, as in "Writing the college application essay is a time of reckoning for the eighteen-year-old high school senior, a young person who is both naive and experienced, both child and adult."

I saw *periodic sentences*, in which the subordinate elements came before the main clause, as in "For the eighteen-year-old high school senior, for a young person who is both naive and experienced, both child and adult, writing the college application essay is a time of reckoning."

And I saw *parallel sentences*, in which the sentence parts were balanced, as in "What is written without effort is in general read without pleasure."

"Those are too fancy for technical writers," I said.

"Well, maybe so," he said, snatching a sentence from the pile and holding it up by its predicate. "But here's one they could use: 'Superconductivity is achieved not by lowering the temperature of certain metals to freezing but by lowering it to near absolute zero.'"

"Well, all right," I said. "I'll take it—not because I think technical writers should abandon the simple declarative sentence but because I think they should use more variety in their sentence types."

CROSS THINGS UP WITH ANTIMETABOLE AND CHIASMUS

Do you like to swing? Can you hear the beat? Hey, baby, let's rock and roll!

For the next three weeks we'll work with six particular rhythms or cadences. Each scheme produces a distinct effect. All six are created by repetition.

Learning to use words to create a harmonious or pleasing sound is probably best done by ear, and a good ear is developed by listening and attending to language—that is, by reading. But as Edward Corbett and Robert Connors explain in *Style and Statement*, there *are* certain techniques that can be studied and imitated.

If you want to get fancy, you can take a seat beside Plato and Aristotle and call these schemes by their Greek names: *antimetabole, chiasmus, anaphora, epistrophe, anadiplosis,* and *isocolon.*

Departures from literal meaning such as metaphor and simile are called tropes. Departures from normal word order are called schemes.

There are four basic types of schemes: schemes of balance (such as antithesis and parallelism), schemes of inversion or unusual word order (as in "Ask not ..." and Yoda's speech patterns), schemes of omission (such as ellipses), and schemes of repetition (such as *antimetabole* and *chiasmus*).

Antimetabole is the repetition of words in reverse order, as in "Everyone who loves his country is a patriot, but not every patriot loves his country."

Chiasmus is the repetition of grammatical structures without repetition of the same words or phrases, as in "It's hard to make time, but to waste it is easy."

Other schemes of repetition include *anaphora, epistrophe, anadiplosis*, and *isocolon*. We'll explore each of these in the next two weeks.

Antimetabole and *chiasmus* depend on the rhythm that comes from repetition, but with a twist—or more precisely, with a reversal. They reverse the order of things in successive phrases or clauses, as in A/B; B/A.

Antimetabole is the repetition of words in reverse order, as in "Ask not what your country can do for you; ask what you can do for your country."

Here, if C = country and Y = you, then the order is CY/YC: "Ask not what your country (C) can do for you (Y); ask what you (Y) can do for your country (C)."

Chiasmus is the repetition of grammatical structures but without repetition of the same words or phrases, as in "It's hard to make time, but to waste it is easy."

Here, if A = adjectives (*hard/easy*) and I = infinitive phrases (*to make time/to waste it*), then the order is AI/IA: "It's hard (A) to make time (I), but to waste it (I) is easy (A)."

Of the two schemes, *chiasmus* generally produces a more formal, consciously crafted effect.

The neat symmetry of both schemes can make simple observations sound profound, as illustrated by the *antimetabole* "The French work to live, whereas Americans live to work" and by the *chiasmus* "What is stolen without remorse, with guilt must be repaid."

These schemes turn up unexpectedly. Once I was skiing with a friend in my Nordic ski club who was telling me about getting her M.B.A.

"The guys outnumbered the girls ten to one," she said. "Unfortunately, we had an odd assortment of possibilities, and all the possibilities were odd."

Now imagine you're a brilliant eighteenth-century neoclassical scholar. You decide a dictionary of the English language would be a good idea, so you sit down and write one—by yourself, without the benefit of assistants. You're smart but sometimes caustic. When an aspiring writer asks you to comment on a manuscript, you find the writing mediocre at best. So what do you say?

Do you say, "Well, it's not very good, and the parts that are good aren't very original"?

Not if you're Samuel Johnson you don't. You respond with an extended *antimetabole*: "Your manuscript is both good and original; but the part that is good is not original, and the part that is original is not good."

Ouch.

The next time you read or hear a good line, check the rhythm to see if *antimetabole* or *chiasmus* is responsible for the effect. Then write your own version of the sentence, imitating the structure but using your own words. Before you know it, you'll be finding opportunities to use these cadences in your own writing.

And if you're looking for some good music while practicing *antimetabole*, I recommend that unforgettable number from Finian's Rainbow, "When I'm not near the girl I love, I love the girl I'm near."

 **EXERCISES**

1. Complete or revise the following sentences using *antimetabole*.
   a. Say what you mean and ...
   b. It's better to let inspiration come looking for you than for you to go out and find it. (Hint: Begin with "Don't go looking for ...")

Do your revisions look something like this?
   a. Say what you mean, and mean what you say.
   b. Don't go looking for inspiration; let inspiration come looking for you.

2. Now revise the following sentences using *chiasmus*.
   a. She skillfully attacked, and he artfully deflected.
   b. I didn't mean to hurt your feelings; I only wanted to help." (Hint: Begin the second clause with "to help was ...")

Do your revisions look something like this?
   a. She skillfully attacked, and he deflected artfully
   or She attacked skillfully, and he artfully deflected.

b. I didn't mean to hurt your feelings; to help was my only desire. (Note that in this example the revised version sounds too formal or stuffy to the modern ear.)

3. Do your own version of Samuel Johnson's *antimetabole*.

> Your manuscript is both good and original; but the part that is good is not original, and the part that is original is not good.

Create paired elements, and reverse their order, not once but twice.

Here, I'll start a sentence for you: "Your excuses are both plausible and amusing, but ..." Complete the sentence with a double *antimetabole*.

4. Using Émile Zola's sentence as a model, write a sentence using *antimetabole*: "The artist is nothing without the gift, but the gift is nothing without work."

5. Create your own *chiasmus*, using this one as a model: "What is stolen without remorse, with guilt must be repaid."

✳ A FURTHER THOUGHT: RHETORICAL DEVICES WILL REKINDLE YOUR LOVE LIFE

Classical rhetoricians like Aristotle, Socrates, Longinus, and Cicero have much to teach us about the artful use of language. Their definition of various figures of speech (divided into schemes and tropes) can help us deliver our message with clarity, emphasis, and style.

Just the other day, for example, my wife and I were sitting by the stone hearth of the Gabimichigami Lodge. We had gone to our favorite Minnesota north woods resort for a romantic getaway.

As the sun fell behind the pines and the light faded from the western sky, I turned to the woman sitting next to me, my companion for twenty-six years, and felt overwhelmed by her beauty, as though I were looking at her for the first time.

I put my arm around her and drew her close.

"Now what do you want?" she said playfully, her voice soft and limp and lazy with fatigue from our day of skiing under the great white pines. Her face was radiant in the firelight.

"I have something for you."

"What?" she asked. She hates surprises.

I held out a copy of Edward Corbett and Robert Connors' *Style and Statement*, a book expounding the uses of classical rhetoric for the modern writer.

"It's for you."

"Oh, Stephen," she said, catching her breath. "It's ... it's ..."

"Stupendous?" I prompted.

She nodded, speechless.

"The next time you have trouble thinking of the proper word, you can use this book for help," I said. "The first section is about choice of diction as measured by the criteria of *purity*, *propriety*, and *precision*."

"Oh, the *alliteration*, the repetition of those consonants ... it makes my heart palpitate," she gasped.

"And mine as well. In fact, alliteration is one of ten schemes of repetition discussed by the authors, as is *anadiplosis* (repetition of the last word of one clause at the beginning of the following clause, as in the lyrics to the song 'Where Have All the Flowers Gone?')."

"Furthermore, *apposition*—which you used in your sentence when you juxtaposed the word *alliteration* and the phrase *the repetition of those consonants*—is a scheme of unusual word order, as is parenthesis (an insertion that interrupts, like this one)."

I could tell she was fascinated, so I went on.

"Each of these schemes or figures of speech produces a particular stylistic effect, as did my sentence 'And mine as well,' which is an example of dependent meaning, a device of fragmentation (common in dialogue) that strengthens coherence."

"What about *polysyndeton*?" she asked.

"You're thinking of the deliberate use of many conjunctions," I said, "a scheme that Ernest Hemingway used frequently and that I myself used in when I thought of your voice as 'soft and limp and lazy with fatigue'?"

"And what about ..."

"... tropes?"

"Yes. Tropes." "In contrast to schemes, tropes are deviations not in the arrangement of words but in their signification or meaning. Some of the more commonly used tropes are *metaphor* ('Our CEO is a lion'), *personification* ('This project is eating up too much time'), *hyperbole* ('I'm working twenty-hour days!'), and *paradox* ('Work is a great way to have fun')."

"Oh, you. You knew I would ask about tropes," she said, slipping in an example of *epanalepsis* (repetition of the same word at the beginning and the end of a clause). "By the way," she said, laying her head on my shoulder, "I loved the *antithesis* (juxtaposition of contrasting ideas) you used to distinguish tropes from schemes when you said 'Tropes are deviations not in arrangement of words, but in their signification or meaning.'"

"And you, my darling—if I may use *anastrophe* (inversion of usual word order) —I love more than you'll ever know."

USE *ANAPHORA* AND *EPISTROPHE* FOR ELOQUENCE

If Patrick Henry had said, "I'd give anything for liberty, even my life," we wouldn't be quoting him today.

Instead, he proclaimed, "Give me liberty, or give me death," to which his compatriots are said to have shouted, "To arms! To arms!" thereby responding emphatically to an emphatically rousing statement.

In both instances, the emphasis came not only from the drama and bravado of the moment but also from one of the simplest and most useful stylistic devices in language: repetition.

There are many types. Simple repetition creates the rising intensity of parallel structure, as it did in Martin Luther King's 1963 March on Washington speech delivered on the steps of the Lincoln Memorial: "I have a dream that one day ... I have a dream that one day ..."

Repetition at the beginnings and endings of successive phrases creates a special kind of emphasis, as it did in Henry's 1775 speech to the Virginia Convention ("Give me ... or give me ...") and in Lincoln's 1863 Gettysburg Address ("... government of the people, by the people, and for the people").

When Marcus Tullius Cicero, Marcus Fabius Quintilianus, and other classical rhetoricians opened successive phrases with repeated words, they called it *anaphora* (such as Patrick Henry's quote above); when they closed successive phrases with the same words, they called it *epistrophe* (such as F. Scott Fitzgerald's advice, "Never confuse a single defeat with a final defeat.").

The opening of Charles Dickens' *A Tale of Two Cities*, which you saw in Week 25, is a well-known example of *anaphora* as well as antithesis.

> It was the best of times, it was the worst of times, it was the age of wisdom, it was the age of foolishness, it was the epoch of belief, it was the epoch of incredulity, it was the season of Light, it was the season of Darkness, it was the spring of hope, it was the winter of despair, we had everything before us, we had nothing before us, we were all going direct to heaven, we were all going direct the other way ...

The following verse from Corinthians is a memorable example of *epistrophe*: "When I was a child, I talked like a child, I thought like a child, I reasoned like a child."

Today we can use the same rhetorical schemes of *anaphora* and *epistrophe* to write and speak both eloquently and memorably. Compare, for example, "I don't want Pop-Tarts for breakfast, lunch, and dinner" with "I don't want Pop-Tarts for breakfast. I don't want Pop-Tarts for lunch. And I don't want Pop-Tarts for dinner. I don't want Pop-Tarts. Period."

Likewise, compare "It was more than liking; she loved him for his money" with "She didn't just like him for his money; she loved him for his money."

Consider these sentences, which have been rewritten using *anaphora*.

> **Original:** Don't know much about history, biology, a science book, or the French I took.
> **Rewritten:** Don't know much about history. Don't know much about biology. Don't know much about a science book. Don't know much about the French I took. (Sam Cooke, "Wonderful World")
>
> **Original:** Today is the day we begin to put our customers first and our competition to shame.
> **Rewritten:** Today is the day we begin to put our customers first. Today is the day we put our competition to shame.

Now take a look at these sentences, which have been rewritten using *epistrophe*.

> **Original:** There's not a liberal and a conservative US; there's a United States of America.

Rewritten: There's not a liberal America and a conservative America; there's a United States of America.

Original: We will work as long and hard as we need to.
Rewritten: We will work as long as we need to and as hard as we need to.

These sentences have been rewritten using both *anaphora* and *epistrophe*.

Original: Nothing tastes better, provides more fabulous calories, or fattens you up faster than corn syrup.
Rewritten: Nothing tastes better than corn syrup. Nothing provides more empty calories than corn syrup. Nothing fattens you up faster than corn syrup.

Original: When I think of my uncle's collection of black velvet paintings, his assortment of multicolored rabbits' feet, and his front-yard flock of pink flamingoes, I am gaga with envy.
Rewritten: When I think of my uncle's collection of black velvet paintings, I am gaga with envy. When I think of his front-yard flock of pink flamingoes, I am gaga with envy.

If you want to write with emphasis, speak with emphasis. If you want to speak with style, write with style.

Whatever that means.

EXERCISES

1. Think of a simple, strong verb such as *need, want, saw, visited,* or *remember.* Use it in a sentence, such as "When we were in Key West, we visited Sloppy Joe's, the bar where Ernest Hemingway met Martha Gelhorn," and keep using it in successive sentences, "We visited ... We visited ..."

2. Using the following sentences by Malcolm X as a model, write a series of sentences with both *anaphora* and *epistrophe*: "Why should white people be running all the stores in our community? Why should white people be running the banks of our community?"

3. Using the following sentence by Ralph Waldo Emerson as a model, write a sentence with *epistrophe*: "What lies behind us and what lies before us are tiny compared to what lies within us."

✳ A FURTHER THOUGHT: GEHRIG, LIKE LINCOLN, USED REPETITION FOR EFFECT

I wonder if Lou Gehrig, like many school children of his generation, memorized the Gettysburg Address. I bet he did.

Whenever I read the New York Yankees first baseman's 1939 farewell speech to his fans, a rhetorical masterpiece, I can't help but connect it with Lincoln's address, one of the great speeches in American history.

Lincoln lamented the loss of 23,000 Union soldiers. Gehrig announced his illness-induced retirement from baseball after having played in 2,130 consecutive games. Both speeches captured the poignancy of the moment.

But the similarity goes deeper. Both men relied primarily on repetition for effect. Compare their closings.

It is rather for us to be here dedicated to the great task remaining before us—that ... we here highly resolve that these dead shall not have died in vain; that this nation, under God, shall have a new birth of freedom; and that government of the people, by the people, for the people, shall not perish from the earth.

Sure I'm lucky ... When everybody down to the groundskeepers ... remember[s] you with trophies—that's something. When you have a wonderful mother-in-law who takes sides with you in squabbles with her own daughter—that's something ... When you have a wife who has been a tower of strength and shown more courage than you dreamed existed—that's the finest I know.

Maybe I'm imagining it, but the underlying rhythm of the successive *that* clauses, presented in climactic order in both addresses, seems too similar for mere coincidence. More specifically, both men used the rhetorical devices of *parallelism*, *anaphora*, and *epistrophe*.

As you know, *parallelism* is the repetition of similar structures, as in Lincoln's *that* clauses and in Gehrig's declaration "Sure I'm lucky" at the beginning of two successive paragraphs.

Anaphora is the repetition of the same word or words at the *beginning* of successive clauses, as in Lincoln's "It is for us, the living ... It is rather for us ..." and in Gehrig's series of *when* clauses.

And *epistrophe* is the repetition of the same word or words at the *end* of successive clauses, as in Lincoln's "government of the people, by the people, for the people" and in Gehrig's "—that's something ...—that's something."

In addition to these three *schemes*, or artful deviations from ordinary word order, Gehrig employs a number of *tropes*, or deviations from ordinary meaning.

Gehrig opens with paradox (apparently contrary statements), heightened by hyperbole (exaggerated language): "Fans, for the past two weeks you have been reading about the bad break I got. Yet today I consider myself the luckiest man on the face of this Earth."

Next he employs *erotema* (rhetorical questions intended to make a point rather than elicit a response): "Which of you wouldn't consider it the highlight of his career just to associate with [these grand men] for even one day?" And then he follows up with five more questions naming the people he admires most.

Gehrig's speech is more than a great moment in sports. It is a great example of rhetorical prowess. Like Lincoln, Gehrig demonstrated a fine ear for the rhythms and cadences of language. And, like his predecessor, he addressed his audience in a distinctively American style—plain talk combined with carefully crafted structure.

CREATE RHYTHM WITH ANADIPLOSIS AND *ISOCOLON*

For the past few weeks, I've been discussing various ways to establish rhythm, all based on repetition. If you thought *antimetabole, chiasmus, anaphora,* and *epistrophe* were fun, just wait. We also have *anadiplosis* and *isocolon.*

Anadiplosis is repetition of the last word of one clause at the beginning of the next, as in "What we need is love; love is what we need."

Anadiplosis is a subcategory of *antimetabole,* which as you know is a crossing or reversing of the order of repeated words, as in "Everyone who loves his country is a patriot, but not every patriot loves his country." In *anadiplosis,* however, the repeated words are juxtaposed.

Compare *antimetabole* and *anadiplosis* in the following sentences.

> **Antimetabole:** "Everyone who loves his country is a patriot, but not every patriot loves his country."
> **Anadiplosis:** "Hard work leads to success; success leads to happiness."

Other examples of *anadiplosis* are "Beauty is truth, truth beauty" (John Keats) and "If you can't be with the one you love, love the one you're with" (Billy Preston and Stephen Stills).

A variation of *anadiplosis* is found in the lyrics of the folksong "Where Have All the Flowers Gone" (written by Pete Seeger and Joe Hickerson).

> Where have all the flowers gone ... young girls have picked them ... Where have all the young girls gone ... gone to young men ...

> Where have all the young men gone ... gone to soldiers ... soldiers gone ... gone to graveyards ... graveyards gone ... gone to flowers ... flowers gone ... young girls have picked them ...

Consider these well-known examples of *anadiplosis*.

1. I am Sam, Sam I am. (Dr. Seuss, *Green Eggs and Ham*)
2. For Lycidas is dead, dead ere his prime. (John Milton, *Lycidas*)
3. Fear leads to anger. Anger leads to hate. Hate leads to suffering. (Yoda, *Star Wars Episode I: The Phantom Menace*)

Frank Zappa also uses *anadiplosis* in the lyrics of "Packard Goose": "Information is not knowledge; knowledge is not wisdom; wisdom is not truth, truth is not beauty; beauty is not love; love is not music; and music is the best."

Repetition of both the same grammatical structure and the same number of syllables is called *isocolon*, as in "How to succeed at business: Have a vision, know your values, and work like crazy," and in "The meal was succulent, but the guests were truculent." Obviously, a little *isocolon* goes a long way.

Winston Churchill used an isocolon for dramatic effect in his 1940 speech given in Manchester, England.

> Come then: let us to the task, to the battle, to the toil—each to our part, each to our station. Fill the armies, rule the air, pour out the munitions, strangle the U-boats, sweep the mines, plow the land, build the ships, guard the streets, succor the wounded, uplift the downcast, and honor the brave.

Here are three well-known examples of *isocolon*.

1. Many are called, but few are chosen.
2. It takes a licking, but it keeps on ticking!
3. I'm a Pepper; he's a Pepper; she's a Pepper; we're a Pepper – Wouldn't you like to be a Pepper, too? Dr. Pepper!

How might you complete the following sentence with an *isocolon*? "What is written without effort is in general read without ..."

You saw that sentence in Weeks 17 and 24. Here's how Samuel Johnson completed it: "What is written without effort is in general read without pleasure."

I don't suggest you use the Greek words when you go out with your friends tonight, but if you're looking for a way to create emphasis through repetition, try using *anadiplosis* and *isocolon*.

EXERCISES

1. Using the following passage from E.L. Doctorow as a model, write a series of sentences using *epistrophe*, *antimetabole*, and *anadiplosis*: "Planning to write is not writing. Outlining, researching, talking to people about what you're doing, none of that is writing. Writing is writing."

   For an extra challenge, make the second sentence in your series a periodic sentence.

2. Using John Keats' line from "Ode on a Grecian Urn" as a model, write ten sentences using *anadiplosis*: "Beauty is truth, truth beauty."

3. Add a second line to your ten sentences, using the next line from Keats' ode, which employs *antimetabole*, as your model.

   > Beauty is truth, truth beauty,—that is all
   > Ye know on earth, and all ye need to know.

4. Using Pete Seeger and Joe Hickerson's lyrics as your model, write the lyrics of a song using *anadiplosis*.

   > Where have all the young girls gone ... gone to young men ...

   If you're feeling inspired, write the music as well.

5. Using the following sentence as a model, write one hundred sentences in Latin using *isocolon*: "Veni; vidi; vici;" which means "I came; I saw; I conquered." (Just kidding about writing those sentences in Latin. Write one in English.)

6. Using the following sentence as a model, write a sentence introducing an *isocolon* with a fragment: "How to succeed at business: Have a vision, know your values, and work like crazy."

7. Read a book by Dr. Seuss, and note all the examples of schemes. How many can you identify by name? Pick your favorites, and do your own versions.

✳ A FURTHER THOUGHT: MORE DEAD (AND BURIED) SENTENCES

A cemetery reveals its secrets at midnight. It is at this hour, as one wanders among the tombstones enshrouded by darkness, that the forces of good and evil unveil themselves.

I met my guide at the appointed place: the Monument to Dead Sentences.

"Come," he said, without greeting. "I will show you the spirit of monotony, and from that encounter you will learn to appreciate the power of variety and life."

As we made our way through the shadows, I was aware of an indistinct murmuring, a low moan that grew into a chant. It was the sound of myriad simple declarative sentences. All were in standard subject-verb order. All were about the same length. None included a subordinate element. None exemplified variety.

"And now you know the secret," said my guide. "To bring your sentences to life, vary your sentence structure and length. From that simple principle, all else follows."

The moon broke through the clouds as we came to a gate marked "Technical Writers." In the valley below, we saw perfect rows of innumerable white markers glowing in the pale light.

"Why so many?" I asked.

"Because technical writers, preoccupied with clarity and precision, often neglect the *sound* of language.

"Now sit there," my guide said, waving a gnarled finger in the direction of a stone crypt. "The truth will come to you with the light of dawn."

I settled into the detritus of dead leaves, my back against the cold stone. As I drifted into a restless sleep, the voices grew more distinct.

1. **Avoid creating strings of simple declarative sentences.** Here is a simple declarative sentence. It makes a statement. It has no subordinate elements. A string of these sentences creates monotony. Monotony steals life from your writing.

2. **Pause for emphasis.** Use a colon or a dash to bring a sentence to a dramatic halt, as in "We met at the appointed time: midnight." A sentence fragment before the colon creates special emphasis, as in "The result: a business boom that has lasted nearly a decade."

3. **Use subordinate elements to indicate relationships and to create emphasis.** Rather than "Janet is head of facilities management, and she is responsible for maintenance," write, "As head of facilities management, Janet is responsible for maintenance."

4. **Follow a long sentence with a short, snappy one.** This long-short combination makes the writer sound decisive: "We have waited years for the right time to expand our business. That time is now." It's a simple technique, and it works every time.

5. **Offer an occasional aside.** Rather than "The vampire bat is an insectivorous mammal. It also feeds on blood," write, "The vampire bat, an insectivorous mammal, also feeds on blood." Mark a parenthetical comment with commas or parentheses. You also can use a dash—or a pair of dashes—to indicate an aside.

6. **Elaborate before or after the main clause.** As in this sentence (the one you are reading), offer a preliminary statement before the main clause. You also can elaborate after the main clause, like this.

7. **Use parallel constructions (and other schemes) to create rhythm and emphasis.** As Mae West once said, "I go for two kinds of men. The kind with muscles and the kind without."

8. **Invert normal order.** Rather than "Word choice is equally important," write, "Equally important is word choice." A subject-predicate inversion creates energy. It also can increase coherence between sentences by moving a reference to a previously expressed thought to the sentence's beginning, where it serves as a transition.

At the first light of dawn, I awoke to a multitude of jubilant voices. I saw subordinate elements dancing hand-in-hand with parenthetical asides and parallel constructions. I saw *antimetaboles* pairing up with *chiasmi*, I saw *anaphoras* with *epistrophes*, and I saw *anadiploses* with *isocolons*. Transformed into more interesting, rhythmic, complex structures, the simple declarative sentences had rejoined the living.

LAY DOWN A BEAT ... AND THEN BREAK THE RHYTHM

There's nothing like a good beat.

In prose, as in free verse, the beat is unstructured, the rhythms natural. In traditional poetry, the beat is made up of a pattern of stressed and unstressed syllables: iambic (ˇ-), trochaic (-ˇ), anapestic (ˇˇ-), dactylic (-ˇˇ), and spondaic (--). These patterns are called metrical feet.

Even here, however, too much of a good thing becomes monotonous. We want to hear a beat, but we also want some variation in the theme. First you establish a rhythm; then you break the pattern.

Consider the beat in this sentence: "I take thee to be my wedded wife, to have and to hold from this day forward, to have and to hold for better, to have and to hold for worse, to have and to hold for richer, to have and to hold for poorer, to have and to hold in sickness ..."

Well, you get the idea. It's too much of a good thing.

Now compare that version with the wedding vow as it was written by sixteenth-century Archbishop Thomas Cranmer.

> I take thee to be my wedded wife, to have and to hold from this day forward, for better, for worse, for richer, for poorer, in sickness and in health, to love and to cherish, till death us depart.

Read the sentence out loud, and listen to its cadence. Note how Cranmer establishes a rhythm and then varies it.

After the first "to ... to ... to ..." comes "for ... for ... for ... for ..." and then he changes it to "in ... in ..." and then he goes back to "to ... to ..." Then comes the shorter, almost abrupt, "till death us depart" (or more commonly, "till death do us part"), suggesting permanence and finality.

It's more than the meaning of the words that makes his wedding vow memorable and enduring; it's also its pleasing sound or euphony.

In the past three weeks, I've discussed six schemes to establish rhythm, all based on repetition. All six can be overused and overdone.

To illustrate *isocolon*, I offered the example "The meal was succulent, but the guests were truculent," and I pointed out that a little *isocolon* goes a long way. Thus the need to sometimes vary your rhythm.

I also offered a sentence by Samuel Johnson as an example of an *isocolon*: "What is written without effort is in general read without pleasure."

To appreciate the importance of matching the two-syllable words *effort* and *pleasure*, try ending the sentence with *joy*: "What is written without effort is in general read without joy."

Here the variation doesn't work as well as the perfectly matched words *effort* and *pleasure*.

But here's an example of how a slight variation in the rhythm does work: "What we hope ever to do with ease, we must learn first to do with ..."

With what? Play around with a few two- or three-syllable words.

Here's how Johnson completed the sentence: "What we hope ever to do with ease, we must learn first to do with diligence."

Do you agree that the variation adds to the effect?

Now, revise the following sentence to create a slight variation in rhythm: "Any fool can make a rule, and every fool obeys that rule."

Here's how Henry David Thoreau completed the sentence: "Any fool can make a rule, and every fool will mind it."

Note the slight alteration in cadence—four trochees, or stressed/unstressed feet ("Any fool can make a rule" or [-ˇ] [-ˇ] [-ˇ] [-ˇ]), followed not by another four trochees but by three ("and every fool will mind it" or [-ˇ] [-ˇ] [-ˇ]). Note how the three-foot variation creates a sense of abruptness and finality.

Be careful, however, not to vary the rhythm too abruptly. If you do, you might jar your reader. Breaking the rhythm too abruptly results in nonparallel structure. Consider these awkward sentences and their accompanying revisions.

Awkward: She was healthy, wealthy, and a philatelist.
Revised: Not only was she healthy and wealthy, but she also collected stamps.

Awkward: To empower our crew members, we need to give them full responsibility for their jobs, work alongside them, and it's important that we listen to their suggestions.
Revised: To empower our crew members, we need to give them full responsibility for their jobs, work alongside them, and listen to their suggestions.

Next, complete the following sentence (which you saw in Week 25) as you see fit, with or without a variation in rhythm: "The difference between journalism and literature is that journalism is unreadable and literature is ..."

You might have finished the sentence with *unread*. Oscar Wilde, however, varied the wording ever so slightly: "The difference between journalism and literature is that journalism is unreadable and literature is not read."

Remember: First lay down a good beat, but when the occasion demands—and your ear tells you to—break the rhythm.

EXERCISES

1. Complete the sentences below with wording that introduces a slight variation in rhythm.
   a. The more serious you are as a writer, the more ...
   b. I never let my schooling interfere with ...
   c. Much of the activity we think of as writing is, actually ...

Here's how William Kennedy, Mark Twain, and Gail Godwin completed those sentences.
   a. The more serious you are as a writer, the more you feel yourself an outsider.
   b. I never let my schooling interfere with my education.
   c. Much of the activity we think of as writing is, actually, getting ready to write.

2. Complete the fourth sentence in this series of sentences using *epistrophe* with a dash and a slight alteration in rhythm to vary the beat: "The big sycamore by the creek was gone. The willow tangle was gone. The little enclave of untrodden bluegrass was gone. The clump of dogwood on the little rise across the creek ..."

Here's how Robert Penn Warren completed the series in *Flood: A Romance of Our Time*:

> "The big sycamore by the creek was gone. The willow tangle was gone. The little enclave of untrodden bluegrass was gone. The clump of dogwood on the little rise across the creek—now that, too, was gone."

3. Look for a passage in your writing that has a singsong effect. Alter the rhythm to vary the beat.

USE ANALOGIES AND COMPARISONS TO ENLIVEN YOUR WRITING

When you leave the literal world for the figurative world, you enter the realm of the imagination. It's there you might find your most promising possibilities for making an enduring impression on your reader.

But where do you start? How do you create an image or comparison that captures your meaning? How do you enter that mysterious, nonliteral dimension of the imagination, the world of tropes, where readers are invited to make their own associations?

As many writers have advised, you work not with the rational, thinking mind, but with the creative, daydreaming mind. Rather than conduct a conscious search, you let go. You abandon yourself. You become absorbed in what you're trying to convey. You follow your thoughts and feelings and see where they take you. Rather than finding the comparison, the comparison finds you.

Comparisons come in three basic types: metaphors, similes, and analogies.

Metaphors, as you know, are comparisons that don't use *like* or *as*. Similes are comparisons that do use *like* or *as*. Analogies, a broader category, are comparisons that might employ metaphors and similes but tend to identify similarities in a logical and literal way.

Your chances of creating a good analogy are greater if you know how to recognize a bad one. Here are some awful metaphors, similes, and analogies I found posted on the Internet that are distinguished by their adolescent humor.

> Her face was a perfect oval, like a circle that had its two sides gently compressed by a Thigh Master.
>
> He was as tall as a six-foot-three-inch tree.
>
> The little boat gently drifted across the pond exactly the way a bowling ball wouldn't.
>
> John and Mary had never met. They were like two hummingbirds who had also never met.
>
> Shots rang out, as shots are wont to do.

Clearly those analogies don't work, although you might argue they're so delightfully bad they're good.

Do you know a good analogy when you see one? Consider the following examples. Which ones work for you? Which ones don't?

1. The young fighter had a hungry look like the kind you get from not eating for a while.
2. He could throw a lamb chop past a hungry wolf. (in reference to a baseball pitcher)
3. She walked into my office like a centipede with ninety-eight missing legs.
4. The majority's reasoning is a five-foot leap over a ten-foot ditch. (in reference to a decision by a state Supreme Court)
5. It hurt the way your tongue hurts after you accidentally staple it to the wall.
6. Ladies bathed before noon, after their three-o'clock naps, and by nightfall were like soft teacakes with frostings of sweat and sweet talcum. (in reference to a small town in the Deep South, sizzling with heat)

The odd-numbered examples are, once again, delightfully bad. The even-numbered examples are from writers renowned for their facility with language.

Example 2, which you saw at the end of Week 3, is from Red Smith, referring to Whitey Ford of the Yankees.

Example 4 is from a state Supreme Court justice dissenting from the majority decision. (Responding in kind, the majority retorted with its own metaphor: "The dissent's reasoning is a ten-foot leap over a five-foot ditch.")

Example 6 is from Harper Lee's description of Maycomb, a town modeled after Monroeville, Alabama, in her novel *To Kill a Mockingbird*. Two factors make her simile particularly effective. First, the distasteful and the tasteful are juxtaposed in the alliterative *sweat* and *sweet*. Second, her simile captures something basic and essential about the oppressive heat by appealing not only to sight but also to smell, a sense that is linked to memory and experience.

> It was a tired old town when I first knew it. In rainy weather the streets turned to red slop; grass grew on the sidewalks, the courthouse sagged in the square. Somehow, it was hotter then: a black dog suffered on a summer's day; bony mules hitched to Hoover carts flicked flies in the sweltering shade of the live oaks on the square. Men's stiff collars wilted by nine in the morning. Ladies bathed before noon, after their three-o'clock naps, and by nightfall were like soft teacakes with frostings of sweat and sweet talcum.

With this skillfully balanced simile, Lee moves from the literal to the figurative, from realistic description to an appeal to the reader's imagination.

You can say it straight, or you can use metaphor, simile, or analogy to make it memorable.

EXERCISES

1. Complete the sentences below with similes (tropes that use *like* or *as*).
   a. Some days the paddling is difficult. Every stroke irritates like a ...
   b. But other days, you float as if ...
   c. Today the boat moved as effortlessly as an ...

In *Wild Shore: Exploring Lake Superior by Kayak*, Greg Breining enlivens his descriptions with three similes, one abrupt and two gentle: *boil*, *in a dream*, and *idle thought*.

Using Breining's three-sentence description as a model, write your own description using a series of similes.

2. In describing Jay Gatsby's mansion in *The Great Gatsby*, F. Scott Fitzgerald writes of music "through the summer nights," and he uses a simile to describe a place where "men and girls came and went like _____ among the whisperings and the champagne and the stars."

What simile do you think he used?

(Card, please.)

Were you thinking *fireflies*?

Fitzgerald's simile was *moths*.

3. Do your own versions of two comparisons by Colum McCann, the first a simile, the second a metaphor.

    a. I was as touchy as a triggered trap.

    b. A couple of jet skis hummed their savage insectry across the water.

If you hate the racket made by jet skis, think of something you find equally annoying and describe it with a metaphor. If you love jet skis, create a metaphor that presents them as one of the twentieth century's great inventions.

4. In *TransAtlantic*, Colum McCann describes the laborious, almost desperate writing process of one of his characters, but I suspect he may have had his own search for the right word in mind when he wrote this passage.

> The best moments were when her mind seemed to implode. It made a shambles of time. All the light disappeared. The infinity of her inkwell. A quiver of dark at the end of the pen.
>
> Hours of loss and escape. Insanity and failure. Scratching one word out, blotting the middle of a page so it was unreadable anymore, tearing the sheet into long thin strips.
>
> The elaborate search for a word, like the turning of a chain handle on a well. Dropping the bucket down the mineshaft of the mind. Taking up empty bucket after empty bucket until, finally, at an unexpected moment, it caught hard and had a sud-

den weight and she raised the word, then delved down into the emptiness once more.

As a writer, can you relate?

At what point does McCann leave the literal and enter the figurative realm in his extended comparison?

Note how he adds another layer of meaning to the first figure of speech, "like the turning of a chain handle on a well" with "Dropping the bucket down the mineshaft of the mind."

Rewrite the last paragraph, replacing the figurative language with a literal description of the elaborate search for a word.

What is lost? What subtle dimensions of the writing process did Mc-Cann capture with his figurative language?

5. Using McCann's passage as a model, create an extended comparison on a topic that's important to you.

✳ A FURTHER THOUGHT: SHOW RESTRAINT IN USING METAPHOR AND ANALOGY

How far can you go in using analogy and metaphor to enliven our writing? How far is too far?

Here are some more examples of intentionally outrageous comparisons posted on the Internet.

Useless as a football bat.

Confused as a termite in a yo-yo.

I'm so hungry I could eat a horse and chase the rider.

Outrageous but amusing.

Here's an example of an analogy from a report that envisions the Twin Cities in the year 2015 written by the Metropolitan Council. The report invited the reader to speculate on the key events that will shape the future of this region. It did so by simple comparison and analogy.

The course of the 20th century was set in large measure by the discoveries made during the last 12 years of the 19th century. Inventors gave us the electric light bulb, the telephone, the skyscraper, the elevator, and the automobile. Those inventions made today's cities possible. What are the inventions and other forces driving change today? How do we prepare ourselves for the future?

The report avoids two common errors: forcing an unlikely analogy and going on too long. Instead, it makes the point succinctly, in a single paragraph of a two-page introduction, and then returns to the main argument.

The metaphors, similes, and analogies that work best are those that reinforce or clarify meaning and appeal to the reader's imagination without calling undue attention to themselves. Those that flop are usually overdone or contrived. They come at you like a big hand appearing out of the blue and grabbing you by the scruff of your neck and tossing you over your neighbor's fence. Yikes.

Remember: A little metaphor goes a long way.

RETURN TO YOUR METAPHORS AND SIMILES

Returning to your metaphors or similes is a trick every good essayist and story-teller knows. Using a figure of speech and coming back to it creates coherence and cohesion. It conveys a sense of thoughtfully crafted structure, and if the subsequent reference occurs near the end of a piece, it creates a tidy conclusion.

A Prairie Home Companion radio host Garrison Keillor uses this technique in his largely unscripted monologues. If he opens his monologue with a reference to a deer in a rut, you can bet the deer will return somewhere near his conclusion. Returning to the image frames his talk, creates a sense of structure, and allows him to wander almost anywhere he likes in the middle without seeming aimless.

In her memoir *Somewhere Towards the End*, Diana Athill uses a metaphor to cap off her explanation of why she thinks society benefits from religion although she herself is an atheist.

> No honest atheist would deny that in so far as the saner aspects of religion hold within a society, that society is the better for it. We take a good nibble of our brother's cake before throwing it away.

In the next paragraph, she returns to her metaphor.

> I have accepted a great deal of Christ's teaching partly because it was given me in childhood by people I loved, and partly because it continues to make sense ... the nearer people come to observing it the better I like them (not that they come, or ever have come,

very near it, and nor have I). So my piece of my brother's cake is a substantial chunk.

And then, at the risk of overdoing it, she extends her metaphor one more step when she comments on her love of religious art. Not only is the piece of Christian cake "a substantial chunk," she writes, but "it is covered, what's more, with a layer of icing, because much of the painting and sculpture I love best ... was made by artists who lived long enough ago to believe that heaven and hell were real."

Whether a person of faith, an agnostic, or an atheist, the reader is likely to find Athill's prose colorful and engaging because of the way she extends her metaphor to develop her point.

As you look for opportunities to use and return to figures of speech in your own writing, keep in mind that they work best when they meet three criteria: They're simple, apt, and novel.

A forced comparison is a distraction, if not a train wreck. It's like the high beams of an oncoming car that blind you when you're trying to follow the hairpin turns on a slick, winding road on a dark and stormy night. See what I mean? When you're working with figures of speech, it's easy to crash.

The high-beams-on-a-dark-road simile may be apt, but the comparison is forced rather than simple, clichéd rather than novel. But returning to it—"train wreck ... it's easy to crash"—might work. What do you think? Still a little much?

When you encounter a figure of speech in your reading, keep an eye out for subsequent references. If you like the example, copy the passage. (It's easy to cut and paste, but typing the text word for word is a good way to get close to the language. I'll spare you additional commentary on the value of handwriting.) If there's no subsequent reference, try your hand at creating your own linked metaphor.

What do you think? Were my figures of speech—*keep an eye out* and *try your hand*—too subtle? Too plain? Probably. But even if they didn't add much, they weren't forced and they did no harm.

As you work with your metaphors and similes, be careful not to mix images that don't go together. In Paul Lehmberg's book, *In the Strong Woods: A Season Alone in the North Country*, the author captures the immensity of a moving glacier with a series of similes and metaphors.

Spreading out like batter poured onto a griddle, it lumbered south over the Canadian Shield and into the Quetico at the rate of an inch to ten feet a day. By cementing uptorn rock debris into its snout and underbelly as it heaved down out of the North, the glacier quarried for itself, cutting, scraping, gouging edges and planes that completely destroyed existing drainage patterns in its track, and the sheer weight of one of these icy leviathans, some of which grew to a thickness of two miles, flattened the crust of the earth.

Lehmberg's description is riveting, but his progression from "batter poured onto a griddle" to "the snout and underbelly" of some unnamed creature (I see a monstrous boar) to "icy leviathans" is somewhat jarring.

The following sentences contain three figures of speech. Try your hand at creating a second metaphor or simile that complements the first one. A few paragraphs ago, for example, I paired "A forced comparison is a distraction, if not a train wreck" with "When you're working with figures of speech, it's easy to crash."

1. The wind had been through / the valley / leaving everything cold / and gleaming / like bells.
2. The sheer weight of one of these icy leviathans, some of which grew to a thickness of two miles, flattened the crust of the earth.

With this type of open-ended exercise, it's unlikely your version will be similar to the authors', but here's how Patricia Kirkpatrick (in her poem, "Hidden Falls") and Paul Lehmberg paired those figures of speech.

1. Walking at the Mississippi, / I was a woman, a ruin / the wind had been through.
2. [As the glacier melted, it left behind] a barren profusion of scoured and tortured bedrock littered with gravel, rocks, and boulders, all awash in the meltwaters of rotting hulks of ice stranded like whales on a beach.

Lehmberg, however, wasn't finished. As he continued his portrayal of how glaciers shaped our northern landscape, he slipped in one more metaphor: "The glaciers had stripped away intervening Earth history and left exposed a moonscape of Precambrian rock—rock of the same age as that buried at the bottom of the Grand Canyon."

Although *moonscape* isn't consistent with the theme of *rotting hulks* and stranded *whales on a beach*, it seems simple, natural, and unforced. I like it.

Whether or not you agree, look for opportunities to create and extend figures of speech in your own writing.

EXERCISES

1. This week's technique is about returning to a figure of speech later to frame your story, essay, or article and create a sense of completion. You can also elaborate or build on your comparison right away.

Complete the following sentences by extending the metaphors or similes.

    a. Feeling a bit like a benign vampire, I recorded their voices, hoarded their photographs. It was as though I had drawn ...

    b. The law has "its epochs of ebb and flow." One of the flood seasons is upon us. Men are insisting, as perhaps never before, that law shall be made true to its ideal of justice. Let us gather up the ...

Here's how Nancy Paddock and Benjamin Cardozo build on their tropes.

    a. Feeling a bit like a benign vampire, I recorded their voices, hoarded their photographs. It was as though I had drawn their life's blood into my veins.

    b. The law has "its epochs of ebb and flow." One of the flood seasons is upon us. Men are insisting, as perhaps never before, that law shall be made true to its ideal of justice. Let us gather up the driftwood, and leave the waters pure.

2. John Mather, senior astrophysicist at NASA's Goddard Space Flight Center in Greenbelt, Maryland, used two metaphors to describe how the Hubble telescope has allowed astronomers to look back in time to when galaxies were forming, thereby giving us new insights into their evolution. Think of some metaphors that might work below, building on the simile *rain on the side of a hill*.

> We thought galaxies formed just like they are. But now we think they grew, they assembled themselves from smaller pieces. It

might have been like rain on the side of a hill. First you get little
_____ that flow together into a larger _____.

(Card, please.)

Building on his analogy, Mather wrote, "First you get little *rivulets* that flow together into a larger *stream*."

3. What images do you think Henry David Thoreau used to extend his metaphor in this famous passage from *Walden*?

> A lake is the landscape's most beautiful and expressive feature. It is *earth's eye*; looking into which the beholder measures the depth of his own nature. The fluviatile trees next to the shore are the slender _____ which fringe it, and the wooded hills and cliffs around are its overhanging _____.

Thoreau's metaphors were *eyelashes* and *brows*.

✳ A FURTHER THOUGHT: SHOULD WE AVOID CLICHÉS LIKE THE PLAGUE?

Like many children growing up in the '50s, I sometimes watched too much television. I remember my Mom telling me, "That's enough TV for today. Go outside and play with your clichés."

Although I may have wanted to see the end of *The Howdy Doody Show* or find out how Hopalong Cassidy turned out, once outside I was always happy to be reunited with my pals, those wonderful, familiar words and phrases like *thunderstruck* and *a level playing field*.

I would imagine myself drifting with *the tides of time*, or being *in the same boat* with Popeye the Sailor, *searching far and wide* for Olive Oyl, and protecting her from that bully Brutus, which meant *pulling no punches* and giving him his *just desserts*.

Sometimes I would sort these colorful expressions into piles according to type.

1. **Alliterative or rhyming phrases**, such as *first and foremost, few and far between, high and dry*, and *holy moly*.

2. **Proverbial expressions**, such as *a bird in the hand is worth two in the bush, an apple a day keeps the doctor away*, and *the exception proves the rule*.

3. **Figurative phrases**, such as *at the end of the day, leave no stone unturned, hit the nail on the head*, and *I'm all thumbs*.

4. **Quotations**, such as *to be or not to be, we have met the enemy and it is us, a day of infamy, the iron curtain*, and *ask not what your country ...*

5. **Allusions to myth or history**, such as *between Scylla and Charybdis, Faustian, Gordian knot, Achilles' heel, Pyrrhic victory*, and *Luddite*.

6. **Foreign phrases**, such as *tête-à-tête, coup de grâce*, and *vis-à-vis*.

7. **Legalisms**, such as *cease and desist, null and void, each and every*, and *suffer and permit*.

Some are words or phrases "clinched by sound alone"; others are images "caught in the popular fancy," as described by Sheridan Baker in *The Practical Stylist* (and quoted by Bryan Garner in *The Oxford Dictionary of American Usage and Style*).

Ah, those happy days with my clichés. But that's another story. Now that I'm grown up (please, no disparaging comments), the only thing I hear about clichés is that you should avoid them like the plague.

But don't you sometimes wonder, if all those familiar phrases are so worthless, why do they refuse to die a graceful death? I'm not saying that every one of them is the apple of our eye, but there must be *something* about them we find appealing.

AVOID VOGUE WORDS AND CLICHÉS

Some trendy words and expressions are merely annoying. That said, those two words (*that said*) are at the top of my list. Unlike useful transitional words such as *therefore*, *nevertheless*, and *furthermore*, they accomplish nothing.

That said, another vogue expression that drives me batty is *if you will*. Have you ever noticed how certain writers and speakers will use that annoying phrase whenever they venture an analogy, metaphor, or simile? No? Well, then you must be, if you will, as blind as a bat, or maybe, if you will, as dumb as a doornail. I'm kidding, of course. In reality, I think you're as smart as a whip, if you will.

Why this peculiar habit of speech? Are the *if-you-will* folks so fearful of figurative language that they feel compelled to call attention to any departure from the literal or the straight and narrow? Are they unconsciously calling attention to what they believe is, if you will, a clever turn of phrase? And why must they insist on doing this 24/7, if you will?

That said, now that I've got these trendy expressions off my chest, if you will, I feel better.

How about you? Are you so enamored of certain words and phrases that you use them ad nauseam?

According to Donald Hall, relying on the easy choices, on trendy words and clichés, causes us to end our search for more precise language prematurely. The risk is that we will stop too soon, contenting ourselves with the obvious and banal rather than continuing our search for just the right word, a novel metaphor, or something fresh.

Here are some sentences to help you practice discriminating between useful clichés and worthless, worn-out expressions. Of course, context and audience normally influence your choice, but have a go at these. Which do you find possibly useful, and which do you find generally unacceptable?

1. We need to begin these negotiations with a clean slate.
2. Otherwise, let's just close up shop and move out lock, stock, and barrel.
3. Given the current economic crisis, many businesses and organizations find themselves in the same boat.
4. If we don't mention the terms disclosed in the fine print of this forty-five page contract, our clients will be none the wiser.
5. Let's nip this in the bud before, like some horse of a different color, it blooms into a foul-smelling rose.

Your eye and ear may differ from mine, but to me the clichés in sentences 1, 3, and 4 are acceptable. Sentence 2 might be all right with one cliché or the other, but piling on two in a single sentence seems like too much of a not-so-good thing. And sentence 5 is ... well, colorful. I hope it gave you a chuckle. I worked hard creating it.

Clichés, of course, can be useful. Because they're common, their meaning is readily understood, if you catch my drift. But if all you do is travel from one tired cliché to another, you risk impressing your audience not with your originality but with your laziness. Rather than profound, you may come across as trite, and wouldn't that be a fine kettle of fish?

 EXERCISES

1. Eliminate ten clichés in the following passage.

> In a twist on airing dirty laundry, Bat Four was arrested by the tribal police for stealing wine and underclothing from three white women campers. When he came before the judge in tribal court, who was all ears, he explained that wine was medicine, sacred medicine for his social medicine bundle. "No

metis would steal medicine because stolen medicine never works right," he explained.

"But there are witnesses who maintain that at the end of the day and then at the time of the stealing you stole their wine and ... whatever, do you now by the same token maintain that you did or did not do this?" asked the judge in the confused language he thought was legal. He smiled over the bench at the white women campers.

"Me pleads the fifth commandment," said Bat Four, not wanting to be caught with his pants down for speaking with a forked tongue.

"The what? Do you think I'm dumber than a doornail or deader than a doorknob?" asked the judge.

"The fifth commandment," he repeated, suspecting the judge was like an apple—red on the outside but white on the inside. His father, he knew, would be proud of him because he told once about white people marking time and covering their lies with the fifth commandment.

Here are the ten clichés you should have eliminated.

1. in a twist on airing dirty laundry
2. who was all ears
3. at the end of the day
4. by the same token
5. not wanting to be caught with his pants down
6. for speaking with a forked tongue
7. dumber than a doornail
8. deader than a doorknob
9. like an apple, red on the outside but white on the inside
10. marking time

Here's how the passage appears, minus the clichés, in Gerald Vizenor's *Wordarrows: Indians and Whites in the New Fur Trade.*

Bat Four was arrested by the tribal police for stealing wine and underclothing from three white women campers. When he came before the judge in tribal court, he explained that wine was medicine, sacred medicine for his social medicine bundle. "No metis would steal medicine because stolen medicine never works right," he explained.

"But there are witnesses who maintain that and then at the time of the stealing you stole their wine and ... whatever, do you now maintain that you did or did not do this?" asked the judge in the confused language he thought was legal. He smiled over the bench at the white women campers.

"Me pleads the fifth commandment," said Bat Four.

"The what?" asked the judge.

"The fifth commandment," he repeated. His father, he knew, would be proud of him because he told once about white people covering their lies with the fifth commandment.

2. Search for *cliché* on the Internet, and compile your own lists of clichés to be avoided and clichés to be used judiciously.

3. Write a short story incorporating all of the clichés on your "to be avoided" list. Give your story to a friend or colleague for feedback without revealing your method of composition. If your friend or colleague really likes your story and says nothing about your language, find another friend or colleague to share your writing with.

✳ A FURTHER THOUGHT: THE FIRST TIME IT RAINED CATS AND DOGS WAS BRILLIANT; NOW IT'S A CLICHÉ

Imagine spending seven hours in a room with thirty or forty attorneys. Actually, it's more fun than you might think.

That's what I was doing in Portland when I presented a continuing legal education seminar for the Oregon State Bar. Contrary to popular opinion, many attorneys are excellent writers. They care about precise communication, they're intelligent, and they're fun to work with. But like everyone else, attorneys live in a world of jargon and poor usage, and despite their commitment to precise expression, sometimes they get sloppy.

Here's an exercise we did with word choice. It involves determining which clichés are imprecise or in some way inappropriate and which add clarity and emphasis despite their being overused.

First, underline the clichés in the following sentences. Then cross out the ones you think don't work, and circle the ones you think serve a purpose.

1. To argue that the Defendant was not only denied a phone call but also spoken to disrespectfully is to go from the sublime to the ridiculous.
2. When the accused confessed unexpectedly, both the prosecuting attorney and the defending attorney found themselves in the same boat.
3. Plaintiff alleges that the powers that be at the Minnesota Department of Labor and Industry improperly denied him health and dental insurance coverage.
4. That a rate hike of this proportion would be disastrous for customers is a foregone conclusion.
5. Blissful ignorance of environmental regulations is no excuse for a callous disregard of the law.

To my ear, in sentence 2 *in the same boat* works well enough, and in sentence 4 *a foregone conclusion*, while not awful, probably should be rejected. The others definitely should go.

The point of sentence 1 is that, of the two purported actions, one is insignificant and one inconsequential, but going *from the sublime to the ridiculous* seems overstated. In sentence 3 *the powers that be* conveys a sense of paranoia or knee-jerk response to established authority.

In sentence 5 *blissful ignorance* and *callous disregard* have a nice ring (their parallel structure, a trope, creates a pleasing rhythm), but closer examination reveals that the two qualities are mutually exclusive. It isn't possible to simultaneously display *blissful ignorance* and *callous disregard*.

If as a writer you serve up one tired cliché after another, you're likely to bore your reader. When in doubt, replace a cliché with a trope of your own making, something novel and apt. In the words of Ezra Pound, "Make it new."

USE YOUR IMAGINATION TO WRITE WITH PERSONALITY AND STYLE

As a warm-up exercise, poet Michael Dennis Browne would sometimes ask his students to write as many outlandish lies as they could think of in the first few minutes of class.

"Don't overthink it," he would say. "Just write whatever comes to mind."

To get them started, he would suggest they begin with something like "My mother wears combat boots to stroll across the green cheese of the lunar surface."

After this freewheeling exercise, he found that his students were more fanciful, expansive, and creative in their exploration of what was possible in their poetry. Whatever self-imposed limits seemed to be holding them back were gone.

What role does imagination play in writing?

On one level, imagination helps you find that unexpected element or twist, that surprise that lingers in your readers' mind, as Colum McCann does in *TransAtlantic* when he depicts this scene set in mid-nineteenth century Dublin: "There was a reek of porter about the streets. A young beggar sang a melody in a tired voice: a police boot sank savagely into her rib cage and moved her along. She fell at the next railing, lay against it, laughing."

The last thing the reader expected was for the young beggar, lying against the railing after having been savagely kicked, to be laughing.

At its deepest level, imagination enables us to associate words and thoughts. If we had no imagination at all, we would lack faith in the value and meaning of words. We would find ourselves incapable of using language or being transported by it. To varying degrees, every writer (and every reader) possesses imagination. To use language is to enter a symbolic world. Every word uttered, every sentence written, is an act of imagination.

But not every writer makes full use of imagination. Not every writer possesses an active, creative imagination. Without that spark, a writer's relationship to language becomes superficial and rigid. To write without creativity is to underestimate the potential of language.

One of the many things I love about Natalie Goldberg's book *Writing Down the Bones* is that it empowers me. As Judith Guest writes in the book's foreword, it gives writers "permission to think the thoughts that come, and to write them down and make sense of them in any way they wish." Goldberg's suggestions for students to be "writing down the bones," as she calls it—for writers to discover "the essential, awake speech of their minds," for getting started and going deeper—are liberating. They let loose what is locked inside. They appeal to the imagination.

A few years ago, I was rereading *The Singing Wilderness* by Sigurd Olson, the naturalist who dedicated himself to preserving the Boundary Waters Canoe Area Wilderness, when I came across this lovely sentence: "The ice on the lakes has secured the shores and islands, has adjusted itself to the form it must keep until spring."

The simple beauty of that sentence took me by surprise. There was nothing showy or ostentatious about it, but that unexpected word—"the ice has *secured* the shores and islands"—captured the scene whimsically and imaginatively.

And then I asked myself, "Why can't I write that way? Why can't I—at least on occasion and when appropriate—move beyond the ordinary and the mundane to the imaginative and the memorable?"

So the next day at work, I looked for opportunities to use surprising verbs. I tried to do so without calling attention to my style—I didn't want to overdo it—but I thought a little creativity could enliven my work environment.

With Olson in mind, I wrote, "Our academic advising services are appreciated by our students, and they have secured a measure of respect from our faculty."

Then I realized the obvious: It wasn't the verb *secured* that distinguished Olson's sentence; it was its imaginative use.

Whenever I sit down to write, I try to remind myself that writing is an act of exploration and discovery. Over the twenty-two years I've been writing my newspaper column, I've learned that a good way to awaken my imagination is to take a few moments to daydream, to allow myself the freedom to roam.

"Writing is not a McDonald's hamburger," Goldberg writes. "The cooking is slow, and in the beginning you are not sure whether a roast or a banquet or a lamb chop will be the result."

So follow your imagination. It may take you to surprising places that delight both you and your reader.

EXERCISES

1. The next time you begin a letter or message with "As per your request, enclosed please find a brochure that describes our services," pause for a moment. Try to think of a more creative, effective way to connect with your reader, and then change your opening to something like "Thanks for your interest in our company. Here's a brochure that describes what we can do for you." Whenever you sit down to write, especially when writing fiction or poetry but even when writing on the job, use your imagination. Go beyond the obvious. Don't be content with *enclosed please find* and *as per* expressions. Be creative. Do the work of trying to find something new.

Replace the standard business expressions below with something fresh.

    a. I'm more than happy to serve you.

    b. Please let me know if you have any questions.

    c. Please don't hesitate to call me.

Did you replace those worn-out expressions with something like the wording below?

    a. I'm eager to serve you.

    b. I'll be happy to clarify any of these complicated instructions.

c. Please don't hesitate to call me—don't hesitate, even though we both know I'm busier and more important than you are, but I'm a generous person who gives freely of my time to people beneath me in the hierarchy of power, people like you, so I hereby grant you permission to impose on my precious time

... Well, I hope you take my point. Perhaps it would be better to avoid that sometimes offending phrase "don't hesitate" and simply write, "Please call me if there's anything else I can do for you."

2. The next time you sit down to write, close your eyes and take a deep breath. Put aside your concerns of the day, and imagine a place you'd like to be. Imagine it with all five of your senses. Spend a few moments there doing whatever you'd like to do. Then open your eyes, and write as many outlandish lies as you can think of for the next two minutes. It doesn't matter what you've written. Now you're ready to write.

✳ A FURTHER THOUGHT: FORGET ALL THOSE RESOLUTIONS, AND PURSUE PASSIONS

I came to a startling realization the other day. Not everyone makes New Year's resolutions.

I should have known. When I think about it, there have been hints in my past.

In the late 1980s, while I was working as associate director of the University of Minnesota's program in creative and professional writing, the program's director asked me what I'd be doing that summer. When I mentioned several projects and a number of trips, he laughed and said, "I don't even know what I'm doing tomorrow."

But how do you ever get anything done, I wondered, if you don't make plans?

I was reminded of Benjamin Franklin's scheme for achieving self-perfection in thirteen steps. I also thought of D.H. Lawrence's scornful response to Franklin's tidy little plan.

> I am a moral animal. But I am not a moral machine. I don't work with a little set of handles or levers. The Temperance-silence-order-resolution-frugality-industry-sincerity-justice-moderation-cleanliness-tranquility-chastity-humility keyboard is not going to get me going. I'm really not just an automatic piano with a moral Benjamin getting tunes out of me.

Let's face it: Some people just don't care for resolutions or self-improvement. But how do they find the discipline to achieve a goal? How do the D.H. Lawrences of the world get anything done? Do they simply follow their passions and whims?

I don't know. But in case you're one of these people, I'm not going to offer a tidy list of resolutions to help you improve your writing. Instead, I offer you the following list of possible passions and whims. Please modify and personalize them as suits your fancy.

1. Quit your job and build a cabin in the woods. Spend two years growing beans, observing nature, reflecting, and writing.
2. Turn off your TV, and lead a life of firsthand experience and wild adventure.
3. Forget about deadlines—take as long as you like to write anything your boss assigns you. Then revise and edit endlessly until you have achieved absolute perfection. Whatever you do, don't allow yourself to be hurried.
4. Quit your job, move to Key West, and write stories and novels about being a man, going to war, hunting, fishing, and falling in love.
5. Read to your children every night before they go to bed. If you don't have children, borrow your neighbor's or volunteer to do storytime at your local preschool.
6. Reject any writing assignments that don't appeal to you. Accept only those that promise rich opportunities for personal expression, inner growth, and self-realization.
7. Quit your job, move to Greece (as it was in the early 1900s), become a shepherd, drink retsina wine, eat goat cheese, and write bad poetry.

8. Learn a second language. Start with an easy one like Japanese or Russian.
9. Read everything your children are reading—from school books to stories, poems, and novels—and make unexpected references to the material, the themes, and the characters over dinner.

I know, I know. Some of these recommendations have little to do with becoming a better writer. But that's the risk you take when you rebel against the straight-shooting, goal-planning Franklin-planners of the world—when, like Lawrence, you refuse to be shoved "into a barbed wire paddock," where you are made to "grow potatoes or Chicagoes."

You lose direction. You wander a bit. But sometimes you find you've arrived where you wanted to be.

ADD A LIGHT-HEARTED TOUCH TO YOUR WRITING

Sometimes you come across something funny when you least expect it.

I was reading Kay Redfield Jamison's *An Unquiet Mind*, a compelling story about how the author's life was nearly destroyed by manic depression—not exactly light reading—when I came across this passage.

> I decided early in graduate school that I needed to do something about my moods. It quickly came down to a choice between seeing a psychiatrist or buying a horse. Since almost everyone I knew was seeing a psychiatrist, and since I had absolute belief that I should be able to handle my own problems, I naturally bought a horse. Not just any horse, but an unrelentingly stubborn and blindingly neurotic one, a sort of equine Woody Allen, but without the entertainment value.

I laughed out loud, and I marveled at Jamison's strength and courage. How could someone describing a potentially debilitating illness—an illness that would cause her mind to race out of control with ideas "coming so fast that they intersected one another at every conceivable angle" and then would leave her numbingly depressed—make a joke about it?

I realized that Jamison's humor, her ability to see the lighter side of things, was integral not only to her story but to her identity and her survival.

And then I wondered about the rest of us. Wouldn't all of us be healthier and happier, as well as more interesting, if we injected a little humor into our day-to-day communication?

Humor is a matter of perspective, a bemused awareness of the incongruous, illogical, and sometimes absurd dimensions of our existence. It's also a matter of timing, technique, and detail.

Jamison's next passage is even funnier.

> I had imagined, of course, a *My Friend Flicka* scenario: My horse would see me in the distance, wiggle his ears in eager anticipation, whinny with pleasure, canter up to my side, and nuzzle my breeches for sugar or carrots. What I got instead was a wildly anxious, frequently lame, and not terribly bright creature who was terrified of snakes, people, lizards, dogs, and other horses—in short, terrified of anything that he might reasonably be expected to encounter in life—thus causing him to rear up on his hind legs and bolt madly about in completely random directions.

Again, Jamison offers a delightful comparison, this time built on wildly contrasting detail followed by a humorous aside—set off by dashes—and an uproarious description of the unfortunate consequences.

Jamison affirmed my belief that, even under the most sobering circumstances, our spirits can be lifted by humor.

EXERCISES

1. Look again at the first paragraph I quoted from Kay Redfield Jamison's *An Unquiet Mind.*

> I decided early in graduate school that I needed to do something about my moods. It quickly came down to a choice between seeing a psychiatrist or buying a horse. Since almost everyone I knew was seeing a psychiatrist, and since I had absolute belief that I should be able to handle my own problems, I naturally bought a horse. Not just any horse, but an unrelentingly stubborn and blindingly neurotic one, a sort of equine Woody Allen, but without the entertainment value.

What makes it funny? Can you identify the specific comic effects? Note the incongruity of her choice between "seeing a psychiatrist or buying a horse."

Write a paragraph imitating Jamison's techniques. Try your hand at incorporating Jamison's incongruity, her outlandish description, and her unexpected comparison of her horse to "a sort of Woody Allen."

Here's my attempt.

> I decided early in my career as a writer that I needed to do something about my tendency to procrastinate. It quickly came down to a choice between seeing a psychiatrist or jumping out of an airplane. Since no one I knew was seeing a psychiatrist, and since I couldn't afford one anyway, naturally I jumped out of an airplane. Not just any airplane, but a reconditioned Vickers Vimy bomber like the one Alcock and Brown flew across the Atlantic in 1919, except instead of dropping a bomb, it dropped me.

2. If you enjoyed this exercise, take the same study-and-imitate approach to Jamison's second passage quoted above.

> I had imagined, of course, a *My Friend Flicka* scenario: My horse would see me in the distance, wiggle his ears in eager anticipation, whinny with pleasure, canter up to my side, and nuzzle my breeches for sugar or carrots. What I got instead was a wildly anxious, frequently lame, and not terribly bright creature who was terrified of snakes, people, lizards, dogs, and other horses—in short, terrified of anything that he might reasonably be expected to encounter in life—thus causing him to rear up on his hind legs and bolt madly about in completely random directions.

How closely you follow your model is up to you, but you may find it useful to imitate Jamison's comic elements point by point.

3. Write a sentence in which you play around with a word, the way sports columnist Red Smith did when referring to the Green Bay Packers' 1958 record of 1-10-1: "They overwhelmed one opponent, underwhelmed ten, and whelmed one."

4. Select any passage you think particularly well written, take a close look at its stylistic traits, and do your own version of the passage on a different topic, imitating the stylistic traits of the original version.

✳ A FURTHER THOUGHT: A SPOONFUL OF HUMOR HELPS THE FEAR GO DOWN

I should have known it was going to be a good flight when I heard a voice on the airport PA system announce: "Would Joyce Elders please expedite her arrival at baggage carousel number two? Joyce Elders, your husband says, if you don't arrive soon, you'll have to walk home."

I was making my way down a busy concourse at Midway Airport on a Friday evening when people all around me—people who a moment earlier had looked tired and expressionless—chuckled and smiled. They were smiling not only to themselves, I noticed, but at each other.

Hearing this voice from a real person, a person with personality and humor, was hardly what anyone expected in this environment. It caught us by surprise. It awakened us.

It was not the voice we are conditioned to hear in airports, where language is routinely tortured into convoluted wording such as, "In the interests of aviation security, all passengers are advised to control their baggage and packages to prevent the unauthorized introduction of unknown objects without their knowledge."

Things got even better after I boarded.

I had just settled into my normal in-flight stupor when I heard the flight attendant say, "Good evening, ladies and gentlemen. My name is Samantha. Please direct your attention to the front of the aisle, where our uncommonly beautiful flight attendant, Sue, will review the safety features on this aircraft."

More than an average number of passengers looked up.

"For those of you who have been in a time capsule for the past fifty years," Samantha continued, "Sue will now demonstrate the proper use of your seatbelt."

A few people laughed as Samantha explained—and Sue demonstrated—how to push the flat metal end into the buckle and how the length could be changed by adjusting the strap.

By the time Samantha got to the part about "in the unlikely event of a change in cabin pressure, a mask will drop down in front of you," I had drifted off again.

Then I heard her say, "First, stop screaming. Then place the mask over your nose and mouth, and breathe normally.

"If you are traveling with a child," Samantha continued, "or with someone who is acting like a child, put your own mask on first, so that you will be able to help the child with theirs."

Next she warned us, "If your luggage is not properly stowed, one of the flight attendants will come back, take it, and you will never see it again."

Nearly everyone was laughing now.

"If you have a cellular telephone," she went on, "I'm very impressed, but you need to keep it turned off at all times.

"I also want to remind you that federal law prohibits tampering with, disabling, or destroying a smoke detector, two-way mirror, or hidden camera in the lavatory.

"If at any time during your flight you need assistance, you can push one of the flight attendant buttons over your head, but it doesn't work and we won't respond.

"We will now dim the lights to show off our flight attendants at their best. I invite you to sit back, but please don't relax. If the flight attendants can't relax, you can't relax.

"Have a good flight."

And we did. We relaxed. We laughed together, and as we laughed we were reminded of our common humanity.

Thank you, Samantha. We depend on your professionalism, but we appreciate your caring enough about people to have some fun with them. And we also appreciate the lesson on how humor can aid communication, a lesson that works as well in writing as in a crowded airplane.

KNOW YOUR OPTIONS FOR COMIC EFFECT

Life is a joke. Unfortunately, the joke is on us.

We're blessed with the gift of life but cursed with the knowledge we're going to die. We're smart enough to know that death awaits us, but powerless to stop its coming.

One response is to recognize the absurdity of what André Malraux called *la condition humaine*. Another response is to laugh. At its most basic level, humor is a reaction to the things we can't control.

In this sense, to tell a joke is to declare your humanity. To laugh is to acknowledge your limitations and even your helplessness. To appeal to another person's sense of humor is to affirm a common bond.

There are two broad categories of humor: lighthearted humor and dark humor (sometimes called black humor). One type of dark humor is existentialist humor, which is based on the view that human life is fundamentally pointless, absurd, and ironic.

A wonderful example is Joseph Heller's *Catch-22*, a novel portraying the absurdity of war. Although "Catch-22" has entered our everyday lexicon as a term referring to a no-win situation involving contradictory or paradoxical rules, in the novel it refers to a particular situation in which a character named Orr, who is "crazy and could be grounded" from flying, is hopelessly trapped.

> There was only one catch and that was Catch-22, which specified
> that a concern for one's safety in the face of dangers that were

> real and immediate was the process of a rational mind. Orr was.
> All he had to do was ask; and as soon as he did, he would no
> longer be crazy and would have to fly more missions. Orr would
> be crazy to fly more missions and sane if he didn't, but if he were
> sane he had to fly them. If he flew them he was crazy and didn't
> have to; but if he didn't want to he was sane and had to.

In some ways, "Catch-22" represents the perfect existentialist dilemma.

As a recovering existentialist, I speak with authority. My existentialist phase began during my junior year of college, when as a student in the Vanderbilt-in-France program in Aix-en-Provence I immersed myself in the writings of Jean-Paul Sartre, Albert Camus, Samuel Beckett, and others, and it extended for several years afterward as I taught a course titled "The Idea of Comedy" at the University of Iowa and the University of Minnesota. Although I never fully embraced the hopelessness of some existentialists, my bout with existentialism opened my eyes to a deeply comic view of life. And it gave me valuable insight into how to make my writing more interesting.

Humor reduces the distance between writer and reader (and between speaker and listener). It makes readers and listeners pay attention, and it helps them remember what they've heard. Because of these attributes, it's a powerful tool, both in writing and in teaching.

On one level, humor provides comic relief. Every novelist, playwright, and screenwriter knows that the audience needs a break when things get oppressively bleak. But humor is more than a momentary break from drama and tragedy. It does more than temporarily boost our spirits and alleviate our sense of hopelessness. On a deeper level, a comic perspective offers insight into the harshness of the human condition. It enlarges our sense of tragedy, and it helps us understand the nature of our existence. Certain realities can be apprehended only through a comic perspective.

"If you're trying to write humor," William Zinsser writes in *On Writing Well*, "almost everything that you do is serious. Few Americans understand this." Comic writers like George Ade, H.L. Mencken, Ring Lardner, Robert Benchley, S.J. Perelman, Art Buchwald, Jules Feiffer, and Woody Allen are not "just fooling around," he points out. They are "as serious in purpose as Hemingway or Faulkner … To them humor is urgent work."

Existentialist humor is only one of many types of humor available to you. To explore other types, let's play with the story of Sisyphus, a figure from Greek mythology and a central metaphor in existentialist thought.

Sisyphus was a deceitful king who was condemned by the gods to spend eternity rolling a huge boulder up a hill, only to have it roll back down. He would never succeed in achieving his goal, and he was condemned to never stop trying. For Albert Camus and other existentialists, his predicament epitomized *la condition humaine*.

Here are ten types of humor you might use in writing about Sisyphus.

1. **Paradox** is an apparently contradictory statement that contains an element of truth. In the hands of a skillful writer, paradox can be a powerful attention-getting device. If we are told, "Haste makes waste," we might agree without giving the statement a second thought. But if we are told, "The swiftest traveler is he that goes afoot," as Henry David Thoreau declares in *Walden*, we are likely to ponder and reflect.

   "If only Sisyphus had realized that frustration is nothing to be frustrated about."

2. **Situational irony** conveys the disparity between perception and reality. Often the divergence is apparent to the reader or viewer but not to the people or characters involved.

   "Never before had Sisyphus come so close to the summit. Tonight he would celebrate his triumph."

   The audience knows better; Sisyphus doesn't.

3. **Verbal irony** conveys the disparity between literal and implied meaning. Easily misunderstood, it often involves saying the opposite of what is meant. Verbal irony is also called **Socratic irony** because Socrates would feign ignorance when questioning his students as a rhetorical strategy. Shakespeare, who reveled in mistaken identities with his characters often appearing in disguise, was a master of irony, both situational and verbal.

   "You can do it, Sisyphus. I believe in you. You're going to succeed. You just need to try harder."

The speaker may or may not believe it; the audience knows better.

4. **Sarcasm** is a form of verbal irony. It involves disparaging or making fun of someone or something.

"My, how strong you are, Sisyphus. What big muscles you have."

5. **Ridicule** is a harsh form of sarcasm.

"Nice try, big guy. Not so powerful now, are you?"

6. **Understatement** (or meiosis) is a form of verbal irony that produces a more subtle type of humor.

"Well, I can think of better ways to spend my time."

7. **Overstatement** (exaggeration or hyperbole) is another form of verbal irony that tends to produce more outlandish humor.

"Now I know how Sisyphus felt. It's taking me forever to proofread my text for this book."

8. **Self-deprecating humor** pokes fun at the speaker. A disarming type of humor, it's the least likely to offend.

"I'm such a quitter. At least Sisyphus kept trying."

9. **Wit** (from the Old English *witan*, "to know") is the clever use of language to produce a comic twist or surprise. According to John Locke, wit is an "assemblage of ideas" involving "quickness and variety." As with all humor, but especially with wit, there is a sudden shock of delight as the audience grasps the unexpected and often unlikely connection between literal reality and comic perception.

"I'd rather roll a stone up a hill than lose my marbles."

10. **Puns** (or paranomasia) are plays on words that are identical or similar in sound but have sharply diverse meanings. Because they sometimes elicit a groan from the audience, puns should be used judiciously.

"Rolling stones isn't so bad, Sisyphus. Just ask Mick Jagger."

Note that all ten types of humor are tropes, or departures from literal meaning. As with all types of humor, there are at least two levels of meaning: the literal and the nonliteral. When you offer a comic perception, you recognize your readers' ability to perceive reality on more than one level. It's as though you're inviting your reader to play the game. In this sense, to use humor is to flatter your audience by recognizing their intelligence.

And as I discussed in Week 38, because of its natural emphasis, the last sentence in a paragraph is a great location to offer a lighthearted observation or quip.

I'll conclude with some words from Samuel Johnson. His little poem illustrates both wit and paranomasia.

> If I were ever punished
> For every little pun I shed,
> I'd hie me to a punny shed
> And there I'd hang my punnish head.

EXERCISES

1. In the opening paragraphs of *Catch-22*, we are introduced to Dunbar, who is trying to escape combat duty by "falling down on his face." Dunbar is in the hospital. Here's how Heller describes his strategy for prolonging his life.

> Dunbar was lying motionless on his back again with his eyes staring up at the ceiling like a doll's. He was working hard at increasing his life span. He did it by cultivating boredom. Dunbar was working so hard at increasing his life span that Yossarian thought he was dead.

Try your hand at using paradox to create absurdist humor. Write a brief description of a character that concludes with a comic twist.

2. Do your own version of the following sentences from Heller's novel, using paradox for your comic effect.

a. The Texan turned out to be good-natured, generous, and likable. In three days no one could stand him.

b. Dunbar loved shooting skeet because he hated every minute of it and the time passed so slowly.

c. Nurse Sue Ann Duckett ... welcomed responsibility and kept her head in every crisis. She was adult and self-reliant, and there was nothing she needed from anyone. Yossarian took pity and decided to help her.

3. In the late 1980s I was wrapping up my career as a full-time university administrator and moving in the direction of becoming a full-time writing consultant. (In those early months after launching my business, I didn't like the title "Unemployed"—it had a harsh ring to it—so I came up with "Writing Consultant.") While I was up north doing some consulting work for President Leslie Duly of Bemidji State University, writer and English professor Will Weaver invited me to go cross-country skiing with him. I was at a challenging period in my life, and Will's easy-going, low-key demeanor was a comfort to me.

The preceding anecdote is enlivened with a humorous aside. (At least that was my intent.) Write your own anecdote or brief narrative episode incorporating one or more of the ten types of humor discussed in this week's material. As you work with your wording, note the importance of getting the timing just right.

4. As Will and I were about to set off in the woods, I paused to read a sign offering some safety tips.

1. Know when sunset is, and time your outing so that you can return to your car before dark.

2. Be aware of changing weather conditions.

3. Dress appropriately in layers.

4. Use extra caution when skiing in areas where ski trails and snowmobile trails intersect, and avoid skiing on trails marked for snowmobiling. They cruise with delight at alarming speeds, and a chance encounter with a slow-moving skier could prove to be unhealthy.

In addition, they pay for and work on their own trails and are entitled to pedestrian-free snowmobiling.

Perhaps in need of some levity, I was delighted by the unexpected humor.

Write your own set of safety tips (or set of procedures) with an unexpected comic element.

5. Do your own version of all ten types of humor described in this week's lesson.

Or, if you prefer, concentrate on the ninth type of humor: wit. Consider the following quips, and then use them as models to write your own versions. I can't guarantee the veracity of the sources, but they're wonderful examples of sharp-witted humor nonetheless.

    a. George Bernard Shaw to Winston Churchill: "I am enclosing two tickets to the first night of my new play. Bring a friend—if you have one"—to which Churchill responded, "Cannot possibly attend first night, will attend second—if there is one."

    b. A member of Parliament to Benjamin Disraeli: "Sir, you will either die on the gallows or of some unspeakable disease"—to which Disraeli responded, "That depends, sir, whether I embrace your policies or your mistress."

    c. Lady Astor to Winston Churchill: "If you were my husband, I'd give you poison"—to which Churchill responded, "If you were my wife, I'd drink it."

✳ A FURTHER THOUGHT: BOB HOPE AND THE MEANING OF STYLE

To write with style is to—do what?

Is it to be good with words, to construct complicated sentences, to concoct improbable metaphors? Is it to make clever observations, to give things a twist, to have an attitude? Is it to be creative, novel, definite, emphatic, witty, or outrageous?

Style is all of these things, but it is something more. Those attributes have more to do with appearance than with style in its deeper meaning, much as the word *lifestyle* has more to do with adornment and material possessions than with underlying values and character.

I was reminded of this deeper meaning of style when I read the tributes offered to Bob Hope at the time of his death.

In an op-ed piece for *The New York Times*, Gary Giddins noted that Hope's career had many highlights—from his ten-year stint hosting radio's "The Pepsodent Show Starring Bob Hope" to his "on the road" movies with Bing Crosby and Dorothy Lamour and his lifelong commitment to entertaining US troops abroad. But there was something about him that transcended his accomplishments.

"Hope was the great comic actor of the 1940s," wrote Giddins, "an original whose persona often transcended lame scripts."

It was Hope's style that was memorable. According to Giddins, "He can still get you with his gangly physicality, his many shades of discomfort, fear or lechery, the trademark gurgle, the off-handed badinage with Crosby, and the luckless romancing with any number of sham femme fatales."

An editorial in the *Star Tribune* declared, "His material was funny, yes, but he was funnier."

Throughout his long career, Bob Hope was who he was. He was a funny guy. He had style. He left a lasting impression.

Consider J.D. Salinger's *The Catcher in the Rye*, a book many people in my generation read in high school. Long after we may have forgotten the protagonist's name, Holden Caulfield, or the story of this troubled, foul-mouthed adolescent whose soft-hearted dream was to stand on the edge of a field of rye and keep younger children from falling off a cliff, we remember the tone of the story and our feeling for the author.

Style is the residue that lingers beyond the details of a lifetime, the specifics of a career, or the episodes of a narrative. In writing, your style is the way you present yourself. It is the impression you convey of who you are. It is the deepest, most authentic connection between you and your reader.

GO BEYOND CLARITY TO ELOQUENCE AND GRACE

Elegance can add power, refinement, dignity, even authority to a message that otherwise might go unheeded. As Joseph Williams observes in *Style: Ten Lessons in Clarity and Grace*, if we never attempted anything but clear, straightforward sentences, "we'd be like a pianist who could use only the middle octave."

To be sure, we need to know the middle octave well. But to write with elegance, to write in a style that is both "distinguished and distinguishing," we need to do more. We need to know how—and when—to accentuate our writing with an occasional high or low note.

As you work to incorporate these fifty-two writing techniques into your practice, bear in mind the following.

1. **Elegance cannot be forced.** It cannot be purchased and slipped into like fine clothes. Writing with elegance comes naturally and gradually. It comes from making the right assumptions about language and from following certain principles of writing.

2. **Elegance need not be complicated.** It can be as simple as E.B. White's sentence in *The Elements of Style*: "These [questions of style] are high mysteries, and this chapter is a mystery story, thinly disguised."

   A simple shift in word order destroys the effect of that sentence: "These are high mysteries, and this chapter is a thinly disguised mystery story." Without the grace note at the end of the sentence, it becomes ordinary.

3. **Elegance depends more on sound than content.** Elegance requires a precise, robust vocabulary. It also requires an ear for language and attention to the cadence, rhythm, and flow of sentence structure. A common device for creating a pleasing sound is to achieve balance and symmetry through coordination.

Compare, for example, these sentences.

   a. Thank you for the commitment, competence, thoughtfulness, and integrity you have demonstrated over the past twenty years.
   b. Thank you for all you have given us over the past twenty years. Your commitment is matched only by your competence, your thoughtfulness only by your integrity.

In many types of writing, the bottom line is clarity. But surely somewhere near the top of the page are elegance and grace.

More than two centuries ago Samuel Johnson, described the most desirable English style as "familiar but not coarse, elegant but not ostentatious."

My, how times don't change.

EXERCISE

"Go forth and write badly."

That was the satiric benediction novelist Alan Burns would offer to his University of Minnesota students at the end of the semester. They would laugh because they knew what he had in mind.

Don't play it safe. Don't repeat the formulas of your previous successes. Be bold. Try something new. Risk failure. By doing so, you're more likely to reach beyond your present abilities and discover something new.

Remember to write in stages. In the first stage, you're the artist. In the last stage, you're the critic.

These fifty-two techniques are intended not for the artistic but for the critical stages. Except for Week 48, "Use Your Imagination," don't try to apply them as you begin drafting. Apply them later in the process. As you draft, let the words flow freely. Follow your natural rhythms and patterns. And then go back and look for missed opportunities.

First you're the artist. Then you're the critic.

✴ A FURTHER THOUGHT: ELEGANCE ADDS POWER TO YOUR WRITING

As you look for occasions to go beyond clarity to beauty and grace, you might ask, what is the point of learning all these techniques and rules of language? How important is structure and word arrangement? What is the point of grammar?

In Muriel Barbery's novel *The Elegance of the Hedgehog*, twelve-year-old Paloma is taken aback when her literature teacher says the point of grammar is "to make us speak and write well."

To offer this explanation to "a group of adolescents who already know how to speak and write is," in Paloma's opinion, "like telling someone it is necessary to read a history of toilets in order to pee and poop."

Paloma doesn't think her teacher's explanation is wrong exactly; she thinks it "grossly inept."

"We already knew how to use and conjugate a verb long before we knew it *was* a verb," she reflects. To her precocious mind, grammar lessons are "a sort of synthesis after the fact ... a source of supplemental details concerning terminology."

More than that, "Grammar is an end in itself and not simply a means. It provides access to the structure and beauty of language. It's not just some trick to help people get by in society."

How do *you* feel about grammar? Is it merely a set of rules that make you look good if you follow them and embarrass you if you don't?

For Paloma, "Grammar is a way to attain beauty. When you speak or read or write, you can tell if you've said or read or written a fine sentence. You can recognize a well-turned phrase or an elegant style. But when you are applying the rules of grammar skillfully ... you peel back the layers to see how it is all put together [and] you say to yourself, 'Look how well made this is, how well constructed it is, how solid and ingenious, rich and subtle.'"

One often hears the contrary argument. Why study English when I already know how to speak? Why study writing when I already know how to write? As long as you understand me, what does it matter if I follow the rules?

There's nothing wrong with using words pragmatically to conduct business or to seal the deal, but isn't there a place in your everyday life for beauty? Do you, like Paloma, "get completely carried away just knowing that there are words of all different natures, and that you have to know them in order to be able to infer their potential usage and compatibility"?

If creating beauty is not your first thought when you arrive for work on Monday morning, consider what is likely to satisfy you at the end of the day. When you look back on a lifetime of work, will you be proud that you nudged the boulder a little higher up the hill or that you did so with dignity, style, and grace?

Isn't that what we all want in the end? Something more than the tricks of the trade and expedience? Something of more enduring value?

We would do well to remember Paloma's concluding thought on grammar: "Pity the poor in spirit who know neither the enchantment nor the beauty of language."

DEVELOP YOUR PERSONA TO BE THE PERSON YOU ASPIRE TO BE

Writing is power. When you write, you assert your concerns, your values, your point of view.

When you give written expression to your thought—when you use these little symbolic squiggles known as letters and punctuation marks to convey your meaning—you create an artifact. And that artifact becomes a record. You make history. You leave a legacy.

With this power comes both responsibility and freedom. Whether you are writing to inform, persuade, or entertain, you should be honest about your intent, clear in your expression, accurate in your information, and respectful toward your readers.

Along with these responsibilities, you have a certain freedom. You are free to assume any voice and the identity of any character that suits your purpose. As long as your reader understands the game, you can play the role of hero or villain, sympathetic supporter or scathing critic, smart aleck or pensive philosopher.

In writing, you can be anybody you want to be. It's a remarkable freedom.

In ancient times, an assumed identity was called a *persona*, the Greek word for the mask worn by actors in the classical theater of Sophocles, Euripides, and Aeschylus. Today we call it an *avatar*.

When you write, your words project an image of how you want to be perceived. That image might closely approximate your true self or it might be a gross distortion, but it's always an image, never the real thing.

Once when I was discussing the concept of persona in a workshop, one participant said, "I understand the idea of persona in fiction, say a novel, but not in persuasive writing. In persuasive writing, aren't the assumed voice and the real person the same?"

Not exactly. Persona might be less obvious in persuasive writing than, say, in fiction, where authors may employ a narrator whose thoughts and words obviously don't represent what they think and believe, but persona still figures in persuasive writing.

Consider the statement "Rapid growth causes inflation." If it suited your purpose to come across as an informed observer, you might hedge your statement: "Rapid growth *often* causes inflation." On the other hand, if it suited your purpose to come across as an expert, you might use an intensifier: "Rapid growth *invariably* causes inflation."

Through a series of choices like that one, you create an image or impression of the person behind the words. Depending on your rhetorical strategy, that impression might be of a person who is well informed or naive, definite or tentative, hostile or sympathetic.

Just as your choice of images is key to your persona, your choice of words determines your persona or the impression you create in your reader's mind. As I advised in Week 48, don't begin a message with "As per your request, attached please find ..." If you asked me to identify the most stilted sentence in business writing, that opening would be my nominee. Yes, the phrase is common. Yes, it's handy. Yes, it's readily understood. But it's also awkward, bureaucratic, and off-putting.

Stilted language creates distance between you and your reader. Natural language makes you come across as genuine and approachable.

Compare the following openings.

1. As per your request, attached please find a brochure that describes our array of personal and professional financial-planning services.
2. Thank you for your interest in our array of personal and professional financial-planning services. The attached brochure explains how we can help you with ...

The first opening is needlessly formal and off-putting; the second is natural and friendly.

Be true to yourself. Think about the impression you want to leave in your reader's mind. The more natural your word choice—that is, the more appropriate it is for your purpose, your reader, and the occasion—the more effectively you will deliver your message.

Compare "I desire to be excused from attending this meeting" with "Please excuse me from this meeting." The natural word choice in the second sentence is not only more personal, but also more concise and emphatic.

Sometimes using natural language involves preferring action verbs to nouns or nominalizations, as I discussed in Week 14. Compare "It is my recommendation that we make a revision in our strategy" with "I recommend we revise our strategy." Again, the natural language conveys a more welcoming, more attractive persona or avatar.

Do you stand in agreement with me? (Do you agree with me?) Should we make a commitment to use verb-based language? (Should we commit ourselves to using verb-based language?) Should we enter into further discussion on this matter? (Should we discuss this point further? Should we talk about this some more?) Are you in need of more examples? (Do you need more examples?)

Probably not.

Natural word choice goes beyond language and techniques of style. Natural word choice shapes the reader's impression of who you are as a person. When a sentence you've written sounds stilted, forced, or overly formal, ask yourself, how would I say that?

Your choice or words should be intentional, not accidental. It should be based on a careful assessment of audience and purpose, and it should serve a purpose. It should offer a clear rhetorical advantage.

Perhaps the most rewarding use of persona is as a developmental tool. Imagine yourself as you would like to be—say, a thoughtful friend, an informed citizen, a sympathetic boss, or a brilliant writer in command of the facts—and then try to present yourself as that person in your writing. And finally, try to become that person in real life. In this way, persona is less a projection than a re-creation of self.

I think of writing as a journey, an opportunity for self-exploration. As you experiment with language, as you study and practice techniques of style and you figure out which ones work for you and which ones don't, you have the opportunity to discover who you really are.

More than that, you are led to ask an intriguing question: Who would you like to be? What persona or symbolic representation of yourself would you like to create and present to the world and perhaps someday be in real life?

John Steinbeck once said he began writing for one "big reason": "I instinctively recognized an opportunity to transcend some of my personal failings—things about myself I didn't particularly like and wanted to change but didn't know how."

What persona would you like to be?

Whatever your choice, I urge you to be a complete person. Reveal not only your thoughts, but also your feelings. Share your insights and humor. Be playful. Write with heart.

Above all, be genuine. "Honesty in story-telling," says Stephen King in *On Writing*, "makes up for a great many stylistic faults, as the work of wooden-prose writers like Theodore Dreiser and Ayn Rand show."

And be sure to invite your reader to share your journey—to think with you, to laugh with you, and to enter your imaginative world.

Returning to where we began our fifty-two-week journey together, your style—your persona, the impression you create of yourself—may at times be based on practicality, expedience, or rhetorical strategy, but it's more than a suit of clothes to be donned for the occasion. Your style is an authentic expression of who you are, your inner being, "the Self," as E.B. White describes it, "escaping into the open."

EXERCISES

1. Revise the following sentences to make them less stilted.
   a. I am making an attempt to make an improvement in my writing.
   b. Please apprise me of what transpired at the meeting.
   c. We need to fabricate a dike around this building utilizing these sandbags.
   d. Such conditions impede progress in finding a resolution to said problem.
   e. Our team leader deems it imperative that we conduct ourselves ethically.

Here's how you might have revised those sentences.

    a. I'm trying to improve my writing.

    b. Please tell me what happened [or transpired] at the meeting.

    c. We need to build a dike around this building with these sandbags.

    d. These conditions impede our progress in solving this problem

       or These conditions are preventing us from solving this problem.

    e. Our team leader insists that we conduct ourselves ethically.

2. Now for the grand prize. Here's an exercise I use in my writing seminars. Replace the fancy language in the following sentence with natural language.

> In the unlikely eventuality that you encounter various and sundry difficulties with the above-referenced project, please apprise me of the situation at your earliest possible convenience.

How about "Please let me know if you have any problems"?

3. Use your imagination to discover who you are.

Don't hide behind your words. Reveal your true, unpretentious self to your readers. Let them in on your secrets, your perceptions, your values, your ways of thinking.

Be honest and courageous. Write about the things that truly matter to you. Always write with the reader in mind, be aware of the impression you're creating of that person behind the words, but as you choose your words, write to please yourself.

At its best, your writing will show the world the person you aspire to be.

CONCLUSION

Congratulations! You've completed your first pass through my fifty-two techniques. Way to go! Give yourself two pats on the back for what you've accomplished and one kick in the butt for what lies ahead.

Now the real fun begins. You're ready to begin your fifty-two-week journey. This time through, take it slow. Devote one week to each technique.

At the end of your one-year journey, you'll find that your writing has improved. Dramatically. Readers, friends, associates, and family members will notice. Your mother will give you a hug. Your father will tell you he's proud. Your teacher will give you an *A*. Your boss will give you a raise. People will stop you on the street and ask you for your autograph.

You'll be more than a good writer. You'll be a remarkably improved writer. You may even be a great writer.

But don't stop there. You've only just begun. Note the date of your arrival on your calendar. A year from that date, review the following Summary of Techniques to remind yourself of what you've learned. If you need to do more work on some of the techniques, or if some seem especially relevant to your current writing, reread those chapters. If you like, do the same review every year for the rest of your life.

Keep at it. It's a long journey, but you can do it. I know you can.

SUMMARY OF TECHNIQUES

1. Listen to your language

Well-chosen words can make your writing memorable. Change the title of Carl Bernstein and Bob Woodward's book from *At this Point in Time* to *All the President's Men*.

2. Write with detail

One of the most powerful phrases in the English language is *for example*. Change "We were confused by the story's ending" to "We wondered why after thirty years of marriage the narrator would leave someone he obviously loved so much."

3. Appeal to the senses

As Joseph Conrad advised, "Don't tell the reader; show the reader." Change "It was a beautiful spot for Dad's final resting place" to "We scattered Dad's ashes in the clear blue water of a wilderness lake."

4. Collect good words

Be on the lookout for words that are just right for your intended meaning. Change "He was grumpy" to "He was irascible."

5. Know when to use a two-bit word

Use a full range of vocabulary, from simple to sophisticated. Consider changing *involve*, *support*, and *believable* to *entail*, *corroborate*, and *credible*.

6. Use the appropriate level of formality

Use words appropriate to your subject, your audience, and the occasion. Make intentional choices between "I can't get ready for your excuses" and "I don't accept your excuses" and between "I must differ with you on this point" and "I have to disagree with you about that."

7. Recognize both genders in your writing

Refer to people in ways that make both genders feel included. Change "A good writer listens carefully to his language" to "Good writers listen carefully to their language."

8. Delete *that* for rhythm and flow; retain *that* for clarity

That is often unnecessary, but sometimes deleting it causes ambiguity. Retain *that* in the following sentence: "His editor believed *that* his explanation for submitting his manuscript one week late was lame."

9. Avoid indirect and indefinite negatives

Replace *not* constructions with more direct negatives. Change "Her reasoning was not comprehensible" to "Her reasoning was incomprehensible," and change "It was not any fun" to "It was no fun."

10. Make every word count

Don't waste the reader's time. Change *due to the fact that* to *because* and *in the event that* to *if.*

11. Eliminate wordy references to time

Watch for this common source of wordiness. Change *prior to* to *before*, *subsequent to* to *after*, and *until such time as* to *until.*

12. Don't trust modifiers

They're the trickiest part of speech to use well. Change *end result* to *result*, *general consensus* to *consensus*, *terrible tragedy* to *tragedy*, and *personal opinion* to *opinion*. Do I need to *continue on*?

13. Use strong verbs to drive your sentences

Verbs add energy to your style. Change "He made a complaint about doing the dishes" to "He complained about doing the dishes."

14. Don't nominalize; verbalize

If you routinely change your verbs into nouns, you'll write with a noun-heavy style. Change "I came to the realization I had this habit" to "I realized I had this habit."

15. Know when to verb your nouns

As Calvin once said to Hobbes, "Verbing weirds language," but sometimes turning nouns into verbs produces a good effect. Change "I find his arrogance hard to take" to "I can't stomach his arrogance."

16. Unstack those noun stacks

Lining up too many nouns in a row produces ungainly constructions called "noun stacks," which can be "unstacked" by starting on the right side and changing the nouns into verbs and modifiers. Change "I displayed a *text revision suggestion anger reaction*" to "I *reacted angrily when she suggested I revise my text.*"

17. Prefer the active voice—but know when to use the passive

The active voice is more direct and emphatic than the passive, but sometimes the passive is better. Change "You ruined this scene with your heavy-handed editing" to "This scene was ruined by heavy-handed editing."

18. Keep your verbs near their subjects

The farther the distance between your subject and your verb, the harder your reader must work to make sense of your sentence. Change "Style with all of its complexity and variations as well as differences in readers' tastes and preferences is hard to discuss" to "Style is hard to discuss given its complexity and variations as well as differences in readers' tastes and preferences."

19. Avoid five types of mid-sentence shifts

Eliminate jarring shifts in tense, person, subject, voice, and modified subject. Change "We *pull* our canoes from the swollen river and *felt* fortunate to be alive" to "We *pulled* our canoes from the swollen river and *felt* fortunate to be alive."

20. Punctuate for emphasis

Pausing mid-sentence gives a sentence shape and personality. Change "The one thing that motivates me is social justice" to "I am motivated by one thing: social justice."

21. Use dashes for dashing effect

The dash is a bold mark that creates emphasis by bringing a sentence to an abrupt halt. Change "I knew it was him, the culprit, when I saw his bloody hands" to "I knew it was him—the culprit—when I saw his bloody hands."

22. Use ellipses to compress your sentences

An ellipsis is the omission of a word or phrase that is suggested by the context. Change the end of the second sentence in "Style, in its finest sense, is the last acquirement of the educated mind; it is also the most useful acquirement of the educated mind" to the way Alfred North Whitehead wrote it: "Style, in its finest sense, is the last acquirement of the educated mind; it is also the most useful."

23. Use semicolons to both separate and connect

Semicolons suggest a connection between two items even as they separate them. For greater suspense, change "Juan was two hours late, and Arriola was getting worried" to "Juan was two hours late; Arriola was getting worried."

24. Delight your reader with the classic setup

The two-step setup has been used by generations of comedians—and writers—to good effect. Note its use in Vladimir Nabokov's statement: "A first-rate college library with a comfortable campus around it is a fine milieu for a writer. There is, of course, the problem of educating the young."

25. Use antithesis to make your point by contrast

Contrary statements draw sharp distinctions and engage the reader by their perplexing nature, as in "Shame is nothing to be ashamed of."

26. Build toward climax

Follow the natural order of things by moving from shorter to longer, simpler to more complex, and less vivid to more vivid. Change "This historical novel is brilliant, timely, and accurate" to "This historical novel is accurate, timely, and brilliant."

27. Trim sentence endings for closing emphasis

To take advantage of the natural stress point at the ending of each sentence, trim excess words. Change "Let's listen to the ideas our customers are offering to us" to "Let's listen to our customers' ideas."

28. Use sentence beginnings for emphasis

Sometimes the wording can be rearranged to take advantage of opening emphasis. Change "Customer service is even more important" to "Even more important is customer service."

29. Subordinate to control your emphasis

Use subordination to vary your sentence structure, to de-emphasize negative information, and to shift your emphasis to positive information. Compare "Although his insights are invaluable, he gets on my nerves" with "Although he gets on my nerves, his insights are invaluable."

30. Expand your sentence repertoire by adding trailing elements

To create more variety in your sentence structure, add a phrase or clause after the main part of the sentence. Change "It's sunny and warm outside. I think I'll go swimming" to "It's sunny and warm outside, a perfect day for swimming."

31. Hit 'em with the long-short combo

Following a long, complicated sentence with a short, snappy one makes your writing sound decisive and dynamic, so let's learn this technique for adding emphasis to your words. Now.

32. Use sentence fragments to punctuate your writing

Fragments can be used for multiple effects, from breaking the rhythm and flow of your sentences to offering compelling observations in concentrated language, as Colum McCann does when he captures the horrors of slavery in seven words: "Some scars on back, two missing toes."

33. End with the thought you intend to develop next

This arrangement creates greater coherence. Change "There are two natural stress points in a sentence" to "A sentence contains two natural stress points."

34. Start with something old; end with something new

For more coherent writing, begin your sentences with previously mentioned information and end them with new information. Change "There are many advantages to proceeding in this order" to "Proceeding in this order offers many advantages."

35. Use paragraphs to frame your thought and set your pace

Like a photographer taking a picture, present your thoughts in units of thought or material. Writing involves deciding what goes into and what is left out of each unit framed by white space.

36. Use three-part paragraphs to organize your thought

Not all paragraphs need be organized the same way, but whenever you think you're losing a sense of organization and coherence, go back to the basic three-part paragraph structure: topic, development, resolution. It's as simple as one, two, three.

37. Write in sentences, but think in paragraphs

Your paragraph is your strategic unit for developing your thought. There may be several points in a paragraph, but every one of them serves to achieve your paragraph's main purpose.

38. Conclude your paragraphs with a click

Save your best line for last, and you'll wrap up your paragraph in a way that satisfies—or delights—your reader. A line like "If it doesn't fit, you must acquit" should come not in the middle but at the end of a paragraph.

39. Use parallel structure to create rhythm

Repeating a grammatical structure creates emphasis and sometimes adds elegance. Change "It's better if you ask what you can do for your country rather than the reverse" to "Ask not what your country can do for you; ask what you can do for your country."

40. Use periodic sentences to create suspense and emphasis

A periodic sentence is one with a series of parallel elements before the main clause, a structure whose delay presents the main point with emphasis and flourish. To change a loose sentence, in which the series of parallel elements follows the main clause, into a periodic sentence, change "The writer is ready for exposure, full of his beliefs, sustained and elevated by the power of his purpose, armed with the rules of grammar" to "Full of his beliefs, sustained and elevated by the power of his purpose, armed with the rules of grammar, the writer is ready for exposure."

41. Cross things up with *antimetabole* and *chiasmus*

Antimetabole, chiasmus, anaphora, epistrophe, anadiplosis, and *isocolon* are six rhythmic schemes that produce special effects. *Antimetabole* and *chiasmus* involve reversing the order of elements, as in "Ask not what your country can do for you; ask what you can do for your country."

42. Use *anaphora* and *epistrophe* for eloquence

Anaphora and *epistrophe* are schemes of repetition. *Anaphora* is repetition at the beginning of successive clauses, as in "I have a dream that one day ... I have a dream that one day ..." *Epistrophe* is repetition at the end of successive clauses, as in "When I was a child, I talked like a child, I thought like a child, I reasoned like a child."

43. Create rhythm with *anadiplosis* and *isocolon*

Like *antimetabole* and *chiasmus*, *anadiplosis* involves a crossing of elements, but with *anadiplosis* the last word of one clause is repeated at the beginning of the next so that the two words are juxtaposed, as in "Beauty is truth, truth beauty." *Isocolon* involves repetition of both the same grammatical structure and the same number of syllables, as in "Many are called, but few are chosen."

44. Lay down a beat ... and then break the rhythm

Having established a beat, break the rhythm and vary it now and then. Change "Much of the activity we think of as writing isn't actually writing" to the way Gail Godwin wrote the sentence: "Much of the activity we think of as writing is, actually, getting ready to write."

45. Use analogies and comparisons to enliven your writing

Go beyond the literal to add depth and color to your writing. Change "Over time you grow accustomed to the threat of nuclear war" to the way President Jimmy Carter expressed the thought: "Our minds have adjusted to it, as after a time our eyes adjust to the dark."

46. Return to your metaphors and similes

Returning to a figure of speech conveys a sense of thoughtfully crafted structure, and if the subsequent reference occurs near the end of a piece, it creates a tidy conclusion. It's a nice way to frame a piece.

47. Avoid vogue words and clichés

Even brilliant metaphors lose their luster over time. Go beyond the tried and true to something of your own creation.

48. Use your imagination to write with personality and style

Don't be satisfied with the obvious. Change "When you're writing something long like a novel, take it one step at a time" to the way E.L. Doctorow expressed the thought: "Writing a novel is like driving a car at night. You can see only as far as your headlights, but you can make the whole trip that way."

49. Add a light-hearted touch to your writing

A playful tone adds life to your writing and elicits an active response from your reader. Change "I'm living beyond my means" to the way e.e. cummings expressed the thought: "I'm living so far beyond my income that we may almost be said to be living apart."

50. Know your options for comic effect

Of the ten types of humor I discussed, I think irony is my favorite because it allows me to play around with the reader's expectations—and intelligence—in so many different ways. The disparity between literal meaning and implied meaning is at the heart of comic effect.

51. Go beyond clarity to eloquence and grace

Elegance cannot be forced, it need not be complicated, and it depends more on sound than on content. In many types of writing, the bottom line is clarity. But surely somewhere near the top of the page are elegance and grace.

52. Develop your persona to be the person you aspire to be

Explore the dimensions of your personality and identity in your writing. By cultivating and consciously projecting an image of the person you'd like to be, over time you might become that person in life.

GLOSSARY OF GRAMMATICAL TERMS

active verb (or active voice): A verb form that indicates the subject is the *performer* of the action, as in "Everyone in our department read the book." In contrast, a **passive verb** indicates the subject is the *receiver* of the action, as in "The book was read by everyone in our department."

adjective: A word that modifies a noun or a pronoun, as in "The book was *wonderful*" and "It was a *complex* problem."

adverb: A word that modifies a verb, an adjective, another adverb, or a whole phrase, clause, or sentence, as in "I read the book *quickly*" and "It was a *very* complex problem."

article: A type of adjective. *The* is the definite article. *A* and *an* are indefinite articles.

clause: A group of words that has a subject and a verb. See **phrase**, **main clause**, and **subordinate clause**.

comma splice: The incorrect joining of two complete sentences or main clauses with a comma alone, as in "I didn't mean to insult you, however, I do think you're wrong."

conjunction: A word that connects and shows the relation between words, phrases, and clauses, as in "A word that connects *and* shows the relation between words, phrases, *and* clauses."

A **subordinating conjunction** (such as *when, while, if, although,* and *because*) introduces dependent clauses and connects them to main clauses, as in "*Although* you missed your plane, you can still make it in time for the opening of the conference."

dependent clause (also called a subordinate clause): A clause that is not a sentence, does not stand alone, and must be joined to a main clause to form a grammatically complete sentence, as in "*Although I wrote an angry response,* I decided not to send it." See **independent** or **main clause**.

dangling modifier: A modifying phrase or clause that does not sensibly connect to any word in a sentence, as in "After reading your reports, it is recommended that you take a writing class." See **misplaced modifier**.

independent clause (also called a main clause): A grammatically complete sentence, one that contains a subject and a verb and that expresses a complete thought. See **dependent** or **subordinate clause**.

misplaced modifier: A modifier positioned incorrectly in a sentence, as in "When well stewed, you add the tomatoes to the pot." See **dangling modifier**.

noun: A word that names a person, place, thing, or idea.

A **proper noun** names a particular person, place, or thing, as in "the *Lincoln Center*" and "the Department of Human Resources."

parallelism (or **parallel structure** or **parallel construction**; sentences with parallel construction are sometimes called **balanced sentences**): The principle that words, phrases, or clauses presented in a pair or in a series must be of the same kind or formation, as in "Our government is of the people, by the people, and for the people" and "Ask not what your country can do for you, but rather what you can do for your country." An example of nonparallel structure is "Our guidelines were found to be inaccurate, inconsistent, and not complete."

passive verb (or passive voice): The verb form that indicates the subject is the *receiver* of the action, as in "The book was read by everyone in our department." In contrast, an **active verb** indicates the subject is the *performer* of the action, as in "Everyone in our department read the book."

phrase: A group of words that lacks a subject and a verb, as in "We found the report *in the top drawer.*" See **clause**.

predicate: The verb part of a sentence. It tells what the subject did or how it was acted upon, as in "He *stomped out of the meeting*" and "She *sought his advice.*"

preposition: A connecting word such as *in*, *on*, *of*, and *with*. **Prepositional phrases** are prepositions and their objects, as in *in the drawer*, *on the floor*, and *with malice*.

sentence fragment: A dependent clause (one that does not stand alone) that is incorrectly punctuated as though it were a main clause (or a complete sentence), as in "Although I disagree."

INDEX